Why the South? Why Egypt?

MELISSA GARCIA

ISBN 979-8-88943-178-7 (paperback)
ISBN 979-8-88943-179-4 (digital)

Christian Faith Publishing
832 Park Avenue
Meadville, PA 16335
www.christianfaithpublishing.com

Printed in the United States of America

Where you are now is not where you'll stay,
but where you are headed is where you will remain until the time
of preparation for what is to come is fulfilled in you!

With all my heart and soul, I want to dedicate this book to my Heavenly Father, my Lord Jesus Christ, and the Holy Spirit. Without the Trinity working in me as one, giving me the strength and confidence to write this book, I would have never become the author of this book.

I also want to dedicate this book to all my trials, mistakes, and failures that took to get to this moment, because without them, I wouldn't have a story to tell or a testimony to share with the world: that through our darkest, toughest moments, God still has His perfect will for our lives in the palm of His hands.

I also want to dedicate this book to my husband and my children who are the very essence of my life. They have given me the motivation I needed to keep going. Every time I look into their eyes, I see a part of me in each one of them, and what God has allowed me to accomplish, I know they will accomplish far more greater works than I ever have, and that's the promise I hold on to from the Lord Jesus Christ, and He hasn't failed me yet.

Finally, I want to dedicate this book to my beautiful, wonderful, amazing mother. If it had not been for my mother helping me through all my struggles and horrible moments that tried to swallow me alive and destroy me, I honestly don't know where I would be. My mother has motivated me in so many ways. She probably has no idea just how much of a hero she truly is. I watched as my mother overcame so many obstacles, but the biggest one was breast cancer. My mother is my hero, and if I have learned anything in this life, it's that no matter how tough life gets, remember where our help comes from. It comes from the Lord, the Maker of heaven and earth.

CONTENTS

INTRODUCTION

We all have a destiny that awaits us. As we travel through life's journey, the moments that matter the most are the moments that are unseen by others. When you find yourself in a season of trials, know that your determination depends on your attitude. It's not so much about counting your blessings but rather cherishing the hidden moments of your trials. If we could take one look into the future and see what God has in store for our lives and if God showed us all we would have to endure to reach that destiny, would we really want to face the trials it would take to get to our greatest victories? Or will we choose to run and hide and ignore the greater calling in our lives? I think, for all our sakes, we are better off not knowing the future and trusting that God knows all things, and as God has hand-picked each one of us to fit the role that each of us has been given, the best thing we can do in this life is place our faith in the Creator of heaven and earth.

Picture God on His throne looking down at us right now, saying, "There is a place where I have designated for you to go that will bring glory and honor to my name and strength for you to grow and prosper." Then picture the Lord taking you by the hand and walking with you every step of the way, and as you cry, He cries with you. As you pray, He listens. When you're scared, He holds you. When you laugh, He laughs hysterically with you. And when you are at the point of giving up, He says in a still, small yet sweet and subtle voice, "Don't give up because you're almost there." Well, this is not a make-believe, made-up fantasy fairy tale; this is the greatest most amazing reality we all can learn to trust and believe in when we choose to accept the truth and the reality that as each one of us on this earth has a purpose from God: to go out and live a victorious life through Jesus Christ. We will have to face an Egypt moment at one point in time or another. In this book that the Holy Spirit laid upon my heart to write, I will show you how to become an overcomer when encountering a season or multiple Egypts or down south moments, because it's in these unfortunate moments in life that God can show you in a moment the most amazing supernatural works that anyone on this earth can spend a lifetime trying to search for but will never find unless they surrender to the will of God in Christ Jesus. So sit back and savor the moment as we dive into all those who had encountered their Egypt moments yet survived and came out stronger than ever to testify to the truth that God is still on His throne and was, is, and will always remain God Almighty for generations to come.

Background
(The Birth of This Book)

I never thought in a million years that I would ever be sitting down to write a book. Growing up, my ambitions and goals never came close to writing or reading because I was never the type to sit still for more than five minutes before wanting to get up and run around. As an active child, I loved to play outside, dance, sing, or just move around at every chance I got. I wasn't the brightest bulb in the box. That was my oldest sister. She loved to read and write all the time. She could sit for hours at a time just reading away. This always came hard for me to do because she was the bookworm while I was the early bird outside before everyone was awake playing and riding my bike around the neighborhood. Yup! That was me. It's crazy how when we're young we have this mindset of living in the present time not worrying about the future and what we will be doing later in life. I was a wild child growing up, and I did not think of ever becoming a book writer, yet in God's plan, He had always seen me this way. This is because God had preestablished every path I would take just to discover my calling later in life. This book was birthed from a simple yet apprehensive passion that God had stirred in my heart to bring forth. The reason I say "simple yet apprehensive" is because, although I know that God is mighty to make this book come to pass, I was not in my right mind to even grasp the concept of what it would cost to sit and write a book, let alone know where I would start. But God, in his immense compassion and mercy, never let me let go of His dream of seeing me finish this book. Writing this book, I wasn't ready or prepared to enter my own down south Egypt moment, but God already knew what I would have to endure and what it would take to finish this book. I can truly stand here after having experienced so many Egypt moments and say with boldness and authority *2 Timothy 4:17*, which says,

> *But the Lord stood with me and strengthened me, so that the message might be preached fully through me, and that all the gentiles may hear, also I was delivered out of the mouth of the lion. And the Lord will deliver me from every evil work and preserve me for his heavenly kingdom. To Him be the glory forever and ever. Amen!*

You and I don't know what the future holds for us, but rest assured that God is omnipresent and knows what was, what is, and what is to come. And when we come to know who God truly is, we also become aware that, however we thought our lives would become like as the word of God says in *Isaiah 55:9*, *"For as the heavens are higher than the earth, so are my ways higher than your ways, and my thoughts higher than your thoughts."*

Before we can ever discover our God-given talents and gifts, we first must be prepared to walk toward our own down south Egypt moments, where in the process of enduring Egypt, we will also discover that those very talents and gifts that God has given us come with a price of enduring all that Egypt puts us through, but with every Egypt moment that God allows us to endure, this will enable us to draw closer to our destiny of becoming whom God has predestined us to become. Sometimes this requires us to completely dismiss any and every thought we have over how we view ourselves now and how others view us from our past mistakes. What God has spoken over our lives will come to pass. We don't need to hear it because if God spoke it, God will bring it to pass, and the one who has already heard it is the one who is making war against us to try and stop the plans of God from manifesting in our lives.

There are times as well when God calls us to rise up and travel toward our down south Egypt moment, not only to wake up the calling on our life but also to shelter us from things or people that try to rise up and take us away from our purpose. We will have to remain in Egypt indefinitely until the time comes when God says those who sought to do harm to you have perished in their own wickedness. I will give you two prime examples from the Bible. The first is Jeroboam. Jeroboam was Solomon's right-hand man. Solomon was David's son who ruled and reigned as king of Israel after his father passed away. After Solomon's reign was nearly coming to an end, God sent a prophet (named Ahijah) to Jeroboam to tell Jeroboam that he would inherit ten kingdoms since Solomon had turned to other idols and gods. He had turned away from fully serving the God of Abraham, Isaac, and Jacob and allowed himself to become perverted through his many wives. One kingdom was left for Solomon's son Rehoboam (which was the southern kingdom that consisted of Judah and Benjamin), but Scripture tells us that when Solomon found out about the prophecy concerning the tribes of Israel and became aware of who would inherit the ten tribes, Solomon rose up and sought to kill Jeroboam. Scripture says, when Jeroboam found out that Solomon was after him to kill him, he got up and fled to Egypt and remained there until the death of Solomon.

Another prime example we see in the Scriptures is Jesus having to go to Egypt and remain there for a while until the death of Herod. This was because when Herod found out the Messiah was born and would one day rule and reign over Israel and become Savior of the world, Herod thought carnally and had all his soldiers massacre innocent male babies two years old and under. When this occurred, an angel of the Lord appeared in a dream and spoke to Joseph (Mary's husband). He said, "*Arise, take the young child and his mother, flee to Egypt and stay there until I bring you word; for Herod will seek the young child to destroy him"* (Matt. 2:13).

As we can see from these two examples, God doesn't only allow us to go to Egypt as a means of bringing out the best of who we are, but also to protect us from those seeking to destroy us, whether it's our ministry, testimony, or even our physical selves. God knows and sees the dangers that lie ahead for us, and as faithful as He is when it comes to Egypt, every moment God allows us to travel toward our Egypt or down south moment will require us to put our own emotions on the back burner and look toward the hills to say to ourselves this: "From where does my help come from? My help comes from the Lord, the maker of heaven and earth." As we get into the different Egypt moments that each person mentioned in the Bible had to go through, we will discover the many different and most fortunate benefits of what it truly means to be called by God to walk through our down south Egypt moments and what a privilege it truly is to be called to the land called Egypt.

CHAPTER 1

The Origin of Egypt's First Encounter

I have a hunch that the enemy is not going to like what I am about to talk about. But this book God has laid upon my heart is a book that will bring change and liberty to all who hear what the Spirit of the Lord is saying. God in His eternal mercy permits us to go through various trials. Some trials can be bigger than others; but one thing I am sure of is, when we find ourselves entering Egypt, it's because God is getting ready to bring you and me through a process that will lead us to a victory so big, the enemy will have to sit back and watch the wondrous powers of Almighty God manifest as He makes a way for us to get to the other side.

When we think of Egypt, we most likely think about Moses and the Ten Commandments and how God made a way for His people to leave Egypt and cross over to the other side through the Red Sea, right? Yes! That was a spectacular moment in time, but before we can get that far ahead, we first must take it back to the first journey toward Egypt that started with Father Abraham. *Genesis 12:10–20*, entitled "Abraham in Egypt," starts like this:

> *Now there was a famine in the land and Abram went down to Egypt to dwell there. For the famine was severe in the land. And it came to pass, when he was close to entering Egypt, that he said to Sarai his wife, "Indeed I know that you are a woman of beau-*

1

tiful countenance. Therefore it will happen, when the Egyptians see you, that they will say, this is his wife; and they will kill me, but they will let you live. Please say you are my sister, that it may be well with me for your sake, and that I may live because of you." So it was, when Abram came into Egypt, that the Egyptians saw the woman, that she was very beautiful. The princes of pharaoh also saw her and commended her to pharaoh. And the woman was taken to Pharaoh's house. He treated Abram well for her sake. He had sheep, oxen, male donkeys, male and female servants, female donkeys, and camels. but the Lord plagued Pharaoh and his house with great plagues because of Sarai, Abram's wife. and Pharaoh called Abram and said, "What is this you have done to me? Why did you not tell me she was your wife? Why did you say she is my sister? I might have taken her as my wife. Now therefore here is your wife; take her and go your way." So Pharaoh commanded his men concerning him; and they sent him away, with his wife and all that he had.

In these ten short verses, we are going to discover many powerful facts about Egypt:

1. Anytime scripture talks about Egypt, it's always about going down to Egypt (letting us know that we are going down to invade the enemy's territory) (*Gen. 12:10*).
2. God never leaves us in our famine state of mind (When we have nothing, God will bring us what we need, and what we need is to trust that His ways are better than our own ways.) (*Gen. 12:10*).
3. Always be one step ahead of the enemy. Abraham was! (The enemy will always seek to take you away from God's purpose by trying to take away what belongs to you)(*Gen. 12:11–12*).
4. *Always know that God is for you, never against you!*

Before I go into detail about Abraham and his family having to go down south, I want to take a few steps back and talk about what God had initially said to Abraham before they made there way down south toward Egypt. This will give us a much clearer picture and set the stage for us to understand just how important it is to take God at His word. God had a plan with Abraham and his descendants: to bless the nations that would come through his son Isaac. *Genesis 12:1–3* says that God would take him and his family out of his own country, bringing him to a land that he has never seen. God also said He would make him a great nation, bless him, make his name great, and be a blessing to others. God would bless those who bless him and curse those who curse him. Wow! That is major.

God has already decreed over our lives all the blessings we will inherit. Every single word that has been spoken over our lives by the Holy Spirit will come to pass. It did with Abraham, and it will with you and me. When the Lord finished speaking, Abraham departed and arrived at the place God had promised him: the land of Canaan. The Lord said to Abraham when he arrived, "To your descendants I will give this land." Notice the words here: "to your descendants." When God decrees a word over our lives, it is never for us to stay with the blessing but rather to be the blessing to others. Abraham knew that because the very next thing Abraham did was build and altar to the Lord. Then Abraham goes on ahead to build another altar at the mountain east of Bethel. I don't know about you, but it seems as if Abraham could almost taste the victory even before he saw it! Abraham believed in God so much, he could not help but lift sacrifices of worship on the altars. What would our lives be like whenever God says, "I'm going to bless you big and make you a blessing to others"? Seeing those prophecies come to pass, would we prepare an altar for worship? I feel deep down in my spirit something big happening. Excuse me while I give God praise and worship. Hallelujah!

Our worship to the Lord should never cause us to stay in one place. Our worship to the creator of heaven and earth should cause us to move and trust. I worship because I know God is not done with me yet. I worship because I know that I need God to move within me, which is exactly what He did with Abraham. God causes abundant rain falls, and He causes great famines to fall upon the earth. Not to harm us but to move us to another level of prosperity. You and I must go down to come up. But when you find yourself going to a place where, just like Abraham, you are afraid for your life, remember that you and I are not alone. God already predestined what you and I would go through from the beginning right down to the end.

Abraham finished calling out to the Lord. I just want to take a brief pause and stop right here and analyze for a moment something very important. According to the scriptures, this was the first altar Abraham erected to the Lord, and when God had spoken to Abraham regarding him leaving his father's house and going to a land promised to his descendants, God spoke only to Abraham. When God gave Abraham the promise of becoming a great nation, God only spoke to Abraham. You see only Abraham knew and was able to recognize God's voice, to the point that he made an altar and a decree not only to follow God but for his entire family to worship the one true living God. Also, for them to become aware through Abraham's worship to God that the God of heaven and earth would never leave nor forsake the house of Abraham but establish his house forever.

So Abraham finished calling out to the Lord, and now he and his family are making their way down south. The Bible says there was a famine in the land they were in, which forced them to head on down to Egypt. The moment they began heading toward Egypt, Abraham stopped his wife and told her, "You are a beautiful woman of countenance and I know Pharaoh will kill me just to get to you so, say you are my sister for my sake that I may live because of you."

For a moment, I want to talk to the wives. The Lord wants me to let you know just how important you are to your husband. Sarai was given to Abraham for two reasons:

1. To be a helper
2. Raise a child

God had blessed Abraham with a beautiful wife, so Genesis 12:14 says. Sarai's act of obedience toward her husband when Abraham asked Sarai to say that she was his sister may have put her in an uncomfortable situation. How many times have we as wives had to come to our husband's defense? I know I have. My husband is my husband, and I will become uncomfortable for the sake of my husband because God has called me not to rule over my husband but to help my husband. You see, Abraham was not the only one who was afraid for his life. Sarai too must have been afraid because she had to be separated from her husband. I do not know about you, but if I am away from my husband for more than a day, I start to feel my heart fill with worry, and that's because ever since we got married, we have taken road trips together as a family. As long as Sarai was in Egypt, God's provision for Abraham's house would continue to overflow in abundance. Genesis 12:16 says, *"He treated him (Abraham) well (meaning pharaoh) for her sake (Sarai)."* Sarai was a woman of purpose and value. God's hand was already placed upon Sarai even before she was in her mother's womb. God was preparing her for something so great that would change the course of her time. She may not have understood her process then, but she sure would later when she had her son, Isaac (the promised son). No matter how hard the enemy tries to keep you down, as God has ordained His purpose, it will come to pass. Remember, women of the Most High God, when you find yourself in a place of loneliness and discouragement, God is only permitting this to let you know that, although it may look like the end, the beginning of your greatest destiny is still to come!

God blessed Abraham with riches from Egypt. Abraham's house was blessed with God's provisions. The little bit they came in with did not compare with the much they came out with. God was not done showing Abraham who He is. He is the God who defends His people and leaves not even one behind. Sarai was still in Egypt, and only a mighty act of God's divine intervention was going to set Sarai free and back to her husband where she belongs. We can see ourselves in Sarai. How she must have felt knowing her family was out there and she is being imprisoned in a place where she longed to be freed from. Only a divine interceding from God alone can save us from our loneliness, despair, intimidation, heartache, and pain. God does not only want to bless us with material things; He wants to free us and rid us of any and every single emotion that does not come from

Him. God wants more than anything for us to walk with our soul—that is, our mind, will, and emotions—fixed on him and only Him. God sees you right where you are, and just like Sarai, God will bring you out so you will know that He is the God who saves!

God always knows how to deal with our situations. Nothing in this life will ever cause God to draw back or stand down from a battle because He is Jehovah Nissi. He is the one who already has it all figured out, and that is why we can trust Him to fight on our behalf. The Lord plagued Pharaoh's house with not just one plague but many plagues. When Jehovah Nissi fights our battles, He just does not come into fight; He steps in to make it known to all people that you do not mess with one of His own and get away with it! Pharaoh knew the instant that those plagues occurred that it was because of Sarai, Abraham's wife. Genesis 12:17 says, "*But the Lord plagued pharaoh's house with great plagues because of Sarai, Abraham's wife.*" And so Pharaoh had no other choice but to let Sarai go. We do not belong to the enemy. No matter what you are facing or what you'll face in this life, as long as you know who's you are, you will always have freedom living inside of you. The enemy knows that God is fighting for you, and that's why the enemy tries his hardest to get you to lose hope and become discouraged. God allowed Abraham and Sarai to feel the separation from one another. There is always a reason why God does what He does. Everything God does is never in vain. Being away from the love of his life caused Abraham pain and agony (the same way the Father feels for us when we were separated from Him due to our sins. It hurts the Father deeply because He loves the human race with an agape love). And Sarai not being able to see her husband caused her to feel the emotion of deep sorrow (just like us not being able to see the Father before coming to Christ, we were deeply sorrowed and longed to be reunited with our true love but while we were being imprisoned by the enemy's lies, our Heavenly Father made a way for us to break free from our bondage and reunite us back to Himself through His beautiful Son, Jesus Christ). Just like Christ took our punishment and was separated from the Father (for a moment) while our sins were being poured out upon Him, His blood brought us back from where we were. In loneliness, discouragement separated from our true love (God the Father), and just like God made away for Sarai and Abraham to become reunited with each other, so has God made a way for us to be reunited with Himself through an act of obedience. No matter how the enemy presents the situation, remember whatever the enemy meant for evil, when we trust God, He will turn it around for good, just like He did for Abraham and Sarai.

The Enemy Has No Grip on Your Blessings

The Bible says Pharaoh commanded Abraham and his household along with Sarai, his wife, to leave Egypt at once. And so, they did with riches of silver, gold, and livestock. They went up from Egypt and journeyed onward to the very place where Abraham first pitched his tent and made an altar to the Lord (Gen. 13:1–4). Abraham called upon the name of the Lord. Our worship to the Lord should never only be about what we get or where he is taking us; it should strictly be because even before you and I were, He was, is, and will always be the Great I Am. The church needs to come back to the beginning when we worshipped God not because there are great events taking place or not because of very well-known singers, preachers, evangelists, prophets, and teachers who come and speak for a few hours. Our worship toward the Lord should be about pouring out every part of who we are as an offering to the Lord so He can receive it knowing that His daughters' and sons' passion is where his heart is, and that is the heart of worship. Worship to the Father is not about what God can do for us; it's about what God has already done for us. He loved us and thought about each and every one of us even before the foundations of the earth were laid down.

Abraham knew that God had divinely intervened on his behalf, and when Abraham came back from Egypt, he ran and went to do the only thing he knew to do: go back to the same altar and call on the name of the Lord Jehovah. Let us all come back to the heart of worship, leaving all worries behind and focusing on what really matters, what is truly important, and that is giving God our time of praise and worship. Call out to God right now. He is listening. He is waiting to hear from you. Don't hesitate to talk to Him because He won't hesitate to respond to your worship. Let us build an altar to the Lord right now and let our voice be the fragrance that makes its way to the throne room of God's tabernacle. Worship His holy name, all you saints. Praise Him because He is a good, good Father. Praise His holy name forever and ever because He is our everlasting Father. As you and I are raising worship to the throne room, He is pouring out His anointing, getting us ready for what lies ahead. God is equipping us for the next chapter of our lives. No matter how that looks like, God's promise for each one of us is found in Joshua 1:9, *"Have I not commanded you? Be strong be of good courage; do not be afraid, nor be dismayed, for the Lord your God is with you wherever you go."*

So here we see the first encounter with Egypt. God, in His divine purpose, made a way even when it seemed as if Abraham was about to lose his wife. This was the first, but surely not the last, encounter that God's people would have with Egypt. As we get into more examples of other people who had a different yet similar encounter with either traveling down south or going to Egypt, we will begin to discover something that we all have in common when it comes to Egypt. As we travel down memory lane of these men and women who had to endure being in Egypt or the south for such a time, I guarantee we will begin to open our spiritual eyes to a whole new view of what going through our Egypt or down south moments really means.

In This Life, We Will Go through Trials

Ever wonder why sometimes we find ourselves going through difficult times, and when we feel like most giving up is when we feel that nudge telling us not to stop and not to give up or give in because we're almost there? It is called the test of trials. It's like when you are hired for a job. Your boss will put you on a trial-basis period or probationary period. This is to see if you have the proper experience or the ability to perform the right tasks that are at hand. As you go into work day by day, hour by hour, week by week, you are being observed by someone who has the power to keep you and/or eventually promote you and make you qualified to keep your position. In the very same way, God would have us go through trial-basis periods in our lives. In order to promote us to the very next chapter of our lives, we are going to have to face the getting-over-the-hurdle moments, climbing-up-the-mountain battles, even the war that rages within our very minds that tells us that we will never make it, or "You were never built to handle such a task as this one. Go back to where you came from. You're a fool to think that you will ever be qualified." If we could just stop and think for just one moment, it's not about us being able to accomplish our goals, achievements, ambitions, satisfactory reports, or our own will but what God has accomplished in us; the goals God has already set before us to achieve; his ambition to constantly pursue us in every way; His satisfactory report that says we are good enough to be in His presence, because of the very blood that was poured out on Calvary's cross by God's only begotten son, Jesus Christ, so the whole human race could come to the knowledge of repentance and live out not our own will, but the will of the Father who is in heaven. God is willing and ready to promote us to the next chapter of our lives if we would do two things: surrender our total and complete lives to the King of kings and Lord of lords and trust that, although we will go through trials, God already knows our end from our beginning. After all, He is the author and finisher of our lives.

Your Courage to Believe God's Plan Will Cause You and Your Family to be Blessed beyond Measure

The two greatest gifts God has given us are the gift of life (good choices) and death (evil choices). *Deuteronomy 30:15–17* says,

> *See, I have put before you life and good, death and evil. In that I command you today to love the Lord your God, to walk in his ways, and to keep His commandments, His statutes, and His judgments, that you may live and multiply; and the Lord your God will bless you in the land which you go to possess. But if your heart turns away so that you do not*

hear, and are drawn away, and worship other gods
and serve them, I announce to you today that you
shall surely perish; you shall not prolong your days
in the land which you cross over the Jordan to go in
and possess.

The very essence of our lives depends upon the choices we make. When we learn to follow the voice of the Holy Spirit, we will be led down the path of righteousness for God's namesake. If we depend upon our mind, will, and emotions, we will surely perish in our own way. We will ultimately lead ourselves to utter destruction. *Matthew 10:39* says, "*He who finds his life will lose it, and he who loses his life for my sake will find it.*" Abraham knew that God would fulfill His promise to them. All they had to do was trust God all the way through, and that's exactly what Abraham did. Abraham pleased God not because of the sacrifice Abraham made by leaving his father's house, but by the faith Abraham had in believing God at His word despite all the opposition Abraham and his household would have to endure to reach the full destiny of God's purpose. *Genesis 15:6* says, "*He believed in the Lord, and He accounted it to him for righteousness.*"

God's grace and mercy were upon Abraham and his house because Abraham believed that God would fulfill his promise however long it took. Abraham had his work of faith cut out for him. After all, Abraham was the only one who heard from God as God spoke only to him. Our job as believers and followers of Christ is to take God at His word and believe God's plan for our lives, and by our faith in Christ, we show the world who our Savior is by shining the light of Christ through our faith in the cross. When the world sees our unrelenting faith in Jesus, the world will come to follow God, just as Abraham's house did; and even if some, like Abraham's nephew, Lot, strayed away from Abraham's house, God's mighty power will come through our prayers of intercession for our family members in the powerful name of Jesus Christ.

Sometimes in life what may look or seem crazy is exactly what God is using or doing to align us to a greater destiny—a destiny that we could never get to without going through our own Egypt experience. God's mighty plan for our lives cannot be stopped by the enemy's opposition. On the contrary, God permits opposition to push us right into our destiny, and even scripture says in *Psalm 30:5*, "*Weeping may endure for a night, but joy comes in the morning.*" We do not know what we will face in the near future. Abraham had no idea he would have to go through Egypt in order to come out with more than he came in with. When we encounter moments like this, our job is to have faith. Easier said than done, I know, right? How can we find ourselves face-to-face with opposition and still have faith? There is a saying that we have all heard before: "Desperate times call for desperate measures." This idiom came from a Greek physician called Hippocrates. His philosophy was that, in desperate times, extreme measures are needed to be taken. Although the Bible does not state when and if Abraham called out to God on behalf of his wife, we can just imagine the agony Abraham must have gone through knowing another man was in possession of his beloved wife, Sarai. What God does for Abraham goes beyond what anyone on this planet could ever do. God plagues Pharaoh's house because of Abraham's wife, Sarai. God saw the agony of Abraham's heart and therefore acted as a protective mother (El Shaddai) coming to save His children (Jehovah Nissi). Even when there are no words to speak, as our tears do the praying and our heart does the shouting, those desperate times that call for desperate measures never goes in vain with God. The Lord sees you right where you are, and an act of faith will cause a great move of God. And when that happens, that means God is positioning us for great victory above our enemies. If God plagued Pharaoh's house on account of Abraham's wife, just imagine what God is about to do with your enemies that have tried time and time again to take away what belongs to His children. Our desperate time that calls for desperate measures is found in *Jeremiah 33:2 and 3*, "*Thus says the Lord who made it, the Lord who formed it to establish it (The Lord is His name). Call to me, and I will answer you, and show you great and mighty things which you do not know.*" Even when it is hard to speak, let your silent prayer rise from the depths of your heart because however it comes out, God hears it, and he will respond.

Enter Your Present and Leave toward Your Future!

Many times God will bring us to the same encounter with a similar situation just in a different setting. Has that ever happened to you? It sure has happened to me. When we find ourselves going through these seasons, God is trying to let us know that the more present we are with our surroundings, the more aware we will be when God brings our future to pass. Where am I going with this, you ask? Well, we just finished looking at our very first encounter with Egypt in chapter 12 where Abraham and his family were forced to go to Egypt because of a famine in the land, and there, God worked a miracle. As they went in with little, God caused them to leave with much more than they had expected. Abraham's faith must have grown ever since because Abraham and his family were now making their way down south toward Gerar. There we find Abraham running into a present situation that he had already encountered previously before. When we find ourselves running into the same situation, that's God telling us, "As I did it before so I will do it again and again and again."

God says in *Hebrews 13:5* and *6*, "*Let your conduct be without covetousness; be content with such things as you have. For He Himself has said, 'I will never leave you nor will I forsake you,' so we may boldly say: 'The Lord is my helper, I will not fear. What can man do to me?'*" True faith comes when we have no other choice but to believe in the One who can deliver us from our present situation, and that's why Abraham reaped the title Father of Righteousness because despite all that Abraham encountered, he did not let that stop him from believing in God's promises. Despite all our present oppositions or our present difficulties or maybe even our present setbacks (which I will talk about later on in a different chapter), all that is required of us (in order to step into our future) is to "*trust in the Lord with all our heart, lean not to our own understanding, in all our ways acknowledge Him and He shall direct our path*" *(Prov. 3:5 and 6)*. God has already given each and every one of us a measure of faith, and as God permits us to enter our present situation, He will surely guide us through to our appointed future with more than we could have ever imagined.

Becoming Less Means Regaining More

As I mentioned before, Abraham and his family were once again heading down south, but this time, it wasn't toward Egypt. Where they were traveling toward was a place down south called Gerar. Abraham was about to lose his wife once again. It was déjà vu all over again for Abraham. *Genesis 20:1* and *2* says, "*Abraham journeyed from there (meaning Mamre) to the south, and dwelt between Kadesh and Shur, and stayed in Gerar. Now Abraham said of Sarai his wife, 'She is my sister.' And Abimelech, king of Gerar, sent and took Sarai.*" Once again, Abraham was separated from his beloved wife. But this time God came to Abimelech in a dream and spoke to Abimelech, saying, "You are a dead man because of the woman whom you have taken, for she is a man's wife." As I was reading this chapter, something remarkably interesting came over me. It was as if the Holy Spirit Himself was pressing upon my heart a revelation of God's Holy Scriptures. When God does something, it never goes without meaning or purpose. When we enter the valley where it is dark and lonely at times, we need to understand one thing: we are not alone and forsaken. We are surrounded by God's light that shines brighter than the day. Our Egypt moments, traveling down south moments, or even our valley moments are only a setup from God to position and align us for something greater than we could have ever imagined. The greatest purpose ever given by God is living in the unknown because in the unknown is where we find that God is always faithful to deliver us out of any difficult situation. His desire is to see His children happy and for us to rejoice in His great plan, even if that means believing without first seeing a single thing. We must first learn that on this journey called life, we are in possession of nothing. As we came naked into this world, with nothing in our hands, so we will leave with nothing. Abraham knew wherever he journeyed God would be with him and would never leave nor forsake him. Abraham trusted in the Lord to see him and his family through difficult seasons. No matter what Abraham faced, he had the faith to believe that God would faithfully deliver him and his household with a mighty deliverance. Whatever you and I are facing, when we surrender it all to the Lord, He will come through for us for His name's sake and deliver us from our enemies.

Every inch of the Bible talks about God's great deliverance. The goal of God is to rescue the human race from Satan's evil schemes, lies, and deceptions. And so the enemy begins by trying to get us to believe the lies and send fear our way to paralyze us and keep us from believing in God's promises. When we begin to feel the spirit of fear trying to take its place in our lives, we must remember God's word and speak life in order to conquer what is trying to keep us back from our destiny. The only way to do this is by walking out God's will and declaring his word. Fear will come! As we have been given five natural/physical senses to act upon as children of the Most High God, we have been given a supernatural sense of faith that extends farther than all other senses. We can act upon in this life, seeing as all five senses rely on our ability to believe and accept what is in front of us based upon what we see, hear, feel, taste, and smell; but our sense of faith is solemnly based upon what we can't see, hear, feel, taste, and smell yet believing God, who has already gone before us, predestined our victories, and has given us different measures of faith to hope and believe in what has already been established in our lives. If we hold fast to our faith, every promise God has spoken and declared over our lives will come to pass. If you and I begin to rely not on our natural senses but on our supernatural senses, doors that have been closed will open, and doors that were opened that lead to our destruction will be closed. When we sow by faith, we will reap the manifestation of an amazing harvest. Remember, just like we have joy and moments of happiness, they will often be interrupted by the enemy's plans to defocus ourselves from reaching God's purpose. Even though we may find ourselves encountering the spirit of fear, remember, God is fighting our battles and we have the victory in Jesus's name! After all, we can see God's hand moving through Abraham, and although Abraham encountered moments of fear, he knew what God did for him and his family down in Egypt. He would continue to do it repeatedly, yes! Even in the south, God can take what the enemy meant for evil and turn it around for good.

From God's Throne, He Throws Down Dreams of Thunder, Shaking the Darkness and Blessing His Children at the Same Time

In a dream, God tells Abimelech he was a dead man for taking another man's wife. Abimelech finds out from God that Sarai was Abraham's wife. Abraham then replies to Abimelech, *"Because I thought, surely the fear of the Lord was not in this place, and they would kill me on account of my wife."* Even though the reality of the matter was, Abraham did not lie to Abimelech (nor to Pharaoh the first time they had previously traveled to Egypt) saying, "Sarai is indeed my sister. She is my sister through the same father but not the same mother." For the sake of his own life, Abraham had to humble himself before Abimelech. But this did not stop the plan of God one bit. Abraham stated that he thought, *Surely the fear of the Lord was not in this place.* We can often find ourselves in a similar situation or thinking the same way as Abraham, simply because, as believers, we might think to ourselves that the fear of the Lord may not be in the place we are standing, and so for fear of what they will do or say we allow the spirit of fear to take hold of our minds. This spiritual atmosphere can take place in our work environment, at school, at a family gathering, or wherever we may find ourselves at that moment. Sometimes we are put in an uncomfortable situation. Not knowing what to say or do (for fear of what others will do or say) can often lead us to say or do the wrong things that can put us in a bind later on. The number one tactic used by the enemy to keep us from the promises of God is fear. Fear makes us say and do things in heist. Fear makes us believe we are conquered. A countless number of times God reassures us that we are not to fear but to be courageous. Sometimes when we are face-to-face with opposition, the best thing to do is humble ourselves before God and trust that He is Sovereign, knows how to fight our battles, and the enemy in the end must release what belongs to the children of God. *Second Timothy 1:7* says, *"For I have not given you the spirit of fear; but of power and of love and of a sound mind."* Our lives are empowered by the Holy Spirit. God has authorized us to sit in heavenly places with Christ Jesus. As we humble ourselves in the sight of

God, He will exalt us and bring us to new heights. God has a plan for every one of our lives; and at times we may need to take a step back and place our faith in the One who knows what was, what is, and what is to come. God cannot lie, and He will not relent in fighting off the enemy so we can see past our fears and doubts and walk right into God's victory. Remember, even though Abraham became fearful for his own life, God already knew the outcome of Abraham's situation and faithfully saw Abraham and his house through once again. After all, this was not the first or the last encounter Abraham's house would have with the south, or Egypt for that matter. If God did it for Abraham and his house, He will surely do it again for you, for me, and for our entire household as we encounter similar situations as Abraham and his wife did. *Joshua 24:15* says, "*As for me and my house we will serve the Lord.*"

CHAPTER 2

The Lonely Road Is Full of Purpose and Meaningful Experiences That Leads to Our Greatest Victory Yet!

We all have a choice to make. I know when I made mine way back when I was in my midtwenties, but before I made that choice to serve the Lord and make him Savior over my life, I had to face many oppositions, and one of the greatest oppositions I faced growing up was rejection. Whatever you're facing today, don't let that stop you from having a relationship with Jesus. He is waiting to hear from you today. If you make the choice to face your issues with the only One who can see you through them, you will begin to count your victories one by one and realize that you, in fact, were never alone, to begin with. God has already gone before us and has predestined our lives. He has already illuminated the road that lies ahead for each believer whose faith is in Christ Jesus. You and I were not conceived from nothing, for nothing, and out of nothing. Whether you choose to believe it or not, the facts remain and are hard to deny that God has formed us in our mother's womb and has given us the gift of life: how we would look like and what we would do for the kingdom of God. We were thought about by the Trinity (Godhead three in one) even before time began. We all have an important role in this life, and one thing I am sure of is that He made us weak vessels so we would come to the reality that one day, when we become aware of our sins, we would come to the foot of the cross, realizing and recognizing Jesus Christ as the Lord and Savior for all humanity. To heed the word of God is to choose life, and to reject the word of God is to choose death. Time is in His hands, but He gives us the gift of choice. By His breath, all humanity was given life, and by the blood of Jesus, all who come to the knowledge of the cross can become redeemed and made new through his sacrifice. The God who has aligned the stars and the planets so beautifully in the vast universe for all to see is the One who has aligned His perfect and beautiful will for our lives. The best time to see God's beautiful, massive, and complex universe is when it is dark out; and I believe God planned it that way to be sort of like a metaphor for our lives. Without those dark moments in our lives, we would never be able to see God's beautiful light shining through us, illuminating His amazing architectural work that only God can accomplish through us if we hold fast to our faith in Jesus Christ. Even before time began, God has shown Himself to be the God who, out of chaos, brought forth calmness; out of disorder, peace; out of destruction, preservation; out of calamity, restoration. And all this goes beyond what our minds could ever comprehend.

The word of God is full of so many wonderful promises. God's word never comes back void. From the time God laid down the foundations, God spoke existence, and existence came to pass. God spoke a word, and the evidence of God's purpose to this day surrounds us. Redemption was already on God's mind even before you and I were brought into existence. As we read the Bible chapter after chapter, verse after verse, book after book, and word for word, we begin to see the undeniable works of God's great redemption plan being knit and woven together like a tapestry or like a beautiful one-of-a-kind masterpiece or a never-ending orchestra symphony playing the songs of life to a never-ending degree. God has made every one of us in a unique way. Because we are all unique, that means the plans that God has for our lives are unique, and if that is so, we must trust that even though it may seem like we are not hearing from God, He is always hearing His children. And in His very own unique way, God will see us through and use us in a unique and powerful way. But before we can get to our God-given destiny, we must understand something very important: that in order to see victory, we are going to have to first travel south toward our very own Egypt. However that may look like, just know that if God has led us down there, He will surely bring us back up with His right righteous hand.

I remember growing up in a household of three siblings. My mother, who was a single mom, had to work hard because my father left when we were little. The only real memory I have of my father was at the beach. I was probably around four or maybe five years old. The vivid picture that stays in my mind to this day is my father holding me up in the air as the warmth and light of the sun hit my back, him smiling at me in the water, and me feeling safe in his arms. That was the last real memory I have of him. I am the middle child. Well, I was the youngest for a while because before my younger sister was born, my mom had three kids from my dad: me, my older brother, and sister. Then about four years later, my mom met a man and got pregnant with my younger sister. Growing up, my mother worked a lot just to put a roof over our heads, clothes on our backs, and food on the table. I grew up in a predominantly White community, and back then, there were not many Hispanics where we lived. As I started elementary school, I was bullied a lot and teased by mostly the girls on the bus or in class. I often felt I was too dumb for anyone to take notice of me. I would have girls randomly come up to me and tell me "You're so ugly" or "You could never be friends with us," and "You look like Mrs. Piggy from *Sesame Street.*" They would pull my hair and make me feel so low about myself. Often, I would find myself not wanting to go to school because I knew what I would have to endure just to get through a day at school. Sometimes I would stay at home from school, and my mom would receive a phone call, and she would know that I was home. When I did stay home, I would hide in the laundry bin hoping my mother would not find me, because if she did, I would get a whooping like nobody's business. The teasing got so bad at school that I would have rather taken the beating for staying home instead of the bullying at school. At home was no better though because we lived in an apartment house with other people, and between them and my siblings, I would also have to endure their teasing remarks and treating me different like an outcast, always leaving me out of what they were doing. Or if I was included, they would treat me like I was just a tag along. But for the most part, I would just get on my bike and ride around the neighborhood by myself looking for things to do. My older sister loved to read, and my brother loved his video games. I was often left to tend to do things on my own. Every weekend my mom would go out clubbing, and I would be left at home to be cared for by my older siblings. Sometimes I would beg my mother to stay with me and watch movies because I knew what staying home at night would mean to me. I remember one night crying myself to sleep after my sister kneed me in the back to the point I would be in so much pain. I wanted my mom to be there beside me instead of having to go through this almost every weekend. Some nights my brother had his best friend come over, and when my mom left (mostly on Saturday nights), he would touch me in inappropriate places. When I tried to tell my brother or sister, he would deny it, and so they just brushed it off as if it was not a big deal. The pain of not being defended for something wrong that was taking place hurt me more than anyone could have ever imagined. As a little girl, I never understood the full meaning of rejection. I only felt the emotional tides that came along with this emotion, and that was a very scary feeling for me.

Growing up, my mother was never really one to stay more than a couple of years in one place for too long so. We moved around quite often. We always lived in apartment houses, and so we shared the backyard and front yard with those who lived with us. My mother use to go to church before we all were born but departed from the ways of the Lord when we were very little. Even though she did not attend church, she did allow us to attend church at the Salvation Army. Cleaning the church was her second job after her first job. She also cleaned houses and a movie theater on the weekends. Going to church was my escape from the hurt and pain I felt from school and home. The best part about being in church (although I never understood the presence of God or fully knew about the manifestation of the Holy Spirit) was the music. Music always seemed to bring me to a place of clarity and peace. Whenever I would sing, I felt like I was distant from everything on this planet. I never understood why I felt that way then, but I sure do now. When we praise the Lord in Spirit and in truth, our inner being comes alive, and fountains of living waters begin to flow from within, causing us to worship the Creator in spirit and in truth. Boy, I really wish I knew that back then because as I began to discover my talent, all I wanted to do was sing, sing, and sing some more.

Every Sunday, we would have choir practice after church, and the same girl would always get picked to do the solos. I longed for just one opportunity to receive a solo part, and when I auditioned, I would get passed by and overlooked. When we experience the pain of rejection as a little child, rejection never stays where we leave it. It will always follow you, waiting for another opportunity to rise once again. There was the opportunity for rejection to once again make me feel less of myself. Being very young and not knowing how to deal with rejection, I began to brush it off because my thoughts were, *No one cares*, just like when I tried to let my siblings know about what was going on all those nights I was being touched inappropriately. As rejection became a part of me, so did anger and bitterness, along with envy. Have you ever heard of the expression "misery loves company"? Being so young, I did not fully understand the presence of God or the move of the Holy Spirit, but looking back now at that point of my life, I see God's perfect hand was holding me, and even though I did not fully know Him, He fully knows me. God fully knew that you would have to endure the things that happened to you in the past, and He knows what you're going through now. And although it may seem like it's unfair because others haven't experienced the harshness of life's blows occur in their lives as you have, remember that if God allowed you to experience what you have gone through or will go through in the near future or what you are going through right now in the present, it's because with what you have gone through, if you are willing to let God take your hurt and pain from your past experiences and weave them into a beautiful tapestry, trusting that God has preserved you for such a time as this, I promise you that whatever the enemy meant for evil, God already has a plan to turn all your unfortunate experiences into a great and wonderful testimony, and this is all because of the very fact that even before you were born, God Himself, in His perfect will for our life, formed us in our mother's womb. Even before He formed us, He already knew us, and if God already knew us, that means that He already knew our character, our intentions, and our will to serve Him.

> *Then the word of the Lord came to me, saying: "Before I formed you in the womb, I knew you; Before you were born, I sanctified you; I ordained you a prophet to the nations." (Jer. 1:4 and 5)*

God Knows the Time and Place, So Why Fret?

A couple of years later, the captains who were overseeing the church at that time were moved to another location, and the new captains arrived shortly after. The girl who always received solos stopped attending the church, and soon after, I began singing each solo. For Christmas, God allowed me to play the lead role in the birth of Jesus. You guessed it, I was Mary. It was quite funny because as I was coming into the scene of Mary walking pregnant toward the manger, I was so nervous I ended up putting the pillow up way to high, and for a woman at the point of almost giving birth, I now know that that pillow should have been a lot lower. For the first time, I started to feel like I was a part of something important, and all I wanted was to be at church every Sunday. Sunday Bible school was fun for me, and after church, we would practice various songs. Every year we would go to a competition either Upstate or at the Salvation Army headquarters in NYC. The event was called Star Light. We all would have our uniforms on to represent our church. I was a part of the sunbeam group and my older brother and sister were a part of the boy guard and girl guards' group. I remember like it was yesterday when my captain came to me and my mom and said that she would love for me to sing a solo act for "There Is a Redeemer" in the New York state competition. I was so excited that I had been chosen that I nearly forgot how nervous I would be until moments before we were called onstage to perform. We practiced every Sunday for about two months. This was the start of something I thought would last forever, but as sure as God's promises are, so is the enemy's plans to try and derail God's children from pursuing their calling.

The boys and girl guards along with the sunbeam girls at church all got invited to attend a Christian concert over at the NYC headquarters. As we arrived, I heard music echoing from within the theater. It was the most beautiful sound I ever heard. My heart was racing, and I was filled with excitement. There that night performing was an all-girl group called Out of Eden. As they performed, all I could do was stay watching in awe as they praised and worshipped God in a way I had never saw anyone worship. There I was standing, a skinny girl with very bushy curly hair just staring at these women. Then all of a sudden, I felt someone put their arm around my waist and whisper in my ear, "One day that is going to be you." When I looked up to see who it was who said those words to me, I saw My Captain looking at me with a big smile on her face. That night changed my life forever!

When God Speaks a Word over You, Remember Who Is Hearing Too!

Proverbs 3:5–6 says, "*Trust in the Lord with all your heart, and lean not on your own understanding, in all your ways acknowledge Him and He shall direct your paths.*" As sure as God has a plan to give us a bright future, a future filled with hope, the enemy also has a plan for our lives. His plan is to kill, steal, and destroy our belief in Christ Jesus. He knows if we start believing what God has spoken over our lives, no weapon the enemy forms against us shall prosper. During our desert season, most of the time things will not make sense. It will seem like all is lost, that you will never get to the other side, God will never pick you, you are wasting your time, and, of course, the feeling of not being qualified to do what God has called you to do. These are all the weapons that the enemy uses to try and derail us from the calling of God. Despite all we must encounter here on this earth, as Jesus conquered the grave, He has seated us in heavenly places and has declared a word over each one of His children's lives that we are made more than conquerors through Him. We can do all things through Christ who strengthens us. As we learn to trust in the Lord in our darkest moments, God will show us the way toward our destiny.

I know of a boy who was rejected, despised, and brought low, only to find that during these encounters, God's sovereign plan was accomplished. It is Jacob and Rachel's son, Joseph. Another encounter with Egypt. But before we get to the part of Egypt, we must first go back to the start of Joseph's life. As we investigate the life of Joseph, we will begin to understand the fullness of what it means to go from rejection to acceptance, from prison to the palace. I believe many who have gone through the pain and hurt of rejection (whether in your job, school, or even in your family) will see a breakthrough just like Joseph did. Despite of the rejections, accusations, and hurt Joseph suffered, He trusted in God's capability to see him through until the very end. *Acts 10:34* and *35* says, "*Then Peter opened his mouth and said: 'In truth I perceive that God shows no partiality. But in every nation whoever fears Him and works righteousness is accepted by Him.'*"

Not Everyone Will Believe in What You Have Seen and Spoken

Genesis 37:1–4 says,

> *Now Jacob dwelt in the land where his father was a stranger. In the land of Canaan. This is the history of Jacob. Joseph, being seventeen years old, was feeding the flock with his brothers, and the lad was with the sons of Bilhah and the sons of Zilpah, his fathers' wives; and Joseph brought a bad report of them to his father. Now Israel loved Joseph more than all his children, because he was the son of his old age. Also, he made him a tunic of many colors. But when his brothers saw that his father loved him more than all his brothers, they hated him and could not speak peaceably to him.*

As I begin reading the second verse, I found something very interesting. If not caught by the reader's eye, he or she would miss some vital information. Just in these very few words, we see something that changes the entire story of Joseph's life. Or is it really about Joseph's life? Why would Genesis 37:2 start with the history of Jacob when we are supposed to be zooming in on Joseph's life? Perhaps God wants us to see a much bigger picture here. Perhaps the story of Joseph goes much deeper than we thought. Or perhaps God from the beginning is saying, "Take your focus off them and put it on me." The story begins with Jacob because it is all about a father's love for his son, not the other way around. God is writing our story, but we must remember one thing: the real story and history and accounts of our lives is not about what we have done here on this earth, but what God has already done to redeem us from the hands of our enemies. Every single chapter of our lives should begin with *the history of our Father in heaven*. As we dive in deeper into the chapters, I believe God, through his Word, is going to speak to us in such a passionate way.

In the second verse, we find Joseph with all his brothers tending the sheep. Joseph was very close to his father, and his father loved him more than all his other sons. We know this to be true because next we see that Jacob (Joseph's father) makes Joseph a tunic of many colors. This clearly looks like a picture of Jesus, the Jews, and God the Father. The word of God in *Psalm 45:7* says, "*You love righteousness and hate wickedness; therefore, God your God has anointed you with the oil of gladness more than your companions.*" And again in *Hebrew 1:9.* Here we see Jacob giving his son something of value, and that causes a distinction between him and his brothers, and for that reason, his brothers hated him. God has given each one of us something of value. God loves us with an unconditional eternal love. And as God has called us to His very own presence, He has adorned us with the oil of gladness. Many will see it and not rejoice with us simply because of their disbelief of what is true and holy. We as Christians have a duty to tell all about the love of God and what Jesus did to save us from the wrath of God. Many will not receive us and welcome the truth because man has loved darkness rather than the light.

For everyone practicing evil hates the light and does not come to the light lest his deeds should be exposed, as it says in *John 3:19* and *20.* When Jesus walked among the Jews, many of them rejected him and did not receive him. *John 1:11* says, "*He came to his own, and His own did not receive Him.*"

When Joseph went to tend the sheep with is brothers, the Bible says, he would bring back a bad report to his father regarding the working status of his brothers. This type of bad report was not to get his brothers in trouble but to accurately give his father a report of any negligence on their part. As we gather more information about Joseph's character, we will see that his reporting back to his father about his brothers were in fact legitimate. Joseph having to report back to his father about the work status of his brothers must not have been so easy for Joseph. Even though Joseph had the deep love of his father, he had the feeling of being alone, rejected, envied, and unwanted by his brothers. How many of us can relate to Joseph right now? Often, we may feel that same rejection from our own family members, peers, coworkers, or even from our own brothers and sisters at church. When we find ourselves feeling that same way too, just remember that sometimes rejection does not always mean something is wrong with you. It could very well be that what you are carrying many cannot comprehend or contain it, and so God is reserving you for a greater purpose such that those who see you now do not have the capability to understand what God is doing in you. So do as *Proverbs 3:5* and *6* says: "*Trust in the Lord with all your heart and lean not on your own understanding. In all your ways acknowledge Him, and He shall direct your paths.*"

CHAPTER 3

Dare to Dream God's Dream!

Now Joseph had a dream, and he told it to his brothers; and they hated him even more. So, he said to them, "Please hear this dream which I have dreamed: There we were, binding sheave in the field. Then behold, my sheaf arose and stood upright; and indeed, your sheaves stood all around and bowed down to my sheaf." And his brothers said to him, "Shall you indeed reign over us? Or shall you indeed have dominion over us?" So they hated him even more for his dreams and his words. Then he dreamed still another dream and told it to his brothers, and said, "Look I have dreamed another dream. And this time, the sun the moon, and the eleven stars bowed down to me." So, he told it to his father and his brothers; and his father rebuked him and said to him, what is this dream you have dreamed? Shall your mother and I and your brothers indeed come to bow down to the earth before you? And his brothers envied him, but his father kept the matter in mind. (Gen. 37:5–11)

Some dreams are meant to be kept in silence until God brings them to pass. But not in this case. God allowed Joseph or permitted Joseph to tell these two dreams to his brothers. I believe it was necessary for them to hear the dream because out of this came the true condition of their hearts. Them hating Joseph so much was a mere representation of the Enemy's hatred toward Jesus Christ. All too often the true condition of our heart shows when we are forced to see reality for what it really is. Joseph had no control over the dreams God put in his mind and certainly had no idea where these dreams would ultimately lead him to one day. Boy, if his brothers did not hate him so much, then they certainly began to now. Isn't it ironic that though his brothers hated him, Joseph did not fight fire with fire? Despite how Joseph was treated by his brothers, we know that Joseph's heart was different from his brothers because before Joseph told his brothers the dream, he said, "Please hear this dream which I have dreamed." This shows a lot about Joseph's character. Joseph knew his brothers despised and hated him. Still, Joseph maintained his dignity by not stooping down to their level. The integrity of Joseph's character will be seen more and more as we go along. Joseph then tells his brothers about the dream, about how they were all binding sheaves in the field and suddenly Joseph's sheaf rises in an upright position and all the other sheaves bowed down to his sheaf. Clearly, this is a picture of Joseph and his brothers prostrating themselves before Joseph. It says that Joseph's sheaf also arose. The key word here is not *arose* but *also arose*. Notice Joseph then goes on to say, "Behold." When we hear the word *behold*, this is none other than an eye-opener for the one hearing or reading what Joseph was saying to his brothers. Remember, this was not just another dream; this was a prophecy from the Lord Himself given to Joseph, only to be fulfilled at the appointed time of God. In taking a deeper look at Joseph's dream, we find that all of them, including Joseph, were binding sheaves. God was painting an amazing portrait of unity here. God's purpose for the body of Christ is to walk in unity. As God unravels His sovereign plan, His intentions are always to bring unity among His children. This dream was not so much focused, or centered, on Joseph but on Christ. This is another metaphor of God's chosen people bowing down on earth before Jesus Christ, proclaiming him as the messiah, the Savior of the world. Every story in the

Holy Scriptures will always point back to Jesus. We know this to be true and accurate because of what scripture says in *John 1:1–3*:

> *In the beginning was the Word, and the Word was with God, and the Word was God. He was in the beginning with God. All things were made through Him, and without Him, nothing was made that was made.*

So here we find that Joseph's sheaf rises and is in the center of all the sheaves. And the sheaves around are bowing down to the sheaf in the middle. I believe the reason Joseph's sheaf arose along with the others is that before Joseph could have gotten to the position he was predestined to inherit, he had to walk the lonely road of humility and rejection only to then become the one who would rise and stand in the gap not only for his family but for the entire world. And if this is, in fact, true, then we also see within this great picture of Joseph as a metaphor for what Jesus, centuries later, would come to do before he was raised from the grave, which was humble himself even unto death on the cross, only to be raised from the grave and through His sacrifice save the entire world from our sins. This truly was a dream to behold. When we attempt to tell others of our dream, we expect them to feel the same way we do, but that is most likely not going to be the case here—at least, not for Joseph. Automatically, Joseph's brothers are filled with more hatred toward their brother because of what Joseph had told them and, in their disbelief and blind eyes, could not speak peaceably to Joseph. I may be going out on a limb here, but it seems to me that Joseph probably thought that by telling his brothers the dream they would somehow accept Joseph into their circle of brotherhood friendship. I think we all can relate to Joseph in some shape or form. We all long to be accepted by someone. Because God had chosen Joseph for a destiny that would change the course of history, this required Joseph to really feel the pain of rejection and loneliness. How do you think God felt when He was rejected by Adam and Eve in the garden of Eden? God blessed them with every-thing they ever needed, and still, they disobeyed God's word. Even through all of that, God still planned to send His only begotten Son (Jesus Christ) to redeem us and save us from Satan's evil powers and to bring us back to His presence. If anyone can relate and sympathize with our pain of rejection and loneliness, it is Jesus Christ. He has all too well felt rejection from his very own people; and still, by His grace and mercy, He chose to use us for His honor and His glory. God has called us to do far greater works exceedingly and abundantly above all we could have ever imagined. But just like Joseph, we too are going to have to experience the pain of sorrow and rejection. It was not easy for Joseph, and it sure will not be for you and me, but remember that although Joseph endured rejection, God never left his side, and He will never leave our side either.

> *Then he dreamed still another dream and told it to his brothers, and said, "Look I have dreamed another dream. And this time, the sun, the moon, and the eleven stars bowed down to me." So, he told it to his father and his brothers; and his father rebuked him and said to him, "What is this dream you have dreamed. Shall your mother and I and your brothers indeed come to bow down to the earth to you?" And his brothers envied him, but his father kept the matter in mind. (Gen. 37:9–11)*

A Confirmed Dream Is a Sure Dream to Come True

Have you ever had a dream and thereafter had a similar or if not the same dream? That is God speaking to you or trying to tell you something. Whether it is a warning dream or an encouraging dream, when God shows you a dream more than once, this is none other than a confirmation. This is exactly what happened with Joseph. God gave him a dream followed by another dream. But this time, the dream did not only involve his brothers but also his mother and father. As Joseph relayed the dream to his family members once again, we find his brothers bothered and annoyed as they could never see themselves bowing down to their youngest brother or the thought of them having to bow down to Joseph one day made them cringe. Imagine one day having to bow down to someone you hate. That day is closer than you think. Remember how I mentioned before how every story in the Bible points back to Christ? Well, that dream that is in every believer's heart will come to pass at the second coming of Christ. Whether you have accepted Jesus into your heart, making Him Lord and Savior of your life (escaping the wrath of God), or hate and rejected Him (having to endure the wrath of God because of your unbelief), the Bible says in *Philippians 2:9–11,*

> *Therefore God also has highly exalted Him and given Him the name which is above every name, That at the name of Jesus every knee shall bow of those in heaven, and those on the earth, and of those under the earth, and that every tongue should confess that Jesus is Lord, to the glory of God the Father.*

The first and second dream Joseph was a metaphor and foreshadowing of the coming Christ. Many will hear the word of God and reject it because they cannot fathom the day of Christ's return. But I tell you right now, just as sure as you and I are living and breathing, so the day will come when God brings all things in heaven and on earth to pass. *Matthew 24:35* says, "*Heaven and earth shall pass away but my words shall by no means pass away.*"

God has called you and me to something big, and because the enemy knows the potential that lies within you and me, he will use anything and anyone to pull you and me off course. The number one lie the enemy uses is deception. If he can get you and me to focus on how other's view our talents and gifts, he can control our very mind into thinking we are "just not good enough," "no one will listen," "you will never achieve your goals" or, the big one, "dreamer you are and dreamer you will always be, nothing more and always less." These are what the enemy whispers to you and me. Many times, we start to believe those lies because that is what the pain of rejection does to us. It causes us to feel like no one hears us, or even cares for that matter. But I tell you that there is one who hears, listens, and never rejects a broken heart or a contrite spirit and His name is Almighty God!

As Joseph told not only his brothers the dream but also his father, the Bible says that his own father rebuked him. The word *rebuke* is an expression of a sharp disapproval or criticism because of one's behavior or action. Apparently, Joseph's brothers and father were able to understand the dream but not grasp the abstract concept of Joseph one day ruling over his own family. The ironic part about all of this is that, although Joseph's father (Jacob) openly rebuked him, he also kept the matter in mind. Whether you preach, teach, sing, play an instrument, have the gift of prophecy, the gift of interpreting tongues, the gift of laying on of hands through the Holy Spirit, remember God has called you and me to do great and mighty works in the Lord Jesus Christ. All who see what God is doing in you will not always welcome you with open arms. They may do as Joseph's brothers did: they may envy you and me. Or like Joseph's father, they will rebuke us openly, but they will also keep the matter in mind.

I know open rebukes all too well. As I would sing at my local church in the praise and worship team, I would hear other sisters and brothers subliminally say things like, "Here the only one who gets the glory is God," which is the ultimate truth, but this was after every time I would sing. Only God knows the true heart of man and only God knows how much worshipping his name means to me; but because of my unresolved childhood rejection, hurt, and pain, I became an easy target for the enemy to come in and bring up my past. We may think we have already dealt with our unresolved issues or it had already disappeared when we received and accepted God's salvation through Christ. Boy, are we greatly mistaken. No matter how much talent or anointing we have from the Holy Spirit, if we have unresolved issues that God has not dealt with, the pain of rejection and the hurt will one way or the other find its way back into our lives.

I want to go back in time to my childhood once again and talk about it for a moment so that you can get a clear picture of what happens when bitterness, anger, and hatred take hold of you as a result of rejection and how eventually, through these negative emotions, they uproot the manifestation of the enemy's plan to try and take us out of God's will for our lives. Then we will get back to Joseph.

When I got older, my mother moved us to Huntington, and slowly but surely, I started departing from the ways of the Lord. By the time I was twelve, I started smoking cigarettes, drinking, doing drugs, cutting class, and hanging out with friends. I allowed the hurt and pain of rejection to take hold of my emotions and began looking for ways to numb the pain. I stopped singing in church, and the passion I once had to praise God was now turned over to the enemy, and I began singing for the world. I looked for any opportunity to sing in school plays and musicals. I now had a mission and a passion to pursue secular music. By the age of sixteen, while most girls were celebrating their sweet sixteen, I was pregnant with my daughter Julianna Marie Gonzalez. And soon after, I was abused physically, emotionally, and mentally by her father. I once again began to feel the pain and hurt of rejection. The bitter root of rejection began springing up, but this time, I started to believe that there was no hope for me. I began drinking more and more, hanging out more and more, going to clubs, just living a reckless life. But even though I stayed away from God's grace, He still had a plan for my life. My daughter's father's mother and great-grandmother never stopped praying for me. They would always say to me, "Jesus loves you," and I would tell them, "I know, I know."

One day when I was in the car about to smoke, I had what I believe was a vision from God. I remember like it was yesterday. Everything went pitch black, and suddenly, I saw the face of Jesus and a crown of thorns on His head, and as the blood came trickling down, I also saw tears coming down from his eyes. At that moment, something happened to me, and I began to ponder that vision time and time again. God had never given up on me. He still had a plan to save me. As I got older, I began pursuing my music career. My brother Willie introduced me to his friend who had a studio at his place, and I started to record music. The type of music I started to record was, of course, what came out of my heart, which was pain, bitterness, sorrow, anger, and strife toward all who had hurt me. I started to make music in other studios as well. I would sing anything from R&B, hip-hop, to reggaeton. Sometimes I would pull all-nighters in the studio just trying to get it right.

In my room one afternoon, something happened that I cannot really explain, but anyway, here it goes. As I was in my room, I heard a voice say to me, "I can make people shout your name." I then began to see my name flashing in lights and hear a multitude of people shouting my name. Thereafter, I heard the same voice say, "I will give you all of this if you will bow down and worship me." Seconds later, I heard another voice so sweet and so gentle say to me, "If you give away your only soul, you will be eternally separated from me." I was convicted that day and started to understand something in that moment for the first time: that even though I forgot about God, He never forgot about me and the plans He still had for my life. No matter how far you have been put in a dry well by your enemies, God's hand is never too short to pull you out. He sees you right where you are and will move heaven and earth just to rescue you. You just have to believe that with all your heart. God's work was already at hand because of those who never ceased praying for me. I felt led by the Holy Spirit to let you know that someone out there is praying for you to come home to the Father.

One day I met a man who heard me singing outside my home, and thought it was the radio (those were his specific words). I thought, just like everyone else, he was going to tell me I had a nice voice and he would be able to get me in the studio to make music; but the words that came flowing from his mouth changed my life forever. He said, "The Lord wants me to let you know that you are on the path of destruction and the only way to be saved is through Jesus Christ!" He then gave me a Bible. I began to read it, and as I began reading, I felt the conviction of God and the love of God at the same time. It is truly unexplainable. After, all I wanted to do was know God more and more, pray more and more, and seek Him more and more. I began recording gospel music. Although I was not a hundred percent there with God, He led me to a small church in New Bern, North Carolina. And there I sang my childhood song "Lord, I Lift Your Name on High." Everyone at that church was full of life, and soon after, the pastor made the altar call. I remember getting up and wanting so earnestly to receive Jesus into my heart, making Him Lord and Savior of my entire life. And so the moment finally came when I surrendered it all into the hands of God. From that moment, I began to see life in a whole different way. My family was not able to comprehend the new me; and so, for the first year or so, they would ridicule my faith. My mother, on the other hand, always told my brother and sisters not to mock my faith because, "Now that she has Jesus, God is the one fighting her battles." My mother understood faith because she too knew the Lord at one point but had departed from His ways. Now my mother and my family, through my act of faith, have come to know the Lord as well.

So you see, God at times allows us to go through the hurt and pain of rejection because that is one of the many tools He uses to bring us from the pit to the palace, from being rejected to being accepted. The rejections I experienced since childhood and up until now have led me right into the arms of Jesus. If it had not been for the redeeming blood of Jesus healing my wounded soul, I do not know if I would have had the courage to right this book, but as *Philip 4:13* says, "*I can do all things through Christ who strengthens me.*"

Joseph faced so many moments of rejection. Some came from his own family members, and others came from strangers in a foreign land. But the bottom line here is, there will always be that someone who you may not see but is praying for you and believes in the power of God to save with a mighty hand. Because Jacob had an encounter with God before, only to behold the mighty strength of Yahweh, he somehow must have pondered over the fact that his son could one day rule over his house. After all, Jacob saw the mighty works of God at hand, enough to know that with God, all things are possible!

Your dreams and my dreams that are given to us by God are only the start of something amazing. Most of us want the amazing part of the dream but are not willing to pay the price to see that dream come true. It can sometimes be a very painful process, but when God is in it, we will win it. No matter how long it takes for that dream to come to pass, never lose hope and never lose sight of the dream God has given you. The seas may roar at you, the mountains may try to stand in your way, the waves of life may try to bring you under, the giants may try to knock you down, and the storm may try to blow you around; but through it all, just remember what *2 Corinthians 4:8* and *9* says:

> *We are hard pressed on every side, yet not crushed; we are perplexed, but not in despair; persecuted, but not forsaken; struck down, but not destroyed.*

Keep this in mind: along with a dream comes a process that will require us to fully trust in God with all our hearts—yes, even unto the nearing point of death.

When We Are Lost God Sends Help

> *Then his brothers went to feed their fathers flock in Shechem. And Israel said to Joseph, "Are not your brothers feeding the flock in Shechem? Come, I will send you to them." So, he said to him, "Here I am." Then he said to him, "Please go and see if it is well with your brothers and well with the flocks and bring back word to me." So, he sent him out of the valley of Hebron, and he went to Shechem. Now a certain man found him, and there he was wandering in the field. And the man asked him, saying, "What are you seeking?" So he said, "I am seeking my brothers. Please tell me where they are feeding their flock." And the man said, "They have departed from here, for I heard them say, 'Let us go to Dothan.'" So, Joseph went after his brothers and found them in Dothan. (Gen. 37:12–17)*

Ever heard of the phrase *teacher's pet?* That was Joseph, because Jacob would always tell his son Joseph to bring back an accurate report of his brothers' work performance, which was part of the reason his brothers hated Joseph. This time they were far ahead of him. Joseph had no idea this would be the day that his life would change forever. When our Heavenly Father sends us out on an assignment to bring back word, we may very well be on our way, just like Joseph, toward our destiny. Notice in verse 13, Jacob says, "Come, I will send you to them." And Joseph replied, "Here I am." This is another portrait of God sending His only begotten Son, Jesus Christ, to go and become the mediator between man and God. We see this in Isaiah 6:8, "Then I heard a voice of the Lord saying, 'Whom shall I send? And who will go for us?' I said, 'Here I am. Send me!'" Jesus Christ not only came to show us the way unto salvation but to become the living sacrifice and Savior everyone needs in order to be saved from the destruction that lies ahead. Jacob told Joseph to go and see his brothers, and Joseph did not refuse but obeyed his father. Joseph had no idea what was about to happen to him. Jacob sends his son out of the valley of Hebron and on his way to Shechem.

"Out of the valley and on his way to Shechem!" Let us ponder those words for a moment. How does our valley look like? Could it be filled with dry bones of resentment or broken bones of hatred, or how about painful hairline fracture bones of having just enough pain that causes you to close yourself in because it seems no one cares or has treated you like the outcast. However your valley looks like, let me remind you all dry bones have two things in common: they lie in the darkest parts of the valley, and they have no life in them. Although they may be in the valley, where nobody else can see them, God most certainly sees them and will cause every lifeless bone to come back to life with the breath of His nostril and the sound of His voice. We trust that if God is for us, who can be against us!

Joseph came out of the valley of Hebron and made his way toward Shechem, but along the way, there was a man who found Joseph wandering in the field. How many of us instead of going straight to our destination begin wandering around? I believe we make our journey depending on how well we listen to instructions. For some, it may not take long; but for many, much like myself, it may take a lot longer, especially because sometimes we become wanderers and God must send someone to bring us back to the right direction. We make the enemy happy when we become wanderers in the wilderness because he knows that if he can distract our minds and lose our focus in fulfilling the plans of God, he has got us right where he wants us. But God is always faithful and will never leave us forsaken! Where God sends His children, He will make sure we get there, even if that means moving heaven and earth just to get to us.

The Bible says a certain man found Joseph. Not a man but a "certain man." Why does God choose to include this word instead of just a plain, ordinary man? First, let us look at the word *certain*. The root word for *certain* is *cert*, which comes from the Latin word *certain*, meaning to be sure, truly established, exact, precise, etc. I believe God divinely set up this appointment with Joseph to guide him right into his destiny, but it would first require him to deal with his rejections. Many times, God's way of helping us deal with our pain of rejection is causing us to go through various trials, and every trial has a test. Every test turns into a testimony if we choose to trust in the Lord. When we trust God in the unknown, He will never let us down but lift us upon His shoulders and carry us through to our destiny, for His name's sake. With God, there are no such things as accidents, only appointments. Where Joseph was, he was meant to be there. Where you are right now, you are meant to be there, because right where you are, God is getting ready to meet with you and point you in the right direction, even if that is to a place of solitude and discomfort and despair. But God knows what He is doing and where He needs you to get to so you can be the one who would stand in the gap for your family. There is One who stood in the gap to see His children saved from condemnation. But before Jesus was able to save us from our sins, He needed to go through the pain of rejection, loneliness, and suffering of the cross. Yours and my destiny have been marked by God for great works through Christ; and for that reason, we will have to endure at times rejection, loneliness, and suffering. But because Jesus has conquered death on the cross, we have been made more than conquerors through Christ. *Second Corinth 4:8–11* says,

> *We are hard-pressed on every side, yet not crushed; we are perplexed, but not in despair; per-*

secuted, but not forsaken; struck down, but not destroyed; always carrying about in the body the dying of the Lord Jesus, that the life of Jesus also may be manifest in our body. We who live are always delivered to death for Jesus' sake, that the life of Jesus also may be manifested in our mortal flesh.

Joseph was now heading up toward Dothan to meet his brothers. Or at least, that is what he thought. He was making his way toward them to do what he always does, bring back a work report to their father. Joseph had no idea the hatred that had been brewing in his brother's minds about him had now made its way into their hearts. Joseph's brothers were now conspiring Joseph's very own death.

Those Who Push You Down into the Pit with Envy Will See God Raise You up with Favor!

Now when they saw him afar off, even before they came near them, they conspired against him to kill him. Then they said to one another, "Look, this dreamer is coming! Come, therefore, let us now kill him and cast him into some pit; and we shall say, 'Some wild beast has devoured him.' We shall see what will become of his dreams!" But Ruben heard it, and he delivered him out of their hands, and said to them, "Let us not kill him." And Ruben said, "Shed no blood, but cast him into this pit, which is in the wilderness, and do not lay hands on him, that he might deliver him out of their hands and bring them back to his father. So it came to pass when Joseph had come to his brothers, that they stripped Joseph of his tunic, the tunic of many colors that was on him. Then they took him and cast him into a pit. And the pit was empty; there was no water in it. (Gen. 37:18–24)

What we can gather from the first few verses is quite clear. The enemy had already begun devising a plan to destroy the purpose of God's will for Joseph's life by wiping him off the face of the earth. The enemy's number one objective is to annihilate the children of God. The enemy knows the power that lies within every believer, and that is why he will stop at nothing until he sees us go down in despair and defeat. Blessedly, the God who sees everything tells us in *Isaiah 54:17*, "*No weapon the enemy forms against us shall prosper.*" And in *Romans 8:31*, it says, "*If God be for us, who can be against us.*" We may not be able to see who is plotting against us from afar, but you better believe that God sure does, and when God has spoken a word over our lives, that word will come to pass. What we may think the enemy is using for our destruction, the God of heaven and earth is using for our greater good. "*The enemy comes to kill, steal, and destroy; but Jesus came that we may have life and that we may have it more abundantly*" *(John 10:10)*. The enemy knows it has nothing to do with your skills, your talents, your intelligence, or even your very own strength. The reason the enemy seeks to destroy us is simply because the greater our belief in Jesus becomes, the more we become a threat to the kingdom of darkness.

Joseph knew how much his father loved him and cared for him, that's why Jacob made a tunic of many colors to publicly announce his love for his son. Joseph's brothers knew that and hated him for it. The tunic of many colors for every believer is the blood of Christ, and the enemy knows that we are marked with the seal of the Holy Spirit, and for that reason, "*the enemy, the adversary, walks about like a roaring lion seeking whom he may devour*" *(1 Pet. 5:8)*. Speaking of lions, this reminds me of another person in the Bible who was placed in a den of lions for his integrity to do what was right before God's eyes.

Three men conspired against Daniel in the hope of getting rid of him as they were jealous and envious toward him. Daniel was faithful to his Father in heaven and always communicated with Him through prayer. This made the three men angry. The Bible says that Daniel had distinguished himself above the governors and satraps because a spirit of excellence was given to him by God *(Dan. 6:3)*.

Daniel's integrity caused him to have King Darius set him over the whole realm, and for that reason, the three men conspired to get rid of Daniel. They knew he was full of integrity and faithfulness toward his God. So the very next thing they did was try to attack his moral standards, which was tied back to his faith in God. When you are a person of integrity, this will almost always cause the enemy to come and try to bring you to a place where he knows you will have to choose between compromising your faith or standing strong, even to the point of losing everything or death. Standing up for the sake of Christ means, others who are used by the enemy will come and test us against our will. The reason this happens is simply because they lack what you have and not being able to walk in that same integrity makes them uncomfortable and, in turn, brings anger and frustration their way, only to become a tool of the enemy to try and bring your destiny to an end. The one thing Satan ever wanted from God was to be God. Since the enemy knows that he will never be like the Most High God, he began devising a plan to make war against God by deceiving a third of the angels in heaven into believing that he could win against God. That's why we see the infiltration of Hollywood and the music industry, being manifest through Satan's lies and deceptions. Lucifer once led praise and worship while in heaven; but the moment he drew back from his integrity and rebelled against God, Lucifer, who now goes by the name Satan. He lost all his holy privileges and has contaminated them. He has now become the prime reason why so many perish in this world today without Jesus Christ. While the enemy is busy trying to gather an army, God has already commanded a plan that involves the army of hosts to stand guard against the evils of this world through His only begotten Son, Jesus Christ. God knows every war the enemy wages against us has already been dealt with when Jesus defeated Satan at Calvary's cross. God already knew what was in Lucifer's heart.

God also knew that the three men would rise up and try to conspire against Daniel. But Daniel did not let that stop him from communicating with his Father in heaven. Daniel was eventually thrown into the lion's den for his integrity to follow after God's laws, but when Daniel entered the lion's den, it wasn't so much a prayer to God that changed the course of action; it's what Daniel did that made the course of action move in Daniel's favor. And that, my friend, is a word that Daniel walked out by faith: integrity. When we know whose we are as opposed to who we are, the enemy would form whatever weapon he wants to form against us and devise whatever plans he may have. The truth of the matter is, God saw it happening way before we did. God already sees the battle won for us. All we have to do is walk with integrity and let God handle the rest. Just picture for a moment the enemy standing right in front of you with a gun aimed right at your heart. What the enemy lacks is the knowledge to fully comprehend that God already caused the bullets in that gun to disintegrate and dissolve. While he is left standing with an empty gun in his hand, you are off celebrating the victory that has been won for you.

The bigger our dreams are, the bigger challenges you and I will face. The bigger challenges we face, the bigger the victory will be. That is the frame of mind every believer should walk in, in order to put the enemy in his place. God has allowed us and will continue to allow us to face difficult challenges so we would cry out to him and solely depend on him for help. Joseph's brothers really thought this would be the end of Joseph's life, but little did they know, they were only helping Joseph get to his God-given destiny. How ironic is it that while the enemy thinks he has the upper hand, God has us in the palm of His hands!

While nine of Joseph's brothers conspired to kill Joseph, one rose to stand in the gap and intercede for Joseph's life. Reuben was the firstborn of Jacob. This is another clear picture of Christ Jesus, the firstborn among God's children, to rise from the grave and stand in the gap and intercede for us when the enemy sought to destroy our lives.

Romans 8:34 says, "*Who is he who condemns? It is Christ who died and furthermore is also risen, who is even at the right hand of God, who also makes intercession for us.*"

So instead of Joseph's brothers shedding innocent blood, they decided to strip Joseph of the colorful tunic his father made for him and put Joseph into a dark dry well, where Joseph would await his time until God moved him to the next chapter of his life. Are you going through a similar situation much like Joseph? Have your enemies stripped you of your shame and pushed you with envy into a place where you feel stuck? Do you feel like it's all over from here, like there is no way out? This was God's plan for Joseph, not to cause Joseph harm but to fulfill His will through Joseph. His brothers hated him, and for that reason, he was forced to become separated from his brothers; but God already knew this would have to happen in order for Joseph's family to be saved. There is a hidden message in all of this. The word *separation* is hitting me deep down into the core of my spirit. I feel so strong by the Holy Spirit to share this revelation with you, as it is ministering to me right at this moment. I want you to imagine Christ being separated from his brothers (the Jews) because the Bible says in *John 1:11*, "*He came to His own, and his own did not receive Him.*" Then in *John 18:36*, "*Jesus answered, 'You say rightly I am a king. For this cause, I was born, and for this cause I have come into the world, that I should bear witness to the truth. Everyone who is of the truth hears my voice.'*" And in *John 19:14–16*, it says,

> *Now it was the preparation day of the Passover, and about the sixth hour. And he said to the Jews, "Behold your king!" But they cried out, "Away with Him, away with Him! Crucify Him!" Pilate said to them, "Shall I crucify your King?" The chief priests answered, "We have no king but Caesar!" Then he delivered Him, took Jesus to them to be crucified. Then they took Jesus and led Him away.*

Whenever I meditate on the word of God, I also come to the conclusion that God has always manifested Himself throughout every event, situation, and tribulation. God has always shown up and made Himself known. We saw God's hand show up to save Abraham and Jacob; and now we are seeing a magnificent manifestation of Joseph being separated from his father and hated by his brothers, who mocked him and wanted him as a dead man. But just like Pontius Pilate did not want to crucify this just man, Ruben stood up in the gap for Joseph, saying, "Let us not kill him. Shed no blood but." Joseph's brothers hated him so much that they sought every way to destroy his life, not knowing that, just like the Pharisees sought to get rid of Jesus, God's plan was already in effect and in motion. When Joseph was brought to Egypt by the Midianites and was separated from his father, the Bible says (in Genesis 37:34) that Jacob tore his clothes and mourned for many days. This is without a doubt another great picture of God tearing down the veil and weeping for His son, as His Son had to become separated and stand in the gap to save us from our unjust ways. I am truly amazed and blown away by how every puzzle piece of God's word fits perfectly together even though at times things just don't make sense. But that's where our faith comes into action. When we begin to see God's will unfold before our very eyes, our faith will grow, and the fountain of God's living water will cause an overwhelming joy to rise up from within our very souls. This is the moment God is telling you to trust in the plans that He has for you. *"For I know the thoughts that I think towards you, says the Lord, thoughts of peace and not of evil, to give you a future and a hope"* (*Jer. 29:11*). It may seem dark now, but help is on the way!

CHAPTER 4

You May be out of the Hole but Not Out of the Process Just Yet!

> *And they sat down to eat a meal. Then they lifted their eyes and looked, and there was a company of Ishmaelites, coming from Gilead with their camels, bearing spices, balm and myrrh, on their way to carry them down to Egypt. So, Judah said to his brothers, "What profit is there if we kill our brother and conceal his blood? Come let us sell him to the Ishmaelites, and let not our hand be upon him, for he is our brother and our flesh." And his brothers listened. The Midianite traders passed by, so the Brothers pulled Joseph up and lifted him out of the pit and sold him to the Ishmaelites for twenty shekels of silver, and they took Joseph to Egypt. (Gen. 37:25–28)*

As Joseph was probably crying and begging them to take him out, they were all sitting and eating. Is that not just like the enemy to go ahead and count his victory before the real battle even begins? While the enemy is sitting back thinking it's all over for you and me, God is just getting started with bringing us through to the next level of our lives. You and I (at some point in our lives) may find ourselves in the same place as Joseph, and we may feel like the enemy has the last laugh, but that is far from the truth. Boy, do I know about being cast out or being forced subliminally out of something you've longed to be a part of, but for some odd reason, people doubt your ability or capability to do what it is you were called to do on this earth.

Well, here it goes. I've had my share of rejection as a child, but I never thought in a million years this could take place where we are supposed to build one another up and encourage one another in the faith. Where God has rescued me from, I have nothing but praise, honor, and glory to give Jesus Christ. Remember when I spoke earlier about my youthful years of becoming bitter, angry, and rebellious? After I had my close and personal encounter with Christ, I began attending church; and soon began to realize, as I worshipped the creator of heaven and earth, that I started to feel once again that same passion I felt when I was a young child. But this time I was fully aware of what it meant to worship God in spirit and in truth. All I kept imagining while I worshipped Christ was me prostrated before His throne, giving Him all the praise, honor, and glory for all He has done. I felt my soul wanting more and more of His presence, and so I continued attending church in Huntington and became a member. I really started pursuing my faith in Christ like never before. I had received Christ into my heart in New Bern, North Carolina. But it wasn't until I started attending church in my hometown that I really started surrendering my faith to the Lord. I remember it like it was yesterday. My pastor and his wife picked me up to go to church one Sunday morning, and the pastor's wife turned around and looked at me and said, "There is a white dove above your head, and whenever you enter a room, whatever darkness or evil force is there must flee because the Lord has bestowed upon you the light of the Holy Spirit." I was probably about twenty-three years of age when my pastor's wife said those words to me. She went on to be with the Lord a year after, but while she was here on earth, the Lord ordained her a prophet. I really didn't fully understand what all that meant at the time, but I received those words into my heart, and when I did, I felt a peace that I had not felt before. So I continued to read my Bible and attend church to the point where my life now was centered and focused on Jesus. I was baptized not too long after, and the real war began to rage when I started having these horrible dreams about Satan and his fallen angels. Me coming from a musical background and then giving up my dreams and passion from pursuing secular music must have really made the enemy mad. I remember this one particular dream I had. I clearly remembered it because it was the night after I was baptized. I was in a large auditorium, and everything was white as snow. I saw far above me risers and angels singing on them. The sound was so beautiful and nothing like I had ever heard before. Then suddenly from a distance, I saw a black image high above swooping across the room. When I looked at the angels, they began to take off their white robes and undress themselves. Under their white robes, they were dressed in all black, and that is when I saw the large image swoop down, almost knocking me down to the ground. As this image got closer to me, I felt my whole body become paralyzed. A force knocked me down to the ground, and I began convulsing profusely. I was mute and not able to speak. In that moment, all I could do was think about the love of Jesus Christ and what He did for me on the cross. The moment that I began trying to cry out the name Jesus, the black image picked me up and slammed me on a table, then began tossing me back and forth. I was crashing into walls left from right, and just when I thought death was near, I let out a huge shout and cried out with all that was left within me the name of Jesus Christ. Immediately after, everything that was causing me pain left in the blink of an eye, and all I felt was an unexplainable love that ran deeper than any ocean or canyon on this earth. I felt so loved and filled with joy at that moment, like my heart was going to burst right out of my chest (in a good way). I saw three doors in front of me, and I heard a voice that said, "The door you pick will be the door that leads to your destiny." I immediately chose the middle door, and as the door swung open, I saw the most beautiful view that no camera could ever capture in one shot. The one thing that stood out to me the most was this enormous waterfall. Its top drew all the way to heaven, and its crystals shined brighter than anything I ever saw on this earth. The trees were so green, and the birds were amazing to behold. The colors of the scenery were so bright and full of life. As I began to walk through the door, that is when I woke up from my dream. All I could do at that moment was call on the name of Jesus and seek comfort. I believe God permitted that dream to let me know that the evil one would stop at nothing to try and destroy my life but as long as I stand fast in my faith in Jesus Christ, I would have the protection of the Holy Spirit all the days of my life.

After about a year, I moved in with my daughter's great-grand-mother, and I started attending church in Brentwood. I began seeking God like I never did before. I would attend every service they had on Thursdays, Saturdays, and Sundays. I would attend church house services. All I wanted to do was live and breathe in the presence of God. I ended up meeting my husband in church, and soon after, we got married. We had three beautiful children. I began singing and worshipping the Lord when I was given a special to sing at the services. I was given opportunities to sing and be a part of the praise-and-worship team. All seemed so wonderful and blissful until I started to encounter moments where others in the group would make comments about me, them getting upset because I was given more than two songs to sing. Just the stares alone were enough to make one uncomfortable. Going to practice was supposed to be a time of fellowship and togetherness, but instead, it felt like all we did was dispute over things that were irrelevant to the purpose of practice. I remember at one practice, there was a woman in the group who rose up with anger, saying, "Why are you just focusing on the ones who have a voice and not on those who sing in the back?" While this was not the truth at all (because I was new to the group and needed to adjust to the note and song), to her it felt like most of the time was being spent on me, and so before we knew it, the leader canceled practice for that night. I went home very confused and perplexed on what had taken place that night. There was another time at practice when another altercation had arose. I had mentioned to the group that praying for fifteen minutes before every practice would help us all be in unity and keep the enemy from trying to disrupt the worship session, but the leader of the group said, "No, that's not the problem." As soon as I heard those words, I knew that this is not where I was supposed to be. And so I went home that night and discussed it with my husband. I had also said to him that my passion for singing was leaving me, and I started to feel that pain of rejection once again. I felt like my opinions didn't matter to the group, and so I ended up leaving the group. The enemy knows the battles that we are fighting in our minds because he is the one who, nine times out of ten, begins them. And so I began singing at church with instrumentals whenever the opportunity was present. There were times when I would ask for a part, and I would get the opportunity, but I was never called up to sing. I began to feel those strong emotions of rejection come over me once again, but this time they were so strong because it was coming from those who I thought I could rely on to build me up, but all the while I was being torn down piece by piece, little by little. I started to feel like I did not fit in, like there was no place for me anywhere in this life. The pain of having to walk this road alone began taking over me. Between longing to serve in the church and finding my identity in Christ, I found myself becoming the envy of many in the church. I became misunderstood by many because as I began hearing the messages, some would make comments on the altar saying, "Those who have good voices think they have it all together," and "Worshipping isn't just about singing really good." It wasn't so much about what they said; it's when they look right at me when they say it. One time I had to get up and walk to the bathroom so no one would see the tears running down my face. At this point, I was just more wounded than I had ever been before; and so, slowly but surely, I was falling into the trap of the enemy's lies and once again started to believe, just like when I was a kid, that I was and would always remain the outcast.

When we don't deal with our inner wounds and lift them unto God, the enemy will use them against us at every opportunity. I held in so much animosity toward my brothers and sister that it was almost as if they drove me into a pit. I was headed straight for it, and I didn't even realize it. I'm pretty sure God did though. I was forced to see life for how it truly is. Even though we live in this life, whether you and I are believers or not, one thing we all have in common is, we all can either lead one's life into a pit or be forced into a pit by others. That was me, long before I knew it. I was in a dark hole filled with hate and anger toward my brothers and sisters in Christ. As I watched how they would stand on the altar week by week, I began feeling so much pain and betrayal that I had no desire to step foot into a church. I felt so distant from my purpose that I fell into a depression, and all I did was cry and weep. As I was in my pit of despair, loneliness, discouragement, bitterness, and resentment, everyone else was going about their business. While my very thoughts to myself were, *Will this pain ever go away?* and *Will I ever see the light of day shine again?* I began self-medicating myself with painkillers I had from my previous C-sections and other operations I had. I often told myself everything was going to be all right, but I knew deep down in my heart that these old wounds of rejection were beginning to manifest once again, and this was only the start of something that would lead me to a distant place, sort of like my very own trip down south or toward Egypt.

It's crazy how when we first have that encounter with God. All we want to do is tell the world about his love and awesome grace. And so we begin by reading His Word more and more, praying to Him every chance we get and just wanting to stay in His presence. But just like me, there will come a point in your life when others won't see what God has put in your path to see, because what God has placed in your grasp, others will become envious, and they will try to rip it right from underneath you, not knowing the real damage they are actually causing to the body of Christ, so I allowed the painkillers to numb my pain to the point of allowing myself to believe the lies of the enemy, that this was the only way for me to cope with life. The logical thing for me to do at the time, which was what my heart truly believed, was to keep self-medicating myself and trying to escape the root of my problems, which was the pain of rejection and longing to be loved like I saw everyone else being loved on in the church. The illogical thing for me to think (because of rejection) was to believe that one day, I would ever feel that genuine love in my life from my spiritual brothers and sisters and that I would be able to experience healing. This was a process I truly was not capable of handling all by myself, and little did I know that this process would lead me to later experience healing like I never had. And in the midst of this process, although I was hurting so much, I never stopped believing in God because through it all, I knew that if God brought me to this point—although the pain was unbearable at times—God would not turn His back on me and just leave me to fend for myself. On the contrary, this caused me to cry and shout out to the Lord for mercy and to hold and cover me in His arms of grace and comfort.

God's plan will always seem farfetched to those who are not in Christ and even to those whose faith has begun to dwindle. God tells us in *2 Corinthians 5:7*, "*For we walk by faith and not by sight*." Our faith in whatever situation we are facing will cause heaven to move on our behalf. If we put our eyes on the situation, we have already lost against the enemy. You see, the enemy works with logic, and God works illogically. Because what may seem like it is, to the enemy is not, and what seems like is not with God, it actually is. Sounds complicated right? Not exactly! When we put our mind set on things we can see, those things will eventually fail us. For example, Joseph loved his brothers, and although they hated him, he still had to work with them and see them every day. Eventually, they manifested their hate by putting Joseph in a dry dark well and left him there until traders came to take him down to Egypt. On the contrary, Joseph could not see God's hand working through all his life moments, but because God is eternal, we can trust that God will never fail us and whatever God is doing, He will always see us through to the other side. *Philip 1:6* says, "*He who has begun a good work in you will complete it until the day of Jesus Christ*." What we can see would eventually fade away with time, but what we cannot see would eventually be made manifest to us if we do not give up but endure until the end.

Rejected without Mercy, Only to be Remembered and Accepted by Grace

Did you know that even in a distant place, you can have favor from God above your enemies? Just because we are not physically yet with our Father in heaven or face-to-face with Jesus, if we are born again and followers of Christ, washed and made new through His blood, then that means we have His spirit flowing through us and His blood running through our very veins and our minds are tied to the mind of Christ. Therefore, we can do all things through Christ who strengthens us. You and I have been designed by God Himself to do great and mighty works wherever the Holy Spirit leads us. The scenario and circumstances may be different, but who we are in Christ should never change. We have been seated in heavenly places with Christ Jesus. Christ has promised us that although we have been crucified with Christ, we no longer live, but Christ lives within us. And so God, through His Son, has established our victory. No matter where God decides to take us, whether it's on the mountaintop or in the middle of the valley, we have the seal of the Holy Spirit who leads us and guides us through with mercy and favor from the Father Himself. The job of the Holy Spirit is to equip us for the challenges ahead and fill us with His wisdom and knowledge so we can fulfill and perform every task that lies ahead. Without preparation from the Holy Spirit, we would all be lost and confused as believers in Christ.

Although Joseph was in a different land, he was still the same Joseph. As he was brought into Egypt by the Ishmaelites (the Word of God says he was bought by Potiphar), Joseph knew that he was in the hands of someone who had so much authority over him; but because God was with Joseph, instead of being treated horribly, God allowed Joseph to experience success. Joseph's success was not only for Joseph to see God's hand moving in him but for Potiphar to take notice that this boy right here was no ordinary young man but a young man with integrity with a willing heart to do what was right in the eyes of God. And so for that very reason, God caused the house of Potiphar to prosper on account of Joseph's obedience toward God. Can you believe that even through all that Joseph went through with his brothers and being sold into slavery, he still maintained his integrity? This must have not been easy for Joseph one bit, but with man, it is impossible, but with God, all things are possible. Despite Joseph's rejection, he still managed to keep his peace of mind and continue walking regardless of his situation. What would our lives look like if despite our current situation we would continue walking and trusting in God's plan for our lives?

I think just about everyone on this planet has experienced a form of rejection at one point in time or another. For some, it may have not taken a toll on their lives and have managed to overcome it, while others become trapped in a whirlwind of emotions that spiral into a web of lies from the enemy. We can overcome these lies by speaking God's word over our lives. This does not mean though that everything will change just like that. In the same way, there is sowing time and harvest; so there will be waiting periods, a time when we will have to endure hardship and sometimes discomfort for a while. This is so we can experience God's love and care through the process. I know it seems like it does not make very much sense, right? I know it may seem like all is lost or like you will never make it out, but God is faithful, and in our darkest moments, God will show us the way and lead us not into temptation but deliver us from the hands of our enemies who seek to destroy us. God already knows the road that lies ahead for every one of us; and because God is all-knowing, he can also see the enemy's plan in trying to kill, steal, and destroy our purpose in God's great plan for our lives. And so God allows the enemy to revolt against us, knowing that every weapon Satan forms against the children of God never prospers, seeing as God has already gone ahead of us and made away. Just because you and I cannot see what God has already gone before us and has done for us, it does not mean that it has not already been established. *Psalm 37:23* says, "*The steps of the righteous man are ordered by the Lord.*" Joseph's brothers thought they were destroying Joseph's life by putting him in a dry well and soon after selling him off to Egypt, but what they failed to realize was they were only a mere part of God's great plan to save even their very own lives from what was to come upon the land in the latter days. Those who have rejected you now will indeed need you later. For example, the kids that are bullied in school may grow up to become lawyers who one day will represent those who have bullied others that could not defend themselves and are now in need of someone to defend them in court. Or how about a doctor or a surgeon who needs to operate on the one whom all their life in school bullied or teased others? God works in mysterious ways. We never know when God will allow the circumstances to change or turn around, but we do know that God is Almighty and does what He pleases, and whatever God does, it is never to harm us but to give us a future and a hope.

> *Now Joseph had been taken down to Egypt. And Potiphar, an officer of Pharaoh, captain of the guard, an Egyptian, bought him from the Ishmaelites who had taken him down there. The Lord was with Joseph, and he was a successful man, and he was in the house of his master the Egyptian. and his master saw that the Lord was with him and that the Lord made all he did to prosper in his hand. So, Joseph found favor in his sight and served him. Then he made him overseer of his house and all that he had he put under his authority. So it was, from the time that he made him overseer of his house and all that he had, that the Lord blessed the Egyptians house for Joseph's sake; and the blessings of the Lord was on all that he had in the house and in the field. (Gen. 39:1–5)*

Joseph was sold by his brothers to the Midianite traders passing by as they made their way down toward Egypt. Joseph was then brought by the Midianites to Potiphar, an officer of Pharaoh, captain of the guard, an Egyptian. Two things happened here: (1) God had already made way for Joseph to get out of the dry well and (2) God has placed the right person to receive Joseph when he arrives at his destination. God has our lives already figured out. He knows who will come into our lives to bring us to where we need to go and who He will use to bring us to the next level of our lives. Grace is given; grace is shown. No matter how many times we think we know how the story ends, God is sovereign, and His ways are always higher and better than our own ways. You may feel stuck right now, but not for long because God has already put the wheels in motion for you to continue moving right along on this journey called life, and the things that are hindered from us at this moment will begin to unravel as we make our way toward and through our own Egypt process. Just as Joseph made it to Egypt, so you and I will too! It may sound like something you do not want to hear about for the moment. I mean, who wants to go to Egypt, right? But I promise you that if you will continue believing in God's promises, you will see that even in your Egypt moment, favor and grace will cover you like a warm blanket on a cold winter night. If God is bringing you toward what seems like is holding you captive, remember that where the Spirit of the Lord is, there is freedom, and if you have already given your life to Christ, you have freedom within you to believe, that although it may seem like all is lost and broken, Jesus is the defender of the weak, and from these ashes, God will bring forth a beautiful beginning to your victory. The test of trials is not to see if we can stand through the storm, but to believe in the One who is standing in the gap for us through the storm. God's mighty hands are guiding us through to the other side.

Their Disobedience Caused the Mercy of God to Rise upon You like the Rising Sun

Every calling and gift from God regarding Joseph was inside of Joseph; it just wasn't the right time for his calling and gifts to be manifested just yet. You and I have gifts and a calling, but that doesn't necessarily mean that they will manifest fast and easy. Joseph wasn't ready to operate in the calling and his gifts just yet because before he could discover them, he needed those who did not understand his calling to revolt against him. There is a great point as to why it is necessary for those who do not understand what God is doing in their life to revolt against you and you're calling. Because of Joseph's brother's disobedience, Joseph has been led away to Egypt but along with Joseph, his calling and gifts went with him as well. When God allows your enemies to drag you down to the valley, he doesn't take away from you the calling that is upon your life. More so, God is using what the enemy meant for evil to turn it around for His greater good. The Bible says in Romans 11:29, "For the gifts of God are irrevocable." No matter how much the enemy tries to make you think that you have no one to put your trust in because you have been betrayed one too many times, that's when you have to remember with all of your heart that God is listening and wants you to talk to Him so He can speak to you and comfort you and let you know that His ways are higher than our ways and His thoughts about what He is doing in us are far greater than our own thoughts.

The Bible does not give a reference as to Joseph's attitude toward his brothers putting him in a dry well and then selling him as a slave to the Egyptians, but we can just imagine how Joseph must have felt. If we truly look at the overall picture of what happened to Joseph at that moment, we will see another revealing picture or a foreshadow of what was to come for everyone on this earth, not just for the Jews as a nation but for us as gentiles as well. I just love how even though we may think we have an understanding of the scriptures, God stops us and says, "Child of mine, I have something I want to show you." As I was typing just now, I felt from the Holy Spirit to share this with you. From the beginning, Joseph's brothers hated Joseph and despised his very presence because Jacob their father loved Joseph very deeply and more than all the others. This made them very angry, and so they devised a plot to get rid of Joseph by putting him into slavery and making him feel ashamed and alone. Although Joseph was kept in Egypt against his very own will, God still had a calling on Joseph's life, and He had deposited in Joseph gifts to be utilize when he was in Egypt. There was a specific reason Joseph was enslaved yet still free at the same time. Perhaps God, in His infinite mercy, was trying to tell us something through this chapter or season of Joseph's life. Our view of what God has done in Joseph's life has become very dim compared to what God is trying to point out here. Jacob loved his son Joseph more than the others, and for that reason, this put a target on Joseph's life and made his brothers hate Joseph. In the very same way, God loves us and has chosen and anointed us for great and mighty works. Thus, we have become a target for the enemy and his fallen angels. Satan has become enraged with us because he knows that as God has called us. He has also equipped us for our calling. Joseph going to Egypt was not only preparation but a metaphor. Just like Joseph had to come out of the well and enter Egypt, so did we when we came out of our mother's womb and entered this sinful world. This was a major turning point for Joseph because Joseph had no idea that the favor from God that was bestowed upon him would bring him, later on, to fully understand why Joseph was used by God to stand in the gap for his people. You and I are still alive today because regardless of what the enemy has tried to do to destroy our life, God has fought our battles time and time again so that one day when it's all said and done, you will be the one, just like Joseph, to stand in the gap for whomever God has called you to intercede for, whether it is your family, country, or nation. After experiencing betrayal, rejection, and loneliness and allowing God to heal you in all those wounded places, you will rise up in the strength of the Lord to do what you have been called to do, and that is to brings those who have been living in darkness toward the light so they can repent and realize that what they thought was turning for their worst moment actually turned them around for their greatest encounter with the Savior of the world, Jesus Christ. You and I were called to bring the lost and confused to Christ. Yes! That means even those who caused you to end up where you are now. When God raises you up like He did Joseph, you'll have them to thank for doing what they did to you, and they'll have you to thank for helping them understand what true repentance and forgiveness looks like. Remember what the scripture says in *Romans 8:28*, *"All things work together for good to those who love God, to those who are called according to His purpose."*

When we are obedient to God, what was already established by God will come to pass. When we are disobedient toward God, what God created with reason will befall us, to let us know what is good was formed out of nothing but what is bad and evil was created for a reason. What God forms is good for us, and that which He created was for Satan and his fallen angels that had chosen to rebel against God. *Isaiah 45:7* says, *"I form the light and create darkness, I make peace and create calamity; I the Lord, do all these things."* God blesses us simply because He is the blesser and shows us mercy when we don't deserve it and grace when we deserve absolutely no grace at all, because He is the One who justifies all things. We, on the other hand, are sinners and disobedient toward the things of God; and for that reason, as God made the garden of Eden for Adam and Eve's pleasure (to see them happy and enjoying one another's company, all because God is love and wants the very best for us) but have chosen to still disobey God and not take him at His word, God had to create calamity and darkness due to disobedience. Those who choose to accept and enjoy God's free gift of salvation through His only begotten Son, Jesus Christ, will partake of all that God has made for us to enjoy. Unfortunately, those who choose not to receive God's great gift of salvation will partake of the calamity that is to come upon the earth that God, with reason, has created for the sons of disobedience, only to be left in total and utter darkness that was created for Lucifer and his fallen angels in the first place.

A Place Destined for a Person Just Like You

Looking at Egypt so far has me thinking Egypt may not be so bad after all. I mean, looking at it from God's standpoint, instead of man's standpoint, makes me realize that Egypt is not just a place where Pharaohs after Pharaohs governed and dictated their rules and regulations but a place where God shows His mighty powers by letting every single person in Egypt know that He is the Alpha and the Omega, the First and the Last, the Beginning and the End. God is above all; and the God of Abraham, Isaac, and Jacob brought Joseph (Jacob's son) to a place that was destined for him to be in for such a time because only Joseph could fulfill what only God has chosen Joseph to fulfill, and that was to save and rescue his own household from what was to come upon the earth and even though his own brothers hated and rejected him and caused him to come to a place like Egypt, thinking that Joseph was living as a slave. The truth of the matter was that, although Joseph went through some pretty intense events while in Egypt, he was being led by God through every season, because in the end, God would take every pain of rejection we face and turn it into a glorious moment in time, which we all have yet to encounter, from the purpose and will God had for Joseph's life. Did it ever occur to you that God has allowed you to endure your moments of rejection and your painful process of going toward Egypt for such a time as this? Perhaps you are the one whom God is raising up to save those who are around you. I am not just writing this book simply because I wanted to write a bunch of words on a page, but I was led by God to write this book and let you know that you have been chosen by God to stand in the gap for your family, friends, brothers, and sisters that maybe you have never seen eye to eye with. God is calling you to step in the gap for them and, in the Lord, do great and mighty works, such that when they see Jesus shining through you, it will cause them to become saved and follow after Jesus. If God raised Joseph from that dry well and moved him toward Egypt, God will surely lift you up and out of where you are right now and move you toward your Egypt moment and toward your destiny that is filled with promises and favor. Regardless of where Joseph's feet were planted, God's favor was over Joseph's life. Joseph was so successful in Egypt simply because God was with Joseph. Joseph's master took notice and saw that the Lord was with Joseph, and everything that Joseph did prospered because the Lord was with Joseph. How about that! When God is in it, we will win it! We need to change our views on some things, and one of those things is how we view Egypt entirely.

I know a little something about being in Egypt (spiritually speaking) and having the favor of the Lord above my enemies (spiritually speaking) despite my circumstances—or maybe a little too much, being that I myself was forced to enter my Egypt process by my very own brothers and sisters in Christ. Sounds crazy, right? It may sound crazy, but it is all so true!

Being overlooked, unnoticed, and misunderstood really ties to how many will (whether by unintentional or tensional reasons) cause you to either run into a pit, or in my case, be thrown into a pit. As I was constantly hoping to be a part of something, I was constantly being rejected and passed over as an underdog. When I first became a member at my church, although being Puerto Rican, I never spoke Spanish because I was never brought up to speak it in my home. Throughout the years and being married to my husband, who is from Honduras, I have learned to speak Spanish quite fluently now. The church was an all-Spanish speaking church for a good while until years later it became a bilingual church for both Spanish and English-speaking members. This became an obstacle in my life because while others were preaching, teaching, and ministering, I was trying to find where I fit in all of it. Many times it was as if I was the outcast of the family, both in my family and in my spiritual family as well. I was often passed by because of my inability to speak Spanish fluently and, for some strange reason, not connecting with my sisters (outside of the church) to have that sisterly bond one should have inside and outside the church, but I remember the times God did open that door for me to speak. I do not know how, but I felt this power from God to speak in Spanish in ways I never thought I could. All I knew is that I wanted more of God's presence but was always being knocked down whenever an opportunity came around. I tried to talk to my pastor about what was going on and how I felt, like I have no purpose for being at the church, but she would tell me, "If this is where God has planted your feet, you must learn to endure what comes your way because God will use you in His perfect timing." And so until this very day (although things didn't get better from there), I still believe that. I remember one night in a service, I was on my knees praying and pouring out my heart to the Lord when suddenly, I felt a hand on my back and the whisper of someone saying to me, "The color robe of Joseph's mantle is upon you." I remember crying out to the Lord with all my heart for understanding because it was becoming all too confusing to me how those whom I love would treat me so unkindly and so unjustly. Not being included and being rejected forced me to fall into a dry well and then be carried off to Egypt. Being rejected and brought toward my own Egypt process was not the most confusing part for me; it was not being able to figure out why this was happening to me. Until now I kept pointing the finger at those who have done me harm when all along God was pointing the finger at me, letting me know that He has permitted these things to occur so He can establish His perfect will in me. I was blinded and robbing myself of seeing the truth.

My friend, brother, or sister who is reading this book right now, when you find yourself trying to blame others for your life's journey, remember, although God does not orchestrate the bad things that take place in this life, He can surely use it and help see us through the storms of life. All God ever wanted us to experience is His freedom, whether that is freedom of redemption, freedom from your past, freedom from your guilt, freedom from your shame, freedom from those who have done you harm, freedom of forgiveness, and the list goes on and on. God's amazing grace and mercy is never-ending, and if we will truly stop and think of the many times we should have perished, we will see God's hand delivering us from that harmful situation. God knew that Joseph could not stay in that dry well for long, and that's why God already made way for Joseph to enter the next phase of his extraordinary life. This was only the beginning of Joseph's life. This is only the beginning of yours as well.

My Egypt process and your Egypt process may look a little different, but one thing I am sure of, when we find ourselves in Egypt, the favor of the living God never comes to an end. He always shines forth for all to see that He who lives within us is greater than he who is in the world. Among the many people living on this vast planet, God has chosen you and me to fulfill His purpose, and although weeping may endure for a night, joy comes in the morning. Even though they mocked Jesus at the cross, Jesus still chose to forgive them and extended his grace and mercy. Even in a place like Golgotha, where Jesus was crucified, God's mercy and favor were still in that place. No matter how dark your life may seem, God can always use it to His advantage.

Valleys Are a Part of Our Seasons

The Lord is my shepherd; I shall not want. He makes me to lie down in green pastures; He leads me beside still waters. He restores my soul; He leads me in the path of righteousness for his name's sake. Yea, though I walk through the valley of the shadow of death, I will fear no evil; for you are with me; your rod and your staff, they comfort me. you prepare a table before me in the presence of my enemies; you anoint my head with oil; My cup runs over. Surely your goodness and mercy follow me all the days of

61

my life; and I will dwell in the house of the Lord
forever. (Ps. 23:1–6)

This particular psalm has been dear to my heart ever since I can remember. When I read this psalm for the first time, I was in a friend's house, and the beginning of this psalm was written on a magnet on her refrigerator. I couldn't help but keep staring at it and wondering why it said, 'The Lord is my shepherd I shall not want." "I shall not want," I kept repeating these words in my mind over and over again. It just did not make sense to me at all. I mean, how can you claim something is yours but not want it? I just could not stop thinking about it; and I am the type of person who, if I can't figure it out, will surely dig deeper until I find the answer. And so that's what I began doing. I looked for other versions of the Bible to help me find its interpretation. I found others that were similar but still of no help. As my last result, I went and found a children's Bible. It was there when I found its exact interpretation. It was like a light bulb lit up on the inside of my mind, and for the first time, I realized that it is in the simplest of things where we find our answers.

The Lord is my Shepard, I have everything I
need. (Ps. 23:1, children's version)

Often, we spend time looking in all the complex places to find what we are looking for, when all the answers to our questions are found in the simple places. Let us face reality. Life is hard and can become very complex and fearful at times. When moments of despair, anxiety, depression, and or even complications (from a spouse losing a job and having a financial crisis come into play, or your kids getting mixed in with the wrong crowd at school leading them to start doing drugs and drinking alcohol) is when we have to know that our solution is not found in the complexity of this world, but in the only One who is the simple solution whom we can without a doubt run toward. We can find simplicity through His yolk that is easy and whose burdens are light. He will show us that all the while we were trying to seek after empty pleasures that leaves us unsatisfied and wanting more until eventually that self-seeking pleasure leads us to a dark place, leaving us more apprehensive than before. God is saying, "In me, you will find the simplicity of what it truly means to rest in me because in me you'll have every fulfillment according to my riches in heaven." It is really that simple and true. In Christ Jesus, we have everything we could ever possibly need to get through this journey called life. The reason we cannot see the truth is that we simply choose not to. This is not a matter of being able to see what we can have, then doing everything in our power to obtain it, but seeing not and believing by faith that who we cannot see has already made a way and is waiting for you and me to straightforwardly profess that He is our shepherd. If we have the Great Shepherd by our side, we have everything our heart could ever desire.

Before we can step into our destiny, we need to be sure beyond a shadow of a doubt that the Lord God is our Shepherd and proclaim His name to the world. God needs to be our way in and our way out. This must be our declaration from minute to minute, hour to hour, day by day, year by year, decade to decade, and from generation to generation. David did not say the Lord is a shepherd but "my shepherd," meaning to belong to another who takes possession of one's life. You and I have been given the immense privilege of being called God's flock of sheep and a greater privilege to declare Him as our great shepherd (*Heb. 13:20–21*). Only those who hear his voice come and follow Him when He calls. Not only do we hear his voice and come when He calls, we also have the privilege to be able to communicate with our Shepherd as well. *John 10:27* says, "*My sheep hear my voice and I know them, and they follow me.*" The God of heaven and earth wants to communicate with us. He wants us to always depend on Him for everything because He is Jehovah Jireh, our provider.

The first step to having a relationship with the Creator is simply turning away from our own sinful life and coming to the knowledge of the cross. Jesus died for our iniquities that all should not perish but have everlasting life. You may very well be in the middle of a storm right now, not knowing what to do. Or you might have lost a loved one and think, *I don't think I will ever get through this*. You may have lost your way in life and think you can never recover from life's downfalls. Maybe you've lost your identity and think you will never find who you are. I have great news! Jesus knows when the storm will end. Jesus knows when you will stop grieving over your loved ones. Jesus knows when the struggles of life will become easier for you to handle, and Jesus most certainly knows your identity because He is the one who made us and predestined us to become someone great on this earth. What we need is to confess Jesus as Lord and Savior and allow the Great Shepherd to rule, reign, and lead us through this life. All Jesus longs for is a relationship with us. He wants us to call upon His name when we feel sad, happy, depressed, sorrowful, joyful, or downcast. Whether in moments of rejoicing or despair, God wants us to acknowledge Him in all aspects of our lives. Making Jesus a daily part of our lives will cause us to see the greater picture. Just analyze for a moment a shepherd leading his flock of sheep. He makes sure they are together, healthy, and attentive to his voice. In that very same way, Jesus, being our Shepherd, only longs to see His flock of sheep together, healthy, and attentive to His voice. The greatest part about all of this is that God promises to never leave us nor forsake us. So when we lose our way or even our identity, with Jesus being the great Shepherd, He will come to find us and bring us back to Himself.

CHAPTER 5

The Enemy and His Followers Have First-Row Seats to Your Victorious Play Called the Victory Is Mine in Jesus's Name!

D o you know that even in the valley you can still have peace? Do you know that even in high waters you can still rest assure that God is with you? Did you know that even in your brokenness God can still restore that which was broken? David in his psalm says, "Yea, though I walk through the valley of the shadows of death, I will fear no evil." But before David mentions the valley, he says, "The Lord makes me lie down in green pastures, He leads me beside the still waters, He restores my soul, He leads me down the path of righteousness." I want you to pay close attention to this next verse because this is the key that unlocks our minds to our understanding. The next verse says, "Yea, though I walk through the valley of the shadow of death, I will fear no evil…" Here it comes! "For you are with me." These are the keywords of acknowledgment that David professed: once in the beginning when he opened his psalm and now in the middle of his psalm. Professing Jesus as our Shepherd is not just a one-time shot. This is continuous and constant. From our highest moment of triumph to our lowest moments of trials, only let our valley moments bring us into a more profound intimacy with God. For His name's sake, everything that God does is simply because He is righteous and will never give us more than we could ever handle.

God knows what we all go through, and for that reason, He will make Himself known, not because of anything we could ever do but what He has already done for us. His righteous act of sending His only begotten Son (Jesus) to die on the cross has paid the way for us to walk through the valley of the shadows of death and not fear, to see the waves of life rising higher than that which our own capacity cannot withstand and still not let us drown, or see trouble coming our way and have God tell us to lie down in green pastures. You see, we capture only a glimpse of a picture that is entirely too big for us to comprehend in one moment. God is omniscient. He knows the end to our beginning because He can see far into our future and knows what we will have to endure just to reach our highest potential in life. Trusting not in the things of this world and putting our trust in God will set us up for a victorious life through Christ Jesus.

The enemy knows the potential that lies within every one of us. That's why his mission is to paralyze us and keep us far from God's plans for our lives. When we make that choice to trust in God, even when we find ourselves in the valley, what God does for us in the valley is found in the very next verse of *Psalm 23:5*, "*You prepare a table before me in the presence of my enemies; you anoint my head with oil; My cup runs over.*" When we are at a table, the first thing that comes to my mind is sitting. God allows us to sit at a table that has already been prepared for us even before we got to the valley because that's His way of letting us know, He has all things prepared for us and all we have to do is come and sit at the table and enjoy with thanksgiving all He has predestined for us to enjoy. The place we least expect God to do the impossible is where He is waiting for you to come and sit so He can show us that even in the valley, He can multiply your blessings and give us a place to sit as the Lord God turns our valley moments into a victorious moment. Everything that you and I will ever need is found right in the hands of our Creator. With God, we will never lack a thing. God is never taken away by the situations at hand or the circumstances of where we find ourselves heading toward because He is the God of heaven and earth, and all its fullness belongs to Him. This reminds me of a story in the book of Luke chapter 9. Jesus had sent his disciples out and had empowered them to preach the kingdom of God and to heal the sick. So they all departed from there and went through the towns preaching and healing everywhere. The Bible says when they came back to Jesus, they told Him everything that had been done. Jesus took the disciples to a deserted place, but when the multitude heard this, they followed Jesus and the disciples. Jesus received the multitude and spoke to them about the kingdom and healed those who had need of healing. Around when nightfall had begun, the twelve disciples said to Jesus, "Send the multitude away, that they may go into the surrounding towns, country, and lodge and get something to eat for where we are is a deserted place." Jesus simply replied, "You give them something to eat." The disciples had no idea what Jesus meant or what He was trying to tell them because their reply was, "We have no more than five loaves of bread and two fish unless we go and buy food for all these people, for there are about five thousand men." Here comes the point of why I am telling you this story. Jesus says to his disciples, "*Make them sit down* in fifty," and they did so. Jesus then took the loaves of bread and fish, blessed and broke them, and gave them to the disciples to set before the multitude. After, there were twelve baskets left over. When we speak about the kingdom of heaven, we must understand something very vital: heaven is a real place, and heaven does not stay still. Heaven is always moving and breathing. The kingdom of God moves within us by faith. If we will just learn to move and operate in heaven's realm, we too can experience God's miracles in those deserted places where we think it's impossible for us to see the kingdom of God at work. Notice Jesus told the disciples to tell the multitude to sit. As we experience our own miracles from God, we need to also let others know about the miracle of being still and knowing that He is God. So many people are hungry for the Word of God, but they have no idea that God wants to show up in their deserted lives and bring them through their valley moment. Let us in the here and now understand one thing: God wants to meet us wherever he chooses to meet us. And if that is in the valley, then trust that God wants you and me to enter and sit as He shows up, illuminating the table He has prepared for you to partake of in the presence of your enemies. Our enemies must watch as God Himself anoints our head with heaven's oil and make our cup run over with heaven's fountains of living water that contain the vitamins of joy, gladness, laughter, singing, and dancing. And in all this, the enemy is having to watch right before his very eyes all that God is doing. If there is something I have learned in this life, it's not when we enter the valley or how we get to the valley, it's simply how we react going through the valley. How will you and I react when we find ourselves going through the deep valley? Will we still give thanks to God knowing that He is in this with us; or will we give in and let the enemy steal, kill, and destroy our hope? The choice is up to us, but as for me, I choose to allow my valley moments to bring out the best in me. As we worship our way through the valley and allow God to show us toward the table, our valley season will surely turn into our mountain season, and as we look toward heaven, we will give shouts of praise to the Lord our God for such a victory that rises high above our enemies. This is what God does for all those who place their trust in His plan. In fact, I have experienced what it was like to go from the valley to the mountain. This truly was none other than a move of God.

I remember back when I was working as a driver's assistant at a bus company. One day the bus driver and I were bringing elementary school kids back from school to their homes when all of a sudden, a boy had to use the bathroom and could not hold it. So the bus driver pulled over and opened the door to let the kid urinate outside. This was a huge violation and an automatic call for me and the bus driver to be dismissed from the company. On that day our supervisor was making her rounds, checking that all bus drivers were doing their routs correctly. It just so happened that our bus was being followed that day. After the boy came back on to the bus, so did our supervisor. Boy, did she reprimand us harshly. The only thing I knew to do was stay silent and say nothing. When we got back to the yard, I was immediately called into the office and was told not to come into work the next day and that I was suspended from work. Of course, I was upset, but when I got home, I closed myself in my room and began to praise and worship the name of the Lord and shout for joy and laugh because I kept reminding myself that He who lives within me is greater than he who is in the world. It wasn't soon thereafter that my mother knocked on my door and said to me, "The bus company is on the phone." Then she told me, "You are about to lose your job, and you're in your room praising God." She handed me the phone, and I remember my supervisor telling me I can come back to work the next day. Why am I telling you this? Because when we find ourselves in the valley of the shadow of death (about to lose our job, a spouse leaves, your house is going up for foreclosure, or you find out a family member was diagnosed with a terminally ill disease), as hard as it may seem for us to comprehend, it is not for us to become discouraged. On the contrary, it is for us to put our faith into action and believe that even in the toughest situations that may be out of our complete control, when we allow God to pour out His anointing and allow him to fill our cup until it runs over, all He asks in return is that no matter where we find ourselves in life, whether on the summit or in the valley, we never let our praise cease but rise up stronger with every waking moment of our lives. God uses the platform we stand on to let the enemy know that he has landed on God's territory because, in fact, the valleys do not belong to the enemy but to God. Wherever we find ourselves, remember we were meant to be there!

I believe it is more fascinating to me when God shows up just when it feels like it's all over and the enemy thinks he has won. It's kind of like when you're watching an action movie. Toward the end, it really feels like the enemy had the final scene. Then suddenly, out of nowhere, the superhero comes out with a supernatural strength to put to death the enemy once and for all. That is exactly what Jesus did when we were without hope.

Before Jesus came to this earth over two thousand years ago, every one of us was lost in sin, and sin was taking its toll on the human race. Jesus Christ, being the Son of God, came down from heaven to show us the way unto salvation and became the living sacrifice we all need in order to save us from Satan's evil power. The enemy knows that without the sacrifice of a Lamb, there would be no forgiveness of sins for humanity. Before Jesus came in the flesh, the only people who could go into the holy of holies were the priest and the high priest of the Leviticus lineage. Every year the high priest would make an atoning sacrifice, first, for his own sins and then the sins of God's people. God's people often (too many times than not) fell into their own sins and always found themselves given over to their enemies as a result. Satan knows God's people would never live entirely by the laws of God because he is the one who comes to deceive the nations and make war with God's people. He knows the morals and ethical laws of God, but he chose to rebel against God, and for that reason, he has chosen to become the source of the main issues that are going on to this day. The enemy will always try to deceive us into making us think he has the upper hand. His main mission is to keep us from seeing the light by keeping us in the dark. The enemy knows if he can get us to stay in the dark, we will never see the light, and in turn, we would never know the truth, let alone walk in the truth for that matter. When Jesus came to this earth, He put the enemy's lies and deceptions to shame by making a spectacle of Satan on the cross. The heroic act of Jesus that took place at the cross was only the beginning of something far greater than even our own minds could ever comprehend. Jesus, being in a tomb for three days, went down to Sheol, took the keys from Satan; and by the power of the Holy Spirit, the Son of God was resurrected on the third day with power and authority, putting the enemy to shame. Now this truth that every believer who comes to Christ has come to know has set us free from the bondage we were once in. We now have the boldness to face this life head-on knowing that the one who came to deceive the nations has no more power to deceive us any longer. The enemy's kingdom has already fallen, and the kingdom of God has already been established in every believer's heart. We have freedom living within us (His name is Jesus) who lets us know that in this life, we may go through so many trials and tragedies, but if we are standing on the solid foundation who is Christ Jesus, we have all the stability we need as believers to keep pressing forth until Christ returns for His bride. Until that day comes, continue pressing forth in the freedom that Christ sacrificed His very own life to give us, because, as scripture says in *2 Corinthians 3:17*, "*Now the Lord is the Spirit; Where the Spirit of the Lord is, there is freedom.*" Amen!

Have you ever received something you thought, *There is no way I could have ever possibly deserved this?* You are right! Have you felt within your heart so much gratitude that your only thought is, *Only God could have done this*? You are so right again! I want to let you know that sometimes God will cause blessings to pour out on our behalf because God is letting us know who He truly is. He is Jehovah Jireh, the blesser, the giver of life, the one who goes above and beyond all measures to give His children all that our heart desires if you and I will delight ourselves in being in his presence. God's goodness is all around us, but we must recognize it, and when we do even in the bad or the worst of times, we will begin to encounter His mercy. To walk in obedience with the creator of heaven and earth is a choice we all must make. Walking in compliance and conformed to his will won't always be easy, but with God leading the way, we are sure to receive His reassurance of who He is whenever we start to lose hope or feel down. God shows us mercy because he wants us to walk in obedience according to His word, and when we do, we will experience the greatest joy and peace like never before.

A Valley Stream Leads to Something Far Greater Than a Canyon

Through the many years of facing difficulties and hard times, I found that every move we make, whether big or small, right or wrong always leaves an imprint of that moment. Our life choices are based upon our actions and our actions are based upon our beliefs, and our beliefs are based upon our determination to seek what is true. The Word of God is the road map that leads us to everlasting life. As we continue walking, we find that the journey in seeking God and living according to His will is not always a walk in the park. It is the exact opposite. When we truly live out our lives for Christ, we will have days when we feel like nothing is happening when so much is happing in God's eyes, and sometimes we will encounter what looks like a setback at times but actually it's God setting us up for a greater victory ahead, and sometimes when we think we have it all together, life throws us a curveball, and that's when we have to learn to stop take a deep breath and bring all matters to our Heavenly Father, who is on His throne just waiting for us to present our petitions before

Him. When we lay our burdens down at the feet of Jesus and cast all our cares upon our Heavenly Father, all these things are setting us up (not back) for a greater purpose in life. Because within the good, the bad, and the ugly, our experiences will mark a difference in our lives and in those around us if we hold fast to the Word of God!

There is a river that runs deep. This river has the power to shape and mold us into something far greater than our natural eyes can see. As we walk by faith, all that we do, say, and think should reflect the very image of God. There is One who came to pave the way, pouring out fountains of living waters, chiseling away at our imperfections, pouring out and causing the rivers of life to overwhelm us with pure anointing; and as we allow God to lead us and direct our paths, we become like streams in the middle of a canyon as God's beautiful creation for all to gaze upon. They will see that the Lord is above all, and by the sound of His voice, creation was put into existence.

Almost everyone on this planet has heard of the Grand Canyon. Its name alone should capture our attention. This canyon stands out from the many canyons on earth. The reason for my bringing up this canyon is that before this canyon became famous for its features, it had to go through a great ordeal. The Great Canyon was once made up of rivers that over the course of time became a *National Geographic* site for all to behold. This mighty canyon that held massive amounts of water slowly began its process of erosion that eventually became what it is today. I want to stress three important details regarding this canyon: (1) it is large, (2) it is deep, and (3) full of many colors. The Grand Canyon had massive amounts of water flowing throughout many regions. When massive amounts of water began pushing down on the riverbed and pressure began pushing up against the riverbanks, erosion took place, which is the process of earthen materials gradually wearing away over time. As pressure is built up by the massive amounts of water, there began the process of chiseling and carving on the river's banks, causing it to form the different elements that we see today. As the hulking waters carved the many layers we see today, we see the different layers in the canyon walls because each erosion responded in a different way, causing slopes and cliffs to form. Gazing upon the breathtaking view of the canyon, we not only see its shape but its vast beauty in all its colors. This is due to the small amounts of minerals found in the rocks of the canyon, most of which contain iron, giving it a red color. Some rocks became yellow and green. The Grand Canyon walls have stripes that represent the layers of sediment stacked on top of each other, showing the diverse image. The general color of the Grand Canyon is red, but each stratum or group of strata has a peculiar tinge of pink, gray, and delicate green; and at its depth, you might even see brown, slate-gray, and violet. As massive amounts of water began cutting channels through the layers of rocks, it caused many avenues to appear. It also left behind streams, which are the result of something massive that once came along before us to carve the many wonderful views we see and love till this day.

Why am I talking about the Grand Canyon? What does this have to do with Egypt and God? Friends, family, brothers, and sisters, this has everything to do with Jesus Christ Himself. If you keep reading, I will show you something so profound about how everything on this beautiful planet was created by Jesus, for Jesus, and through Jesus! As we gaze upon this massive planet called Earth, we can only see so far out until we see a line on the horizon. Every beautiful scenery we see is only a glimpse of how glorious our God truly is. Out of nothing, God spoke something into existence. Out of nothing, God formed something with His precious hands. Out of nothing, God sustained something with His power. You see, you and I are God's greatest creation, and being that we were born out of conception means that before we were conceived, we had no life expectancy until God the Father thought about us, and by His word, we were conceived. By His hands, we are formed, and by His power, we are being sustained on this planet called Earth.

In the beginning, was the Word, and the Word was with God. He was in the beginning with God. All things were made through Him, and without Him, nothing was made that was made. (John 1:1–3)

Before you and I came into this world, God already knew us and knew what we would be doing on earth. God has predestined every one of our lives to glorify His beautiful name; but before we can discover all that God has planned for us, we must first go through a massive process of being shaken, pressed down, and measured on all sides. This is what every believer in Christ Jesus will have to experience and endure. The effects of what was and what now has been made of because of the massive waters that ran through the Grand Canyon, we see a beautifully carved portrait of God's glory in His creation. If God took the time to recreate something that was so massively submerged in mighty waters, how much more will God take the time to recreate our lives that have been submerged under the massive trials and crises we have all undergone in this life? No matter how difficult our lives may get, God always knows what He is doing. For us to view the entire picture, we must first learn to endure the process of reformation. It may feel like the pressure is being built upon all sides, but it's only God's way of breaking off bits and pieces of what God Himself is chiseling away at because he knows this is what is going to cause the right piece to fall in line with all the other necessary pieces that have endured throughout the process.

Take Joseph's life for example, before God could ever allow his family to see the fullness of God's grace and mercy, Joseph had to go through a heavy process and endure many obstacles that only Joseph would have the capability to endure. Joseph emerged in loneliness and rejection and was forced to remain in a dark well for a time until he was brought to Egypt, only to be pressured by Potiphar's wife to do something immoral (a temptation Joseph never fell into); and although Joseph was put into prison for such false accusations, this was God's way of reforming and preparing Joseph for a future filled with beauty for ashes, dancing for mourning, and laughter for sorrows. In life, what may look or seem common on the surface of things is put through the process of being refined until all that is left standing is a breathtaking view of what God reformed and recreated in us. All will come and see that the good works God began in us He is faithful to complete. And now when everyone looks at you and me, they will glorify the One true living God through your testimony and my testimony of how God reserved you, just like He did with Joseph, and promote you and me to a place of honor and not shame.

Kept and Preserved for Such a Time as This!

The path we are walking on may have its difficulties; but overall, if God is the one directing our path, rest assured that no matter the difficulties that lie ahead, He will give us the strength to endure if we trust in His word and have faith. We live life not knowing what is up ahead. We can plan and still not know how everything will fall into place. We may have an idea, but we will never really know the outcome until we arrive. Sometimes things are planned out for the best but can turn for the worst very quickly. When we have a dream or a vision, we tend to think for some reason that to get to that dream or vision, we won't have to face the hard reality that with a dream comes dream killers and with a vision comes vision stealers. For example, when Joseph had those two dreams, I could have just imagined Joseph thinking, *I am going to gain respect from my brothers once they hear what God has shown me*. But boy, was Joseph in for a rude awakening when he discovered that his brothers hated him more, saying, "Do you truly think that we would ever bow down to you?" How hard it must have been for Joseph to know and understand his dreams but having yet to go through the tough process of enduring the greatest battles of his life. You and I have been chosen and destined for something great, but along with great dreams come great trials and afflictions. Everything on this earth belongs to God, and if we are on this earth, we will have to go toward or pass through them—yes, even the territories that are not always the easiest to pass through. When God causes us to reside in a place (for a time) that may seem dark and lonely, just remember this too shall pass and your greatest victory lies closer than you think.

There are places that we look at and think, *God could never use me where I am* or *Where I am God could never raise me up to establish His work* or *In the condition I am in, God would never want to use me*. It's in those moments when God is saying, "Press into my Spirit. Seek me in every way, and I will show you who I am. I will begin to do great and mighty works through you. By my Spirit, you will begin to do and see unimaginable works." God often causes us to look deep inside ourselves to see the most prized possession that lies within our very being. God is not looking at our capabilities or incapabilities. As a matter of fact, God is always working off His ability to establish His mighty works through us. The center of our attention should never be focused on whether we can follow through or not but on following the one who can see us through our darkest moments, because the One who has brought us thus far has promised us that He would never leave us nor forsake us. So we, as children of the Most High God, can stand with boldness and say, "The Lord is my helper. I will not fear. What can man do to me?" (Heb. 13:5–6).

God is about to take your darkest season and turn it into your brightest season. Everything that has happened to you thus far is because God has allowed it to come to pass. Even God knows that without trials, there's no triumph. Don't worry as God Himself has already counted your steps and knows the intent of your heart. He has already established His very work in you and has declared over your life the good works the Lord has begun in you, and He will carry it to completion until the day of Jesus Christ's return, according to Philippians 1:6. This is where our confidence should lie: in His word. You are where you are meant to be because God has brought you forth. So whether you are going into a storm not knowing the magnitude of the raging winds that lie ahead or in the middle of the storm watching as the waves of life rise higher than you could have ever imagined or your coming out of a storm and the debris of what the storm left behind has brought you to your knees, losing everything you spent your whole life, trying to hold on to, just know that although you may feel like the storm served without a purpose, the greatest purpose the storm served was to show you just how strong you truly were to keep holding on to your faith in Christ. And in turn, the very storm that tried to knock you down would be the very storm that will carry you right into victory. And when the next storm comes, having built resilience from the last storm, you will start to look at your storm tracker as an opportunity to become a storm chaser instead. A storm tracker can only see the storm coming from afar from the Doppler radar, but a storm chaser sees the storm ahead. And no matter how big or how fierce it may look, the storm chaser faces the storm head on by chasing it down and dissecting it through different measures of methods and strategies until finally what was to be discovered while going through the storm becomes accomplished and completed by standing firm in the midst of the storm's high-velocity winds and turbulence, only proving and letting us know that if the last storm couldn't destroy us, the storms to come will have no hold over us, because He who lives within us is greater than any storm we face. And through each storm we face, we become more and more resilient and stronger, and any giant or the tallest mountain we face will have to come crashing down and disperse in a thousand pieces right before our very eyes. If you are about to face the most challenging storm, giant, or mountain in your life, remember, with God, there are no such things as accidents. And along with your most challenging storm comes your greatest victory ever to be seen, marked not just for your generation but for thousands of generations to come. You are where you are meant to be; and in due season, if you faint not, you will reap an unimaginable harvest, just like Joseph did when he found himself in Egypt's prison ward for something he never should have been there for. But God stood by his side and gave him three things: favor above his enemies, grace during adversity, and mercy in the middle of his trouble. When we acknowledge these three things and believe that God is in our midst, we begin to see the hand of God move in such a powerful way. Whether we find ourselves (figuratively speaking) in a dark and lonely well, in Egypt's prison ward, or in the palace, we can surrender the process to God and watch as he moves us from glory to glory according to His everlasting word.

Without a doubt, one of my biggest heroes in the Bible is Joseph, because this was a young man who conquered so much in his life despite the rejections from those who hated him. Joseph kept living life because God kept giving him life, and even when it seemed like all was lost with Joseph, God showed up time and time again. Joseph had every right to be upset and angry, which I'm sure he was at times; but Joseph, unlike his brothers, never held it against them or to be so angry that it would rob him of his greatest victories. Even when Joseph wanted to still hold a grudge for what his brothers did to him or for Potiphar's wife falsely accusing him of attempted rape, he must have found it deep down in his heart to ask God to release him from that grudge and remember what God did for him in the midst of betrayal and treachery. If you can keep your eyes fixed on the One who holds your future, just like God saw Joseph through to his purpose and raised Joseph to a higher power, so God will raise us up to do great and mighty works through Christ Jesus. There is a key to having success in life, there is a magnificent reaction that takes place when we discover our identity in this life. The only way we can identify with whose we are is when we surrender who we are into the hands of God.

Before we can even begin to fathom the greatness of God's goodness, we must first look at ourselves and confess that we are all broken vessels before His presence and that we need His grace and mercy to lead us all the days of our lives. We need to understand that although we see the beauty of God's creation, we will still see parts that God created through a lens that is so far yet still so close. Even what may seem plain to the natural eye, when we start to view this life through heaven's eyes, we will begin to see restoration in the places that, through the natural, could only see brokenness and desolation; whereas through the supernatural eyes, we could see conservation; and reformation; whereas through the natural and naked eye, we could only see deformation. But our God has the power to take whatever the enemy meant for evil and turn it around for the greater good. When God calls us to walk a lonely road, He not only sustains us but begins to refine us in ways we could never possibly understand. This is where faith kicks in, and we can do one of two things: we can stay put and drown in our sorrows, or we can allow those tears to become the very river that takes us to our destiny. God allows us at times to cry rivers of tears so that when we have run dry, God will say, "Now my dear daughter (or son), it's time to jump into the river of life, where all your sorrows become joy and your morning is turned to laughter." We all have the potential to enter our God-given destiny, but few are willing to step into the battlefield to fight the good fight of faith, for a destiny that has already been won for us through Jesus Christ. Abraham, without knowing his destiny, chose to trust God, not only for his destiny but the destiny of his household. Isaac chose to follow in his father's footsteps because Abraham trusted in the promises of God and saw enough in his lifetime to know that God is who He says He is and fulfills all that He has promised to fulfill. Even though Abraham had to endure Egypt for a moment, God already knew that Egypt would be a place of development and transformation. Let us think of Egypt as a waiting period wherein no matter how rough things may get in Egypt, God is turning it all around for good. Whether you are in Egypt or you're coming out, remember with God, all things are possible and that God has all the power to raise you up during chaos and use you to bring hope and light to those who need saving. All we must do is humble ourselves in the presence of God and release all those emotions that try to trap us and take us under. We release them into the hands of God, and keep the calling that is within us, asking the Holy Spirit to lead us and guide us into all truth.

There is a lesson to be learned with every chapter that comes to an end in our lives. Whether it is good or bad, we must all take a hard look at ourselves and think about who we are and what we have been created to do on this journey called life. The reason many won't recognize their calling is that they have no foundation. Do you know you can achieve everything this life has to offer and still have no direction? How many people on this earth have worked so hard to achieve rewards, money, fame, riches, cars, and so much more; but when they are alone, they are without direction? In fact, you would hear a lot of fortunate people say things like, "If it had not been for such and such, I don't know where I would be right now" or "Without such and such, I would be lost." The point is, no one in this life (whether rich or poor) has a sense of direction. If we all had a sense of direction, we would all become followers of Christ Jesus, but that isn't the case. We have all been led astray because of our own desires and our own pleasures, which in turn have caused us to become separated from the only One who can lead us back to eternal life. In the book of Genesis, the stories that we read about are filled with true life events that took place, and it all had to do with us as humans losing our way. And God, in His eternal mercy, raised up men empowered by the Holy Spirit to bring forth direction and to warn us of our evildoings. God has always been there for us, pointing us back in the right direction, but the problem is, we've become so consumed with where we are trying to get to that we miss where God is trying to point us toward. Direction is the keyword here. Noah was moved by God's voice directing him to build an ark. Abraham was directed by God's voice when God told Abraham to leave his father's house and go to a place where God would make him and his descendants a blessing. Upon hearing God's voice, these men were able to rise and trust that the voice speaking to them was the leading director of all time who would lead not only them but the generations to come into all truth—all because they chose to walk in obedience, trusting that the voice speaking to them was none other than the voice of the Holy Spirit (God Himself). We will encounter so many moments when it will be hard to hear the voice of God since we are constantly at war with the mind's battlefield. But when we have Christ living inside of us, we will always find that still, small voice that has the power to triumph over a thousand voices telling us, "Do not fear for I Am your God. Do not be afraid for your help draws near." And when we learn to be still and know that He is God, we will begin to see and hear all that God is trying to tell us through His unchanging Word. Maybe you have gone through something so tragic in your life, causing heartache and suffering, and it brought you to a moment or season of not being able to hear God's voice. Maybe you have chosen, because of the bad events that have occurred in your life, to purposely block out the voice of God from your life. Whatever the case may be, just know that even when we stop pursuing God, He never stops pursuing us. God has one mission, and that is to bring us back into His loving arms through Jesus Christ's sacrifice on the cross, so He can embrace us and communicate with us through His Word. God is never caught off guard by our trials and afflictions. On the contrary, if we make that choice (and as hard as it may be) to release our hurt, pain, struggles, faults, and failures, God will begin to heal us and cause us once again to hear His still, small voice as He whispers gently to us, "I have never left you nor have I forsaken you. The plans I have for your life are not to harm you but to give you hope and a future."

God knows the process we all will have to face before we can reach our destiny. God's plan for our lives will never be to harm us or to see us destroyed but to let us know that when these unfortunate events occur, He is the first one on the scene, willing and ready to revive us and take us through our healing journey. The moment we find ourselves in a situation where it seems impossible, that should let us know that God, who is the creator of heaven and earth, is waiting for us to surrender the impossible state of mind for the possible state of mind, which God is able to do exceeding, abundantly above all we ask or think, according to the power that works in us. We have been given the power of the Holy Spirit to do above and beyond what our minds can comprehend, and when all may seem lost, it is never lost; it is actually found in Jesus. Just when you think it is all over, God comes through at just the right time to let us know He has been watching us this whole time, and the whole time He has been allowing certain things to occur because He knew that in the end, it would all work out for the greater good. All for His honor and glory. Just look at how the God of heaven and earth used Joseph to raise up and establish the promises of Abraham. It was not only necessary but vital for Joseph to endure everything he went through. The hurt and pain today won't compare with the joy and laughter of tomorrow. The pain was real for Joseph. The rejection of his brothers was real and tangible. The loneliness was real for Joseph. The reality of being falsely accused by Potiphar's wife was the reality of Joseph's life, but through all those unfortunate events, God showed Joseph favor above his enemies and never left Joseph's side. Not for one moment was Joseph ever abandoned by his Heavenly Father but watched over and led by God's Spirit until Joseph reached his destiny. You may think God has forgotten about you and you have been left in the dark to advocate for yourself, but if you will stop take a deep breath and believe with all your heart that God is faithful, God will always come through when we cry out and call on the name of Jesus, no matter how far gone you think you may be. God's arms are never too short to pull you up and out from where you are. He will pull you up and out and bring you to the next phase of your life, if you will be willing to do one thing: never give up in believing God's promises for your life.

We all have a place in our minds that we would love to get to someday. For some, it may seem so close, while for others, it may seem so far away. And when we think about that place, whether near or far, we get happy and excited because we know that place exists, and our dream is to eventually get there one day. But there is only one problem, that before we can arrive to our dream destination, we must understand and conclude that everything in this life has three things: seed, time, and harvest. Anytime we are about to embark on a new adventure or a new chapter in our lives, we need preparation and determination to keep pursuing our goals and dreams. When we plant a seed in the ground, we won't see the manifestation of that seed right away. We know what kind of seed it is, and we know that with the proper care, it will grow to become what it was meant to be, but with all that in mind, we still forget that it must go through a process before we can see the finished results. Wouldn't it be nice to already arrive at our destination without the struggles? If you said yes, let me just say that would be the most practical answer but not the most logical one. The Word of God says in John 16:33, "In the world, you will have many tribulations, but be of good cheer, I have overcome the world." We all have a battle that we face every day of our lives, and it rages against us and tries to pull us away from God's purpose. The type of battles we face is like no other battle. We see all around us finished works of what people all around the world have accomplished, but we don't consider the battles that took place to accomplish those works. As humans, we face, day to day, a spiritual battle of wanting to conquer ground but not stepping on the territory to claim it. We want it handed to us on a silver platter, rather than face the reality of what it truly means to treasure and value the walk of life. When Jesus came to this earth over two thousand years ago, He knew that bringing the message of salvation would be no walk in the park. Jesus already knew what He was stepping into when He made that choice to come off His throne and rescue us from our sinful ways. From the time the seed of the Holy Spirit (who is Jesus Christ) was conceived in Mary's womb, there continued the battle between God's people and Satan. The seed (Jesus Christ) came to bring heaven into existence by showing us a whole new way of living. The entire course of time on earth was being shifted as heaven's atmosphere was invading earth. But even Jesus knew that in order to bring change, there would have to be a time and space for everything to fall through according to heaven's calendar. Remember when I talked about knowing the seed but not its manifestation right away? Well, scripture tells us in John 1:11 that He (Jesus) came to His own, and His own did not receive Him. Rejecting the very seed that brings life is a very dangerous thing. Not knowing the seed that is before you can very well cost you your life. And not receiving the seed that was given to you can lead you to a life of eternal condemnation, where you will be eternally separated from God. Here in this verse, the Holy Spirit was talking about Jesus and the Jews. The Jews who saw the seed born of the Holy Spirit come into earth did not believe Jesus to be the Messiah, and so they rejected Jesus. But the verse thereafter goes on to say, "But as many as received Him, to them He gave them the right to become children of God, to those who believe in His name." This is no ordinary seed; this is the seed that gives life, the seed that has altered the course of times history. Jesus was, is, and has become the seed who God chose to become that firstborn seed that would be trampled upon, sacrificed, and put into the heart of the earth, only to be raised up, as a seed breaks forth and begins to uproot and break through the surface of the ground for all to see: the Son of Man high and lifted up, crowned in glory and everlasting truth. Jesus is our harvest and our exceedingly great reward. If the Son of God endured seed time and harvest, let us answer this question: who are we not to go through seed, time, and harvest? For us to reach our God-given potential, we will have to endure the time of the seed and the time of waiting in order to encounter our greatest times of harvest. None of us is exempt from these three rules of life, but rest assured that as God has established these three rules of life, and this goes without saying, to God be the glory, honor, and power because in and through our down south Egypt moments, we can encounter the most miraculous events God has predestined for us to endure, encounter, and enjoy if we hold fast to our faith in the Lord Jesus Christ.

God Can Use the Worst of Things to Bring Out the Best of Things

Joseph from his youth had gone through some intense moments in his life. He went from rejection to almost being killed to being sold into the hands of the Egyptians and to being falsely accused, thrown into prison, kept and held against his own will. This was pretty much his whole life growing up. But I truly believe with all my heart that God allowed the worst things to happen to Joseph to bring out the best things in Joseph, and boy, did it work. It appears, reading about Joseph's life and all he endured led him to the very place (the staging ground) that God would use to demonstrate his mighty powers through Joseph. It is almost like Egypt is the grand old opera theater and the best part is yet to come, where the great finale is just minutes away, and we are all waiting in anticipation to see the end results of what God started in Joseph that has now led up to this incredible moment that will make you cry tears of joy. We don't know why God has chosen to use Egypt many times to display his mighty powers, but as far as we know, every time God allowed Abraham to go down to Egypt or for Isaac to travel down to the south and Joseph to be left in Egypt, it wasn't to harm them but to let them know that no matter the places they needed to travel through, the Lord God Almighty was with them. God's promises to us are found in His every word. He has promised good to us. No matter the battles we face daily, if we know that God is for us, no matter what tries to come against us, the power of God's mercy will always defend us from the enemy's schemes. The enemy won't devise a scheme unless he knows the value of the potential that lies within us. Joseph was not put in the dry well before he shared the dream but after his brothers heard the dream. The enemy knows the great potential that lies within us more than we believe it ourselves. The greatest part in all this is, even when we lack courage, God always has enough to share.

We all are humans, and as humans, we are not exempt from feeling the emotions of being scared and lonely at times, and in all truth, it's not about what we feel in the moment that can take us away from stepping out and into the unknown. When it's all said and done, it really boils down to us making the mistake of holding on to those feelings and emotions of fear and letting them cripple and paralyze us from taking even one step out into the unknown. You see, because God already knows that when we are up against something bigger than ourselves, we will begin to feel the pressures of life build up; but if we know whose we are, we can quickly bounce back to the reality that God has not given us the spirit of fear but of love, power, and sound mind. We can release all—and I mean, all—the cares of the world into the hands of the almighty and all-knowing God. He will take over and become our shield and buckler, defending us from the enemy, letting him know that the enemy can certainly try, but no weapon that the enemy forms against the sons and daughters of God will ever prosper. Just because we cannot see what goes on in the spiritual realm does not mean that nothing is taking place. On the contrary, more is taking place in the spiritual realm than is taking place in the natural realm.

Those dark places or valleys that we must walk through sometimes are never dark places but places that God is illuminating for us to see that he has never left us nor forsaken us; but because of our ability to hold on to bitterness, pain, anger, resentment, and rejection, that is all we can see. And for that reason, we begin to believe we are in this alone and that God is nowhere to be found. So we stay trapped in thinking there's no hope when all along, the very place God has allowed us to be in is where our blessing in disguise has been hidden the whole time. As we continue to explore who God truly is, we will begin to realize that everything that happens on this earth happens for a reason and that every season later in our life would depend on how we react to the season we are in now.

As we journey on in this life, we are going to encounter moments where even when we are doing the right thing, others will come and tell us words that tear us down and make us feel discouraged from going on and fulfilling the promises and destiny God has called us to finish. Discouragement will come from all different avenues, and without them, everything would come simple and easy. Life is full of obstacles and challenges, but when we truly put our faith in God, we will be able to push through and make it to the other side with gratitude and indulgence. Just know that the harder the battle, the sweeter the victory will be. We must continue to persevere in this life with these words written and engraved in our hearts: "*If God is for us, who can be against us*" (*Rom. 8:31*). This means, if God has already established our steps in this life to accomplish what He has set out for us to accomplish, there is nothing and nobody in this life that can take us away from fulfilling God's great plan for our lives. That to me is a victory you and I ought to be celebrating every day of our lives.

We have read so far about those who have physically had to go down to Egypt and how God fulfilled His purpose through them. But now thinking about it, even though some may have physically had to go down south or to Egypt to see the hand of God move in a supernatural way, there were others in the Bible that had their own metaphorical encounters of Egypt in their own minds. When I think of Egypt, the first thing that comes to my mind is a staging ground for God's presence to manifest. Yes, it's true we may get scared and lonely when we are going through our Egypt or down south moments, and that's because as we have been given this physical body, we have also been given all the emotions that make up how we react to certain situations. What I mean is, it's okay to be afraid, but it's not okay to stay afraid. You see, we have the supernatural ability to change the current circumstances of our lives just by speaking truth into our very being that was destined to believe what God has spoken from eternity so it shall come to pass. If we allow ourselves to dwell on Satan's lies, we will become paralyzed and not be able to move on to the next phase of our lives. If you want to show the enemy up, just reject those feelings that come your way and replace it with God's promises. This will give the enemy no power over you, because from the moment you start to speak truth of God's word over yourself, the enemy will be nowhere in sight. After all, what does the darkness have to do with the light? Absolutely nothing at all. Start shedding light on all those dark places and allow God to lead you every step of the way, that even when you encounter moments of having to metaphorically enter Egypt or travel down south, remember that when God leads you, He always leads with a purpose in mind. The bigger the calling, the greater the challenge will be. The greater the challenge, the stronger God will be to sustain us until the very end. And that even when we become weak, His strength becomes our perfect and tangible motive to continue walking through the season we are in until we reach the end of that chapter and God allows us to face another season stronger than before.

Every time we are faced with a challenge, we are being faced with an opportunity to do something great for the kingdom of God. When God lays upon our heart to do something out of this world, it is going to require us to put our whole trust in God's perfect plan because what may seem farfetched to others is His way of letting us know how He operates by taking the foolish things of the world only to put to shame the wise (*1 Cor. 1:27*). God takes the weak things of the world to put to shame the strong. Being in a place of discomfort for so long can cause us to draw back and give up, and that's exactly what the enemy wants us to do. Hearing from God during adversity and trials isn't always the easiest thing to do because of all the other voices that often tell us all the things we are doing wrong, but the voice of God will always speak truth into our spirit. Even when it gets lonely and troubles build up on all sides, remember all that God has done for you before. If He did it then, He's only getting us ready to do it again. I have learned that when God calls, we must respond and not delay. God knows what lies ahead of the task that is before us or the assignment He has laid before us to complete. Your assignment may look different from mine, but we are all working toward the same goal to build upon the foundation of Christ's sacrifice and resurrection so the world will know that even though the world is full of darkness, God has already made away for us to come back to the light, who is Christ Jesus, and find meaning and purpose once again.

CHAPTER 6

•••••——•——•——•——•••••

Prayer before Request Equals Favor above Our Enemies

There is an urgency for those who are in Christ to mourn for those who still do not know about the love of Christ and what Christ has already done for them. So many people are in distress because of everything going on all around them. Those of us who have received salvation through confessing our sins and have believed in our hearts that Jesus is the Savior of the world have been called to tell the world about the amazing grace God has to offer through His Son's sacrifice. Before you and I came to Christ, we were desolate and without hope; but when we found the truth and we held on to it ever since, we found love, hope, and faith. God has called us to go out into the world and tell others about that same hope, love, and faith so that which was broken and torn down can become lifted and transformed through the blood of Jesus. You are that one God is calling and saying to rise up, pray, and intercede for those who, without even knowing, are waiting for you to come and make a difference in their lives through love and compassion and to soon know what freedom looks like when we shine the light of Christ in the midst of their darkest days, and then they too will begin to experience that same encounter we had when we first surrendered our lives to the Father's will. It's called saving grace, and we all need it and are desperate for it. Only those who heed the calling will recognize and accept the truth as well as inherit the most precious gift of all: salvation that can only come through Jesus Christ! Maybe, just maybe, you have been in Egypt or down south for so long, enslaved by the things trying to take you under that you haven't noticed that where you are right now is God's way of calling you to come out of that place and into the promised land. My prayer for everyone reading this book is, if you are currently fighting a battle that isn't yours to fight, give it to the Lord and surrender your life to Him so He can begin to deliver you out of Satan's power and in to God's divine presence. If you know Christ but are stuck in a pattern you think you'll never get out of, I want to let you know that, if you do not become fainthearted, soon you will see God's hand move in such a way that what you thought would destroy you is working out for your benefit. My prayer is for God to illuminate your heart and mind from being held captive by Satan's lies and cause you to see the truth of God's word come to pass in your life. I am believing God on your behalf for that immense miracle, and if I am believing it, you should too because the word of God says in *Matthew 18:19* and *20*, *"If two of us agree on earth concerning anything that they ask, it will be done for them by my Father in heaven, For where two or three are gathered together in my name, I am there in the midst of them."*

We will speak a lot more about Joseph and how God took a young man and turned him into an intercessor for his people. And just as Joseph had to step in the gap, so will you and I, but I also know of another man out of the book of Nehemiah. When Nehemiah found out that the survivors who were left from the captivity in Jerusalem were in distress and reproach along with the temple being burned up and torn down by the Babylonians, he sat down and wept and mourned for many days before God in heaven *(Neh. 1:2–4)*. Nehemiah turned to the Lord and started praying and interceding. His prayer to the Lord reached the throne room of God. There is truly something powerful about a bold prayer to the Lord God Almighty. Nehemiah held back nothing from God. He knew that in order to touch God's heart, he would have to do some serious praying and calling out to the Lord. Nehemiah's prayer starts in verse 5 and ends in verse 11:

> *And I said: "I prayed, the Lord God of heaven, O great and awesome God, you who keep your covenant and mercy with those who love you and observe your commandments, please let your ear be attentive and your eyes open, that you may hear the prayer of your servant which I pray before you now, day and night, for the children of Israel, your servants, and confess the sins of the children of Israel which we have sinned against you. Both my father's house and I have sinned. We have acted very corruptly against you, and have not kept the commandments, the statutes, nor the ordinances which you commanded your servant, Moses. Remember I pray, the word that you commanded your servant, Moses, saying, if you are unfaithful, I will scatter you among the nations; but if you turn to me, and keep my commandments and do them, though some of you were cast out, to the farthest part of the heavens, yet I will gather them from there, and bring them to a place which I have chosen as a dwelling for my name. Now these are your servants and your people, whom you have redeemed by your great power, and by your strong hand. O Lord, I pray, please let your ear be attentive to the prayer of your servant, and to the prayer of your servants who desire to fear your name; and let your servants prosper this day, I pray, and grant him mercy in the sight of this man. For I was the king's cupbearer."*

Prayer is the key element to seeing God's hand move in our lives. Before we think to do or say anything that will ultimately lead to our blessings or to our destruction, we must call out to the Holy Spirit for guidance and direction. Since we all don't know what tomorrow holds, we ought to pray every day to the one who holds tomorrow and our destiny in His hands. Not knowing where to go and what to do should be the least of our worries because if we trust God, we also must trust that He is in control of our lives and that God will work all things out for our good. I want to pause just for a moment and zoom in on this verse taken out of Romans 8:28, which, if not fully understood, can often become misunderstood. When scripture says, "All things work together for good," this does not mean everything every time will turn in our favor so we would feel good. While that may be a part of the truth, many will take it out of context. When God says, "All things work together for good," what He is actually saying is, "Even when it looks bad, I'll bring you healing and restoration through my ability to see you through your toughest moments in life." For example, when you lose a loved one, it hurts, and it's painful, and the pain becomes unbearable in that moment, and although we want our loved ones to come back to us, God says it was (his) time to leave this earth. But I believe, when we surrender our pain to His will, God can give us a supernatural comfort if we allow Him to become the shoulder we cry on as we get through that particular period in our life. We can't see the hidden design behind what God is doing, but if we hand our afflictions to Him and begin reciting His promises back to Him and trusting in His word, we will see His promises come to pass. There will be days when you are okay and other days when you are reminded of those precious moments that'll lead you to cry rivers of tears, but it's in those moments when we don't understand what God is doing or where He is taking us that, when we trust in His word, it will cause us to rise up with God's supernatural peace and strength to overcome the season we are walking in. Perhaps your ministry couldn't have started until your loved one went on to be with the Lord in heaven. Or perhaps until you were persistent in your prayer life with God, you were not able to move on to the next chapter of your life. Whatever the case may be, God always works all things together not for our good pleasure, but for His greater works. God is the potter, and we are His clay, and every tear that falls from our eyes God uses to mold and shape our vessels as He sees fit, and as those precious tears fall into the hands of our Heavenly Father, He allows us to experience a flow of joy as God turns our teardrops into a river we can swim in, and we will be glad in knowing that all joy that comes from God never reaches us void or empty but always serves as a means for us to continue seeking God, even in our Egypt moment.

God has already established a good work in all of us, but it's up to us to fight the good fight of faith no matter where we find ourselves, and sometimes, we may not even have to travel toward our Egypt moments. Sometimes our Egypt moments and those used by the enemy will come to bring distraction to our lives. The enemy knows the potential that lies within every believer's heart. That's why he sends out his ranks to discourage and distract us from fulfilling the assignments that are before us to complete. The enemy loves it when we face hard times because this gives him an opportunity to try and distract us from truly focusing on the things that matter in life. The enemy is the father of all liars. He will try and use others to distract and disrupt us from completing the task at hand so that we will give in and give up. Remember this, the enemy never fights fair, and as long as you and I continue steadfast in our prayer life with God, no matter what weapon the enemy tries to form against us, it will never prosper.

Prayer and submission are the most powerful tool God has given us to fight off the enemy. We have been seated in heavenly places with Christ Jesus, which means that our communication level always stays in range with heaven. When we find ourselves being attacked by the enemy, heaven is already waiting for us to call out for help and make our matter known to the king. It's sort of like on earth when there is an emergency that requires immediate attention. We dial 911 and make our emergency known to the dispatcher. In turn, the dispatcher notifies EMT. As the rescue response team makes their way toward the scene of the accident, with its ambulance lights and sirens sounding, every vehicle on the road must part either toward the left or the right shoulder and let the ambulance pass through. This is how our God operates in the spirit. When we call upon the Lord and pray for help with urgency, God Himself calls down angels to come to our rescue. As our response team rushes down from heaven to come to our rescue, every evil spirit that is in the way must part to the left and to the right and watch as our Lord and Savior comes to our defense. No matter how big or how little you think your problem might be, put it through to God's prayer line, and he will never put you on hold or hang up on you but will listen and stay with you every step of the way. I want us to understand something very important here. When God allows or permits us to go through various trials, that's His way of telling us, "I want more of you. I long for you to turn to me and realize that I have been calling you to come to me so I can show you great and mighty works which you have not seen before." Nehemiah probably never thought in a million years that God would call him to rise up and lead others to rebuild the temple of God. Your calling and my calling will require us to step out in faith because where God is calling us. The enemy is sure to follow and wreak havoc on us. A willing heart to serve the Lord is a heart the enemy is after to try and stop the plan of God from being fulfilled.

While Nehemiah was called by God to come back, along with many others who were with him, to rebuild the wall, opposition arose for Nehemiah and the children of Israel. An Ammonite by the name of Tobiah, along with Sanballat, was used by the enemy; and he became indignant with the Jews and tried to discourage them by mocking their every move as they tried to rebuild the wall. How many of us have gone through something like this? God has called you to do something, and all you hear is the enemy whisper in your ear, "You're a fool if you think that was God telling you to do that" or "No matter how much or how hard you try, you will never have the capability to fulfill the task at hand." All those thoughts are just evidence that something greater lies on the other side of your calling and the enemy is just trying to stop you from pursuing that great call on your life. That great call on your life is what the enemy is after; to kill, steal, and destroy it completely.

But there are armors God has given us to fight with. The defensive armor God first gives us to put on is the belt of truth. Knowing and accepting the truth sets us free from the enemy's lies. The truth of who God is is enough for us to walk with the belt wrapped around us, and not only around us but also secured tightly, with no means of ever becoming loose because the truth is what every believer needs to live by every day of our lives. But knowing the truth isn't enough for us to just walk in. We also need to put on another piece of armor that is vital to the spirit and goes hand and hand with the truth, because this specific armor must attach itself to the truth. This is the breastplate of righteousness. In all truth, we must guard our heart and soul by living a righteous life through Jesus Christ. What does living a righteous life in Christ look like? It's not a perfect life. It's not a life without errors and mistakes. It's not even living life to a degree to where we think we are so right that it makes us think we don't need a Savior, but righteousness is knowing that we are deserving of condemnation. But God, in His mercy and grace, has made a way through the righteousness of His Son, Jesus Christ, to take all that was wrong in us and, through His precious blood, cleanse and sanctify us through a righteous act on the cross, bringing us to our knees and causing us to fully understand that righteousness only comes through Christ's sacrifice that made all things right and has caused us to now live a righteous life through Jesus and not for ourselves, because the word of God says that our works are like filthy rags. It's only through the righteousness of God's work can we understand what truth really means. Knowing the truth and walking in the righteousness of God's calling brings us to the next piece of armor, which is the armor that causes us to bow down before the presence of God having shod our feet with the preparation of the gospel of peace. That, in season and out of season, we should always preach the gospel that brings peace to all who put their faith in Christ Jesus. And soon after, having shod our feet with the gospel of peace, we must rise and take hold of another piece of armor. But before I go any further, I just want to point something out that the Holy Spirit laid upon my heart to share with you. As I was talking one night with my husband regarding the armors of God, it was then that the Holy Spirit spoke to me and gave me clarity to fully understand what it really meant to be dressed with the full armor of God. He said to me that when we first put on the truth (gird, the belt) and live righteously (with the breastplate) before God, this enables us to bow down and shod our feet with the gospel of peace, prostrated before the presence of

God. Once we have come up from praying, God gives us that peace, and in turn, we now have the capability to pick up the next piece of armor, which is the shield of faith. When we pick up this armor, we are letting the kingdom of darkness know that from the former position, we can now rise up and take the shield that enables us to now walk by faith in knowing that whatever we prayed to the Father, He has heard us and has given us peace and the faith to overcome and He guards our heart against the enemy's fiery darts and with all and above all our heart is protected with the shield of faith. When we hold up that shield, we are declaring to the enemy that above all that is occurring, we will still choose to put our faith in the one who has already defeated him at the cross.

Soon after holding the shield, we put on with confidence in Christ the helmet of salvation. Many think and believe that the first place the enemy targets is the mind. While this may be partially true, the reality is that, these armors that God has provided for us to walk in have been strategically assigned for us to put on in an orderly fashion. The reason for this is, before we can put on the helmet of salvation that guards our mind, we first must guard our heart. With this being said, God knows that above all else we need to stand in truth and in righteousness. How do we do that? Well, scripture tells us in Proverbs 4:23 that we need to guard our heart above all else. We all need to understand that the first target the enemy goes for is, in fact, not the head but the heart. This is because the heart is the most delicate organ we have, and if the heart becomes distorted so does the entire body. Just like we need oxygen and blood flow in order for the heart to remain alive, we also need to guard and protect our hearts from the enemy's deceptive ways of trying to distort our hearts by penetrating those fiery darts of lies and deception that in turn causes us to become weak in the faith. Once we fully understand the concept of what it means to protect and guard our heart against the enemy, we can then move on to what the word of God says regarding the helmet of salvation and why this next piece of armor is so vital for us to understand. The helmet of salvation is placed over the head in order to protect the head of the soldier on the battlefield. When we place the helmet of salvation over our minds, we are doing something so important that even the enemy knows this, because after the enemy has done everything to distort and destroy your heart, the very next organ he goes to attack is the mind. This is because the enemy has one last chance to try and distort the very thing that he has left in his book to do, and that is our salvation. Satan stages most of his battles in our minds because that's where he wages most of his wars when he knows that we have guarded our hearts in faith.

So that the enemy has no chance or opportunity to enter these delicate places, we all must guard and protect ourselves from the kingdom of darkness with the armor of God. We must learn to protect our heart and mind by filling them with God's word and speaking the word that has the power to tear down strongholds that try to exalt themselves above the knowledge of God's word. This brings me to the last but most effective armor of all. There is one armor that if we go to battle without, we are sure to lose against the enemy, and that is the sword, the Spirit, the Word of God. We need to pick up the sword and fight back when all seems lost or when we are face-to-face with the enemy. Our war is not carnal but spiritual. When we begin to fight and wage war in the spirit by faith, we must believe that God is fighting for us; and no matter what is going on in the natural, just remember, in the supernatural, God is making a way for His children to see victory every single time. We as children of God walk from victory to victory and from glory to glory, knowing and believing by faith that if God is for us, who can be against us? In other words, if God is the One fighting for us, it's a done deal, and the enemy knows that. That's why he tries to come and discourage us into thinking no one is on our side so we might as well quit and throw in the towel.

That's what the enemy was trying to do with God's people, but boy, did it backfire on them. Because Nehemiah knew exactly what to do with the matter at hand; and that was trust in the truth, do what was right, continue to bring peace and reassurance to the Israelites, continuing in the faith that the wall would be rebuilt regardless of opposition, even knowing that the enemy was rising up. Their salvation was found in the Lord of Host, and that the Lord of Host would save them from their enemy. And last but not least, Nehemiah would come up with a strategy to keep the enemy from invading their territory. In a few short words, God's people dressed themselves with the whole and full armor of God. I want to remind you once again that God hears our prayers in times of adversity. In fact, He is waiting to hear from us right now. If you're at the point of breaking down and the enemy is face-to-face with you, it's your time to reach out to God with all you have left and watch as God comes through for you.

Your Weakness Is Evidence That You Need God to Step In

I remember growing up, as a child, my brother loved watching wrestling programs; and from time to time, I would sit with him and watch for a while. They used to have this one particular event where the wrestlers would partner up and have a tag-team match with their opponents. As one team member started to fight, the other teammate would be outside the ring, ready and willing to come in when his partner was worn out and weak. The only problem was, the one standing outside the ring could not step in until the one inside the ring tapped his hand to let him know that he can't go on any longer and he needs him to rescue him from the opponent. The moment his partner feels the tap, he barges through the ring to take out the one who tried to take his teammate out. God is our partner and friend. God is on our side just waiting for you and me to touch Him and let Him know that we are weak and worn out from the enemy's low blows and need Him to step in and take over. It's an all-or-nothing battle, but the Bible says in Ephesians 6:13 that when we have done all we can, just stand. There is no way the enemy can withstand the very presence of God when He shows up to rescue us. We can wear every part of our armor and think we are ready for battle, but if we have no prayer life, we are like one body with no help up against our opponents that is ready to charge at us like wild bulls or like a man or woman in a ring with no one to tap when we become weak and restless. Nehemiah and his crew knew what it was like, because while they were all rebuilding the wall, their opponents were throwing low blows and trying to weaken them to the point of giving in and giving up. Nehemiah knew this was something out of his control, and therefore,

Nehemiah prayed to the Lord for God to step in and bring the enemy's plot against them to nothing. Isn't that just like our God?

The wall was close to being finished, and the parts were all coming together. This really made Sanballat and his people even more infuriated, and so now they not only sought to mock them but kill them because they thought by getting rid of them that would stop them from continuing the work of finishing the wall. What the enemy failed to realize was that Nehemiah's prayer already reached God's throne room and God had already established a plan. If there was a time when God's people had to work together as a fortified nation, it was now. There is something so strong about unity. But did you know that we can have unity and still fall into utter destruction? Let me explain what I mean. For example, in the tower of Babel (Gen. 11), as Nimrod dictated to the people how they should build a tower, they began to build a tower that would reach as high as the heavens. Yes, they were all in unity, but the problem with this picture was that their intentions were all wrong. They only wanted to build a tower to make a name for themselves. There was no true unity, only pride and selfishness. And so for that reason, God, from His throne, caused the tower of Babel to come crashing down; and instead of unity, there was confusion among the people as they all scattered abroad in dissolution. Now let's look at the day of Pentecost (Acts 2) when the disciples were in the upper room waiting for the Holy Spirit to come down from heaven to remain on the earth until the day of Christ's return. The Bible says they were all of one accord in one place. The disciples had just witnessed what Jesus had gone through to save the human race. They witnessed a selfless act of righteousness on the cross wherein Jesus Christ before told them that these things needed to come to pass for them to become witnesses of his amazing love, and therefore, the only one who can give testimony to the truth is the Holy Spirit Himself. So as they were all waiting in unity to build upon the foundation (who is Christ Jesus) who was slain before the foundation of the world was laid down, they were also waiting with love to go out and speak of an unconditional love that would spread like wildfire and bring transformation to the entire world after the Holy Spirit came down from heaven to testify of this great love, which instead of confusion brought clarity and instead of pride brought humbleness. When there is unity with no love, that is only a recipe for disaster. When there is love and unity, there is a movement that will change the course of time, just like on the day of Pentecost. And this type of unity only comes when we pray and seek God's face. The moment we begin praying, the enemy will try and make us think he still has the upper hand and will continue to try and discourage us by making us think he is in control of the situation, just like he tried to do with Nehemiah and God's people. But the truth is, God has already gone before us and lit up the pathway for us to see, that whatever plan the enemy has devised against us has been brought to nothing. God's wisdom is what we need to get through our toughest most challenging times in life. As we pray to the Lord, we must lay it all out to him and become transparent with Him. We must never hold anything back, because when God comes through for His children, He promises to never leave nor forsake us. God always comes through with all His strength and power to defend us from the enemy because our God is a waymaker. When we pray like Nehemiah who prayed and interceded for those who need our intercession and trust in God even in the most difficult times of opposition, when all is said and done in the unity of love, the victory that we so long to see will come to pass. God will stop at nothing to get our attention. Even in a dream, God can capture our attention and cause us to respond as He knows what the outcome of our current situation will come to in due season.

Ask by Night, Receive by Day

When God speaks, we must be attentive to hear His voice and humble ourselves before His very presence. We must be able to stand transparent before Him and pour out our hearts with sincerity and confess with all boldness that we declare Him Lord and Savior of all. Every one of us has been marked with a great calling from God, and because we have been marked by the Holy Spirit, we also have become a main target for the enemy. But as God has called us (through Jesus Christ) to lead others to Himself, we must first learn to follow Jesus's ways. Before we can even fathom moving ahead into this great calling, even before we can step into that opportunity of becoming who God has predestined for us to become, we must first answer the question God has asked us to ask. Sounds a little confusing, right? Don't worry I'll explain what I mean. The Bible tells us, in 1 Kings 3:5, that the Lord appeared to Solomon in a dream at Gibeon. God did not ask Solomon what he wanted but said to Solomon, "Ask! What shall I give you?" God specifically told Solomon to ask, so instead of God asking Solomon what he wanted, God told Solomon to ask God what he needed. The great question here is not what we want but what we need, and that was the point that God was trying to bring to Solomon's attention. Of all the things in the world you could ever want, what is the one thing you need the most? This type of question cannot be answered lightly. When God is telling us to ask, this is perhaps because he wants us to look deep within our souls and dig deep into the calling that is before us. Our circumstances should not dictate how we are feeling in the moment, because at that moment, we may be scared and frightened of the road that lies ahead. And for that reason, making the wrong choices could ultimately result in our downfall later in life. In 1 Kings 1, Solomon's father, David, proclaims his son Solomon to be the next king of Israel. Solomon must have been aware of the great responsibility that lay ahead as he was about to take on the biggest and toughest burden of walking in his father's footsteps. What Solomon was thinking must have been deep because Solomon goes on to tell God, in verses 6 and 7, that his father did a great job as king. "But as for me," he says, "I am a little child" (paraphrased). It appears Solomon was becoming open and transparent before God. Having an open heart with God is what God longs for. God never fails to reach us at just the right moment. Whether in a dream, a vision, through scripture, or through a prophet, one thing is for sure, when our calling is made manifest to us, the one thing God will require of us is this: "Ask! What shall I give you?" Be very careful how and what you ask God for because it could very well be a test of your faith. God speaks to us sometimes in ways that we will never comprehend but will ultimately bring us to that place of solitude and tranquility. And so Solomon says to the Lord, "I know that you have chosen me to be king for my father, David's sake, but I am not capable of leading your people, and so all your servant asks for." Or in other words, Solomon was saying, "What you can give me is understanding to discern between good and evil in order to judge rightly." Solomon, before asking God for what he truly needed, placed his petition before the Lord and became an open book for God to see (even though God already knew) his humble heart. For that reason, God gave Solomon great wisdom to lead and judge His people with understanding. The Bible tells us if we lack wisdom and knowledge, to ask God and He will give it to us freely (James 1:5).

When God opens that door for you and me to walk through, we must humble our very selves before the presence of Almighty God. And when God speaks to us, we must pour out our hearts to him and remind ourselves that we are but dust from the earth and all power, strength, and authority comes from our Heavenly Father. Before asking him for what we need, since He already knows what we need, all we must do is to be real and transparent with Him, and He will hear us and help us. So the point of the matter is, no matter where we find ourselves in life, the main focus is not on how we got to where we are; it's about where we are going and what we need to do to prepare ourselves for the moment after. The steps and measures we take are determined by the attitude we have and, in turn, will reflect the actions we take while walking out this journey called life. Prayer is one of the biggest and most vital ways of communicating with God, aside from our praise and worship. Our time spent with God will bring us that much closer to where God wants us to be. He is the only One who can position us to be at the right place at the right time and keep us in His perfect will, even if that means having to encounter down south moments of trials or a season of Egypt's afflictions. Rest assured God's plan for our lives is never to stay in one place long enough to destroy us but to launch us toward a destiny filled with so much success and victory.

Not about Me, Not about My Story, It's All about God's Glory

I know you've already heard bits and pieces of my life growing up and how I faced many challenges of rejection, but there are so many things I left out, not because I don't want to share them with you. On the contrary, we must never be ashamed to share our testimony with others because, although there may have been some horrible moments that we've all experienced, we must expose them and bring them to the light so God can heal us and then give us the courage to stand up and talk about them because through our testimony, God Himself becomes glorified through what He has done for us. What I am about to talk about won't be easy for me to put into words, but I believe with the help of the Holy Spirit leading and guiding me, I will be able to share with you all a testimony that will glorify our Father in heaven. God is no respecter of one man because what He does for one He will most certainly do for another.

Growing up, I found life to be most challenging when face-to-face with our innermost vulnerable feelings of rejection, regret, and depression; and it settles into the point of feeling hopeless and helpless—all because that's what we have been accustomed to feeling and dealing with almost all our lives (speaking for all those who have encountered these moments). The feeling that never goes away even when you try your hardest to fight it off is the pain of rejection. As a little girl, I often tried to fit in where I could get in, and for that reason, I ended up believing the lies of the enemy. At such a young age, the enemy had a target on my life to destroy me even in my mother's womb. When I was in my midtwenties, my mother told me the story of when she was nearly ready to give birth to me and how the umbilical cord was wrapped around my neck and the doctors were going to have to do surgery on my mother or else I was going to die. At the time, my mother was attending church, so she knew to go right to the pastor and ask for prayer, and that's exactly what she did. By God's grace and miracle—the doctors were not able to explain what happened—but the umbilical cord that was wrapped around my neck miraculously was no longer around my neck, and my mother gave birth to a nine-pound healthy baby girl. Oh, but this wouldn't be the first or the last time the enemy would try and destroy my life. Through different methods, the enemy tried to destroy my life through fear and rejection. One of the biggest tactics the enemy used to make me feel like I was worth nothing more than a piece of meat or just a space being occupied on this earth was through sexual relations against my own will.

As I mentioned before, I was sexually molested as a young girl by my brother's best friend. I'm not sure how long after but my mother would bring us for the holidays to visit her family in Philadelphia. My aunt had a husband who would touch me in inappropriate ways, which would make me feel so uncomfortable, but I would be too afraid to tell anyone. After all, no one believed me the first time it happened with my brother's friend. I would cringe and squirm every time he would put his hand behind the seat and grab my thighs. I remember one night we were all in the living room and he asked my mother if he could take me to Chuck E. Cheese for a while, but my mother said no, and to this day, I am thankful to God that my mother said no because only God knew what his true intentions were that night. I believe with all my heart that God intervened on my behalf that night so something terrible wouldn't occur.

I want you to think back and reflect for a moment on a situation that you thought could have occurred but God saw you through and intervened on your behalf, or maybe you did experience something traumatizing that left you in the dark. I want you to know whatever happened to you does not define you for one second. God was there, and whatever happened to you, it happened to Him, and it hurt Him very much, but vengeance is of the Lord. Your job is not to make it right by seeking your own vengeance or keeping those unresolved feelings within you, but to press into God so He can begin healing you. You're not responsible for what happened or for what could have happened, but you are responsible for allowing God into those broken places so He can make them whole again. When we hold on to unresolved issues, they become like a snowball rolling down a massive hill, and sooner or later that issue we were holding on to begins to hold on to us, snowballing into a huge destructive ball, heavy and coldhearted. This is when we begin trotting on dangerous territory and start to do things that we may not realize at the moment is a direct cause of the real problem. Sort of like the main issue being the root beneath the surface attached to the seed that, when broken, if not nourished properly and taken care of at an early stage, will grow or uproot with bitterness and eventually become rotten and disregarded as something that was never tended too; and until we allow the only One who has the power to restore come into the picture to take what was contaminated and making it new, restoring and purifying that seed, we will continue to experience no life from within oneself. I don't know what you have gone through or what you're facing right now, but I do know God is willing and ready to help you get through your toughest moments. With God, all things are possible, and the first step to the beginning of your healing process is confronting the issues and exposing them and bringing them to the light. The next step is trusting (through God's word) that everything God has spoken over you is true and will come to pass. Whatever brought you to this point in your life was no accident. It is an opportunity for you to know just how much it pained God to see you go through what you've gone through and for you to come into the reality that God has an amazing plan for your life and also for you to fully see the overall picture of what God has predestined for you. Unfortunately, because we live in a fallen and broken world, we are not exempt for encountering tragic and horrific moments of pain and rejection from others, but rest assured that whatever the enemy meant for evil, God has already restored a plan to turn your darkest season around to a brighter season if you will open your heart and begin to allow God to illuminate those dark areas in your life. Even the deepest darkest moments of our lives leave us crying out for someone to save us, and I believe that you reading this book and having gotten this far is because your soul is crying out for Jesus to save you and to rescue you from your past. He is here, and He is just waiting for you to open your heart to Him and become a vulnerable being before his very presence. Do not let yourself become vulnerable to the enemy's lies any longer. When we are in a vulnerable state of mind, we begin to detach ourselves from others, and everything that has meaning in life becomes a distant future with no means of ever reaching our highest potential, and we become drawn toward the very things that have the power to drag us under. That's exactly what was happening to me in Philadelphia with my aunt's husband. I never told anyone about it and just kept it within me, not knowing how much it would affect me later in life. This was the bitter root that had begun to rise up from my heart, and without even knowing, this would become the bitter root of rejection and pain that would soon permeate throughout my heart and cause me to be led down a dark, cold, and lonely road of confusion and entanglement of an occult that I hadn't been aware of but Satan was well aware of, because the enemy feeds off our fear, rejection, and pain to accomplish his number one mission, and that is to completely finish us off and destroy the calling that is upon our lives.

As years passed by, I began exploring other areas that the enemy had already planted in me to explore, and that was the occult and witchcraft. My older brother and sister and I, along with our neighbors, would always play with the Ouija board and call on the dead spirits and have contact with the unknown. We would go to the beaches and do séances. At the time, it didn't seem very harmful to me until I started seeing demonic figures in my room. One time I was sitting on my dresser when suddenly, I saw a green hand come out of the closet wanting me to follow it into the closet, and I remember running into the bathroom where my mother was getting ready to go out to the club, and I begged her not to go because I was so terrified of what I saw. Because we had opened up the demonic portal and given access to the enemy, strange things started happening soon after. There was another time when my siblings and I, along with our neighbors upstairs, were all in my brother's room playing the Ouija board and started communicating with the spirits. We discovered that someone had died from a horse accident a couple of blocks down the road from where we lived. At first, we didn't know what to make of it; but one day, early in the morning, we all decided to walk downtown toward Northport village and hang out. We started walking, and we passed by this house that looked abandoned and had a ranch, so we all decided to see if anyone was there. We were not prepared for what we would have discovered that day. To our surprise, as we approached the fence, there was a man there; and we asked him about the ranch and the horses and if there were any accidents that occurred. He told us that, yes, years ago there was a girl who was riding a horse and had fallen off and died. We knew then that we had tapped into the dark realm of the spirits, but when you are young and have no knowledge whatsoever of the demonic realm, you begin to explore more and more thinking that no harm can actually be done to us, just like what we see in horror movies on TV or in the theaters. But the truth is, the demonic realm is full of horrors we can't even begin to imagine. The enemy is not playing around. He wants our souls and will stop at nothing to claim them if we give him access to it. As a little girl, I was being led by demonic spirits to explore more and more into the kingdom of darkness. My older sister met a friend, and he was deep into the occult, and so he started showing us how to tap into black magic. We would find abandoned psychiatric wards to perform séances in, and soon after, I began engaging in these practices. It was as if I was becoming more and more attracted to the dark side, which brought me to a place of rebellion.

When I reached my high school years, I began getting into trouble with the teachers, acting out and getting detention almost every other week. I remember one time I had gotten all-day suspension, and that is when I met a girl who introduced me to a deeper side of black magic and she taught me how to get a boy to fall in love with me. We hit it off very well that day, and after school, we left in her car, and from that day, we just kept hanging out with one another. I started ditching school just to hang out with her and her cousins. But this time, I had already started drinking and smoking cigarettes, but was about to discover another form to numb the pain that was still lingering within my soul. I still remember it like it was yesterday. I was supposed to go to school that day when my friend called me in the morning and told me to stay home because she was going to pick me up and take me somewhere. She came twenty minutes later, and we left and went to Central Islip on our way to her cousin's house. We went upstairs, and I noticed there were a lot of people there, and they were all acting very strange. Music was playing in the background, and it looked as if they were all having a good time. There was a balcony in the back, and as I was making my way over toward the backyard, I heard my friend say to me, "You want a hit." I didn't know exactly what she was talking about, so I said, "No, thanks." I just lit a cigarette and went inside after. When we were all sitting on the couch, I noticed they were all laughing and looked to be having a good time, so I gave in and said to my friend, "Let me take a hit of what you have." So we went to the backyard, and that's when I tried marijuana for the first time. From that point on, I found myself wanting that temporary high because it made me forget about the problems I was facing in school and at home. But little did I know that this was part of an ongoing plan that the enemy had to kill, steal, and destroy my life. The enemy will strategize a plan to get you to a place of vulnerability so he can whisper in your ear all the things that will drive you to think you're in control, but the truth is, you're only allowing the enemy to take control of your mind and your life. As far as the enemy is concerned, he's only after one thing, and that's our precious soul. If the enemy can keep us focused on our own way of thinking, then he can gain access to us and keep us from acknowledging the underlining root of what's really going on. Satan will then continue to play the puppet master of our lives and bring us farther from God's plan and lead us down the road of destruction. The enemy wants us to stay stuck in a bitter pattern of guilty feelings because through these feelings, he can manipulate every situation. He would have us think that every temporary pleasure he puts before us to tempt us will deal with the source or the root of the problem, when in all reality, even Satan knows that the temporary pleasures of this world lead to the path of destruction. For that reason, he comes up with a plan to try and keep us from knowing the absolute truth of God's word. And those who choose to follow after Satan's lies and deceptions (like what I had done), instead of acknowledging what Jesus went through on the cross to save us from our own sinful ways, will begin to allow the working of Satan's power to take over our lives; and in turn, we begin to live a life full of confusion, deception, bitterness, and loss of our true identity. This is exactly what happened to me. The enemy would stop at nothing just to try and claim my life as his own, and so that's why he devised a plan to try and take me away from God's plan and purpose for my life. From the beginning, Satan sent his demons to attack me with rejection, making me feel forsaken, bitter, lonely…the list goes on. But this time he sent someone who was deep into the occult to really keep me from discovering the truth about who I really am and what I was called on this earth to do. Like many others, I fell for the enemy's lies and tricks, and because of that, I continued living a lifestyle that only brought me pleasure for a moment but would soon after leave me more bitter and hurt than before. Oh! But that didn't stop me from becoming rebellious and caused me to cut school, get high, and get into trouble, or even tapping more into the realm of the demonic occult.

One day after cutting school, I went to the mall with my friend and got a book on black magic, specifically on how to make a boy fall in love with you. We went back to my friend's mom's apartment and began setting up the séance, putting candles all around and taking out the Ouija board and began calling out to the dead spirits by placing our two fingers on the planchette to form words from each letter on the board to then make contact with demonic spirits. We must have tapped into the demonic realm because soon after the atmosphere changed and we began to feel a sensation of terror come over us. It was like someone was tangibly in the room with us. We began testing and talking to the demonic spirit through the Ouija board. The spirit that was communicating with us was a woman. We told her if she was really in the room with us, to turn off every candle in the room; and sure enough, within seconds, every candle was blown out. We got up in total shock and quickly turned the lights on. We then packed up the board and remembered the book we got at the mall, and so we then set up everything according to what the book of black magic had required us to do and say. The book said we needed red lipstick (for the passion part of the séance), a piece of paper (for the declaration part of the chant), and a lighter (to ignite the fire as I recite the chant out loud). The book told me to write on a piece of paper the boy's name who I wanted to fall in love with me, and with the lipstick, I was to draw a big heart around his name. I then took the paper and hung it way out of the window, took a lighter, and lit the paper on fire while declaring the boy's name three times out loud. As I was chanting his name, suddenly, my friend yelled, "Your hair is on fire." She ran and got a bucket of water, and that was the end of that.

Have you ever heard the saying, "It's all fun and games until someone gets hurt"? This saying is something the enemy doesn't want you to learn because he will paint everything as if it is magic in the air and make us think that the dark and demonic world is just a place of fairy tales and fairy dust that magically makes everything glitter and sparkle to the T. But the reality is that the demonic realm is a cause for destruction, and that's why the Bible says in 2 Corinthians 11:14, "And no wonder! For Satan, himself transforms himself into an angel of light." Satan will never disguise himself as someone who you would want to run from, but someone whom you would, in the beginning, feel attracted to, because his number one objective is to, at first, bring you to the dark side with false and temporary, quick pleasures that this world has to offer. Then, like a fly being led to the web, we become caught and entangled in Satan's web of lies. Satan then begins taunting us with fear and guilt, causing us to keep away from even trying to know the truth that has the power to set our souls free from the enemy's lies and deception. Satan causes more than half of the destruction of the human race. He comes only to kill, steal, and destroy. Satan is named the destroyer numerous times in the Bible.

> *For the Lord will pass through to smite the Egyptians; and when he sees the blood upon the lintel, and on the two side posts, the Lord will pass over the door, and will not allow the destroyer to come into your houses to smite you. (Exod. 12:23)*

> *And when the people saw him, they praised their god: for they said, our god hath delivered into our hands our enemy, and the destroyer of our country, which slew many of us. (Judg. 16:24)*

> *Shining morning star, how you have fallen from the heavens! You destroyer of nations, you have been cut down to the ground. (Isa. 14:12)*

These are just a few of the many times Satan is called the destroyer in the Bible.

As a follower of Jesus Christ, I am now fully aware of all the dangers of tapping into the occult lifestyle. This is no thrill or joyride like the movies paint it to be. As I have stated before, the demonic realm is after one thing and one thing only, our soul. If you have been contemplating entering the occult, you will be entangling yourself into a web of lies and deception that will ultimately claim your only soul and lead you right down into the pits of hell, to be eternally separated from God. Where you once had hope and an opportunity of accepting God's gift of salvation on this earth, when you have taken your final breath will, all come to a sudden end. You will find yourself in a place, only to be condemned forever and ever. While you are here on this earth, living and breathing God's air, there is still an opportunity for you to turn from your sins and turn to God and receive His only begotten Son, Jesus Christ, who came not to condemn the world, but to save the world through His ultimate sacrifice on the cross. Where light does not exist, love does not abound and the weight of God's mercy and grace is nowhere to be found, and this place is called the abyss, a place where one can never be freed from. The only thing you will feel, my friend, is the horrible and devastating repercussions of the actions you took while on this earth, rejecting the only salvation that had the power to save your only soul, and that is the power of the gospel of Jesus Christ. The Bible says that *"the wages of sin are death, but the gift of God is Salvation"* (*Rom. 6:23*).

When talking about the wages of sin, it leads me to believe that in this life, there is only so much that we can do that one day we will have to be held accountable for. Let's take a candy shop for example. Almost everyone on the planet loves candy, right? We go to the candy shop and grab a bag, and we start filling it with all the things we like, right? We continue to fill the bag, some with caution and others with none, not realizing that every pound has a price. So the more we fill the bag, the higher the price becomes. And so when we are done filling our bags, we make our way over to the cashier to give our filled bags to the clerk. The cashier takes the bag, and he or she weighs it on the scale to find out how much we would pay. The heavier the bag, the higher the cost will be. In the very same way, our sin has a price on it, and that price is death, and when we take our final breath here on this earth and have not received the gift of eternal life from Jesus Christ, our lives are like that bag of candy being weighed on the scale, and the only one who will pay for it is us. I have a question for us to analyze. What is our bag filled with? Is it filled with self-righteousness and pride, or how about self-righteous works? All these things are what keep us from entering the kingdom of God. Those are the very things that cause the price of the bag to become heavy and burdensome, which in turn will keep us from receiving eternal life. Just picture for one second someone coming over to you and saying, "I'll trade you the bag you have been holding on to, which has a high price that you are not able to pay your way out of yourself, for a bag that I will give you that has already been paid for in full. Only this time everything that you fill it with has already been sanctified and purified by what I have already gone through just so you could enjoy the many tasteful opportunities I have for you to indulge in." The point I am trying to make here is that Jesus paid the price for the wages of our sins when He chose to come down from heaven and pay our debt on the cross. Jesus Christ, the Son of God, came down to this fallen and broken world to offer himself up as a sacrifice well-pleasing to the Father, just so to provide a way for us to inherit the eternal gift of salvation, which could only be offered through a selfless, self-sacrificial act of obedience on the cross. Then Jesus, who was, and is, without spot or wrinkle would therefore be able to save us by giving us the gift of eternal life. And anyone found in Christ has had their wages of sin paid in full. The more we fill our hearts with the things of this world, we are just like the person holding the bag at the candy shop just filling the bag without knowing the price of what he or she is holding on to is the price they are not able to pay for. Don't allow yourself to fill your lives with decaying promises and things that can only bring pleasure for a moment. After all is said and done, the things that looked good to our satisfaction will ultimately, over the course of time, lead us to our own destruction.

When I think back to all the times I should have been dead, my heart begins to feel like it's about to explode. Even though I couldn't see God's hand moving on my behalf then, the evidence points to the fact that I'm still living and breathing today, and that is because God has sustained me this far and has preserved me for such a time as this. God wants every reader to know (including myself) that regardless of our background, what we have done in the past, or what the enemy has planted in our minds all those years, God still has a plan for our lives; and He is certainly not done with us yet. Our beginning can't start until we come to the end of ourselves. Jesus is the author and finisher of our lives. I can't write a book until I make the choice to not hold back the truth and pick up the pen and start writing. You and I can't expect God to follow through with His plan for our lives if we are not willing to give Him every part of our lives. Every chapter of our lives is being woven into a tapestry of many colors, and some colors may be brighter or darker than others, but one thing is for sure, when we are broken and a mess, God can see the finished work before we can even begin to see a glimpse of our lives being transformed. We are so dear to God that every promise He has ever spoken over us will come to pass, when we take the time to seek His beautiful face and believe what God says about us in *Jeremiah 29:11*, *"For I know the plans I have for you," declares the Lord, "plans to prosper you and not to harm you. Plans to give you hope and a future."*

As I had mentioned before, my mom worked several jobs, so after school, I didn't really have someone to look after me besides my older siblings; and even then, they were often attending to their own things. So I would just go to my neighbor's house and hang out there. I had a friend who was so much older than me. I started drinking and smoking at an early age. I was introduced to my first boyfriend by my friend who before I left the ways of the Lord used to go with me to church. We all would hang out at the Commack movie theater and the mall. We hit it off well at first. We would spend a lot of our time talking on the phone, and I would sneak him sometimes into my room when my mom was working, but my older sister would always rat me out. We were together for quite some time until he wanted to move to the next level in the relationship, but I refused. That, of course, didn't stop him from trying anyway. But every time it looked like it was going to happen, I would back out and tell him I didn't feel comfortable, and I just wanted to go home. After a while,

I started to notice a change in him not coming around as often as he used to, and we didn't talk on the phone as much either. I knew something was wrong, but what happened next I did not expect to affect me the way it did. He cheated on me—and not just with anyone! I had a friend who worked with me at a children's summer school camp. We got along so well and continued to be friends until I found out one day that she went behind my back and slept with my boyfriend, and to make matters worse, she was pregnant by him. This put such a hole in my heart, and I was horribly depressed for a very long time. I was not only betrayed by my friend and boyfriend, but I was also later told the reason he did what he did, and it was all because I wouldn't give him what he wanted, and that was my virginity. It took a long time for me to get over that situation. But this only caused me to do what I have always done even as a little girl: keep quiet and not talk about it and find ways to cover up my true feelings. So I started going to teen clubs and pulling all-nighters with my friends. I eventually became numb to the pain and started allowing all the bad influences to take their toll on my life. At this point, I didn't care about anyone but myself. I would take the bus or train without my mother knowing and hang out wherever and whenever I wanted. I became like my own boss so to speak. There were nights when I would be out drinking and getting high, to the point of not knowing where I was. I was in a pattern of feeling good and having the feeling of pain and rejection simultaneously keep me in the state of bondage, which constantly reminded me that nobody really loves me and nobody will ever love me. So I would just keep drinking and smoking until I reach the point of not thinking about it, but by then, I would have my head in a toilet.

There was one time when I went to the Bronx with my friends, and we all went to Skate Key. It was a roller-skating place. We hung out for a while there. One time, catching the train back home, a man approached me and asked for my telephone number, which I didn't have at the time; so he gave me his instead. I called him about three days later and met him at the mall. He picked me up, and we went somewhere to drink and smoke. I had no intentions (because I was still a virgin) of doing anything, but he had different plans up his sleeve. So he began to touch me, and I began telling him no and to take me home. He got upset and didn't want to take me back home. About the third time, I told him to take me home. He left me on the corner street to walk all the way home by myself. When I look back at that moment, I knew God's hand was there even though I couldn't see it. He protected me when I didn't even deserve His protection. He still cared about me. Think back to a place when you knew danger was at your door but somehow God intervened on your behalf and rescued you from a situation that could have led you to your death, only to perish with no hope of seeing eternal life with Christ Jesus.

As I had mentioned before, I had an older friend, and she would take me almost everywhere with her to get drunk and high, but most of the time, I would spend the night at her mother's place and would just drink and smoke until the next day. There were times though that I would find myself in the house of some guy my friend had met, and he would have a friend for me to hang out with. We would all get drunk and high, and the next thing I knew she would go off with whoever she was with and leave me by myself. I would be scared because the next thing I knew, whoever I was with would try to make a move, and I would refuse, which in turn would make them angry (this wasn't just one time). There was a time when we were downstairs in the basement of one of her guy friends' home. We were all drinking and smoking. Then she left again, and I was alone. The guy that stayed with me tried to make a move on me, and I told him no and that I was a virgin and was not interested in doing anything with him. I truly thought that something terrible was going to happen to me that night, but to my surprise, I heard banging on the door. That night I had never been happier to see my friend's older brother come through the door and take us home. I may not have seen and understood then, but I sure do now. It was God protecting me from something horrible that could have ended tragically.

As the years went by, I eventually got worse. I became more rebellious toward my mother. At fifteen years old, I stole my mother's car when she was at work (she had two cars at the time) and drove around town with my older sister sitting in the passenger's seat. I had no idea what I was doing or where I was going. My mother had no idea, and I now believe that God's saving grace was upon my life and still is to this very day.

There were a lot more things that I did, but if I began to write down every little detail, this book would have a different name and would become a lot longer than intended. I will, however, share with you the years after I had my daughter at seventeen years old.

I met my daughter's father through my older sister. She worked at the bus company with him and his mother. My sister introduced me to him, and we went on our first date and really hit it off well after. He was nineteen when I met him, and he owned his own car, and we really got serious with one another. He would pick me up on the weekends, and he would come and see me almost every night at my mom's house. My ex-boyfriend found out about us, and one night while we were hanging out at my mom's place, he showed up with some of his friends, ready to fight my daughter's father. Suddenly, I saw my daughter's father pull out a screwdriver and stab my ex twice. I was standing at the doorway when I saw my daughter's father run inside my mom's house. Then I heard my ex scream, "He stabbed me. He stabbed me." From that night on, we became inseparable, and a couple of months later, I moved in with him and his family. I got pregnant soon after. Life took a turn for the worse a couple of months into the pregnancy. I started to feel abandoned by him when all he did was hang out with his friends and leave me at home. Our first argument led him to run my face into the doorpost, cutting my eye, causing it to bleed and swell up badly. I quickly ran outside and hid in his car. Minutes later, he came outside and apologized for what he had done, but this wouldn't be the last time something like this would occur. As time went on, it became a daily routine, and before I knew it, I was entangled in his web of lies and had no way of getting out. It was like a spinning wheel going around and around at its maximum, and even if I tried to get out, I feared I would fall down all on my own. I was being controlled by him and manipulated by him in every way. Then came a time when I was eight months pregnant, and we were both arguing about something. I raised my voice, and suddenly he put his fist up and tried to hit my stomach, saying, "I'll end this pregnancy now." I quickly put my arms over my stomach and ducked down as fast as I could, and his fist hit the wall. I knew at that point I was in serious trouble. But I still had no place to go if I left. I believe the reason I survived those moments was that his mother never stopped praying for us. As a woman of God, she would always try to talk to us about Jesus and say, "Come to church with me and find the Lord." Every so often I would go with her, but because of my hurt and pain, I would have a hard time believing that God cared about me or wanted anything to do with me. Because of the guilt and shame that I felt, believing the enemy's lies was enough to make me reject such a beautiful salvation that Jesus won for me on the cross. So every time there was an altar call, I would remain seated from all the shame and guilt that was weighing me down.

After my daughter was born, I had a lot of support from my mother and his mother, but for me, things were becoming a life I never dreamed about. I began drinking more and partying more, just trying to escape from life's responsibilities. I allowed myself to become consumed in a world of destruction. I eventually started taking the drug ecstasy and eating mushrooms. Things got so bad for me that at one point I found myself living with my daughter's father outside in a car and would have to go to the gas station to brush our teeth. I hurt almost everyone around me, and it got to a point where, because of my selfishness to seek my own fleshly desires, everyone around me slowly started abandoning me. I was in my darkest season with no direction, and I wanted so badly to get out of that life. Eventually, I got away from my daughter's father, and years after, I started pursuing music once again. I began recording music in the studios and pulling all-nighters. My brother had a friend who had his own studio, and so I would spend weekends with him and his crew just recording multiple tracks at a time. I started becoming promiscuous and letting the spirit of lust and seduction really take over me. Wanting to become famous seemed like a dream that one day I could achieve if I just did whatever they wanted me to do. I also believe that a part of my living that way had to do with me being controlled by my daughter's father for so many years, which caused me to think that this is what life was like. It was the only thing I was used to. It felt like there was no hope for me to ever change my ways. This was my life, or so I truly thought. I couldn't take care of my own life, let alone my own daughter, my own flesh and blood. So I did the only thing I knew in my heart was right to do. I ended up having joint custody with my daughter's great-grandmother (on her father's side). I would come and pick her up on the weekends and every summer vacation and holidays as well. I began putting my dreams and desires above my real responsibilities, and for that reason, I couldn't care for my daughter in the right way. I wasn't able to care for her because I was too busy trying to numb the pain. Also, I still couldn't believe that I had a child of my own. For the first few years, before I gave joint custody to the great-grandmother, it was my mother who got up in the middle of the night to feed and change my daughter even though she would have to be at her job at four thirty in the morning. My mother has been a huge blessing in my life, and I don't know what I would do without her. To this day I still call her a superwoman because although I didn't know it then, I sure know now that God has been the one giving her all that super strength she needed to endure everything I put her through. After my daughter's great-grandmother had taken her into her custody, I began pursuing music full time. I started going to the gym almost every day just trying to get into shape. I eventually tried going back to school to get my high school diploma, just trying to do it all on my own strength, but I failed repeatedly. After so many attempts, I gave up and quit. I went back to drinking and smoking and just hanging out all night. There was one time when I went to a friend's house and was hanging out drinking and smoking when I received a phone call from someone telling me that if I could get to the city, I would be able to record a track. So being that I had no way of getting there, I talked my friend into letting me borrow his car. He didn't want to in the beginning, but eventually, he gave in and gave me the keys. I left and made my way to the city with marijuana in the car, and as I got up to the toll booth, I realized I didn't bring any money with me. I had no license, and in Suffolk, I had a warrant for my arrest. The next thing I knew I was in handcuffs and brought to the nearest precinct where I stayed all night. I saw the judge later on that evening. I called my mother, but at that point, she didn't want to deal with me. The guy who lent me his car was saying that I stole the car, so my mother didn't know what to believe. I remember getting out of the precinct the next day and having a friend drive me back home. I eventually was brought back to court with fines of over a thousand dollars, and if I couldn't pay it within a matter of time, they were going to lock me up in prison. At that point, I felt like there was no hope for me at all. I just wanted them to lock me up and throw away the key. It was in that moment that I realized for the first time just how deep of a pit I was in and the only One who could rescue me from that point on was God Himself. Still, I felt the guilt suffocating me like a bag over my head.

As time went on, I went back to the one thing that I loved to do the most, and that was singing. I eventually started leaving behind the secular things of the world and started really pursuing God's Word and seeking His will. The more I read the Bible, the more in love I fell with Jesus. Eventually, I started leaving behind everything, including the friends I had, and the things I used to do I had no desire to do anymore. I started working with my mother and siblings at the bus company. I took my Bible with me and read it wherever I went. On the bus, on my break time, and even when we were waiting for our run to start, I would be in the trailer house sitting at the table just reading, reading, reading. About a year later, I got baptized, and all I wanted to do was tell everybody about God's saving grace.

Years after I got saved and born again, I fought so hard in prayer to get my daughter back because her great-grandmother (even though she knew I was a changed woman and everyone telling her that Melissa is a new woman in Christ Jesus) did not want to let her go. She fought with everything to keep my daughter with her. I believe that financially, my daughter was of benefit to her, and so she didn't want to give her up. During these years of trying to get her back, I met the love of my life. He soon became my husband, and we began praying together with the same prayers each morning, and that was for my daughter's great-grandmother to let her go and allow her to come back to me. It was so hard in the beginning. There were nights when I would cry and couldn't sleep. I would continue to press on in the faith and hope that one day my daughter would be with me again. The day finally came, but my daughter came back to me with a price, and it wasn't until my daughter's great-grandmother's husband passed away that she finally gave in and said, "I will go to court with you so you can take your daughter back." I hadn't thought about it in this way until one day my daughter's grandmother came to me and said, "I love my mother, but I must say this to you. My mother for various reasons had her heart hardened like Pharaoh and did not want to let your daughter go. But just like Pharaoh had to encounter the loss of something to understand the meaning of losing something so precious, so my mother had to go through the same thing, and just like Pharaoh soon after allowed God's people to go free, so my mother, in the same way, allowed your daughter to come back to you." I cried and cried, mostly tears of joy because my daughter was back home with me but also because my heart broke for my daughter's great-grandmother and her great loss.

Looking back at that moment makes me realize something: we all have moments where our lives should have ended; but by God's great grace(whether we choose to believe His existing presence is real or not), we were spared and delivered, only to count our blessing and then share them with others so others will see what God has done and for them to glorify His awesome name or eventually, for the nonbelievers, a believer will speak out after hearing a nonbeliever say, "I don't know how I survived that event in my life," and the believer can say with great faith, "This was none other than the hand of God protecting you from the harm that was in front of you."

We don't know why we go through what we go through at various times in our lives; but when we choose to put our trust in God, despite our circumstances or unfortunate situations, we will overcome them by the word of God, if we stand up and depend on God to fight our battles as we fight the good fight of faith. Whether we feel like we've been in Egypt for a lifetime, bound by our sin like a slave to this present world, find faith in Christ, hold fast to your faith in Jesus, and be of good cheer because the best deliverance is yet to come!

Life is full of ups and downs. Failure is a part of life just like success is. Even though we have obtained moments of success, we also will have to face moments of failure. You win to lose, but you lose to win. If we always win and never lose, then we would all be perfect and have no need of a Savior. That's the point we think we are winning when all along we are losing because we grow up not knowing the truth, and in order to win in this life, we must lose who we are and find it in Jesus Christ. You can be the most famous person on this planet and have the greatest success story of all, but if you don't have Jesus, your success becomes temporary and without use for everyone else who is lost just like you. We can spend our entire lives thinking we are winning, but when it is all said and done, it will all boil down to one thing: our salvation.

Our salvation cannot be defined by how much money we have in our bank account. Our salvation cannot be defined by how much recognition we have from the public, our salvation can never be determined by how many good works we have performed, and our salvation most certainly cannot be defined by how much head knowledge we have of God's word. Salvation is a gift from God sent to us through His Son, Jesus Christ. Salvation is only obtained through an act of selfless love that only Jesus was able to fulfill. "Well," you say, "many people have performed tons of selfless acts of love on this earth." Yes, while that may be true, every one of us is not without sin. We have all sinned and all have fallen short of the glory of God. But there was, is, and will always remain One who came to this earth who, without sin, became sin on the cross so you and I could be redeemed from the powers of Satan's lies. One of those lies is, we can get to heaven by our works. *Isaiah 64:6* says, "*That our works are like filthy rags.*" The only reason Jesus's sacrifice on the cross was valid before God was not only because of a selfless act of love but because Jesus Christ had not one ounce of sin in Him. And for that reason, He was to be the perfect spotless lamb to be slain from the foundation of the world without stains or blemishes. The Lamb, who was slain to cover us with His precious blood and redeem us back to the Father, has won it all for us. So it's not until we come to the realization of what salvation really means that we will continue to lose in this life and eventually perish in our own sin.

CHAPTER 7

A Spectacular Deliverance: One Step for God but a Giant Leap of Faith for Man

I have watched enough action movies in my past to take notice of something very spectacular that happens at the climax of every action movie. Have you ever watched a movie where the main character is running from those trying to catch him and, all of a sudden, after climbing a flight of stairs and finally reaching the incredible height of the rooftop of a building, he finds himself at a crossroad between surrendering his life into the hands of his enemy or taking that giant leap of faith? He does not know if he will make the jump or not. So he takes that giant leap of faith anyway, and suddenly, we see him gliding through the air and we're waiting in anticipation to see if he will make it to the other side or fall to their own destruction. But just when it looks like he isn't going to make it, something supernatural happens and what seemed almost nearly impossible for him was made possible by a decision that was taken in a split moment. I believe in the same way our life moments are at the mercy of faith. We all must make a choice at one point in time or another. Some of those moments allow us time to think it over and make a wise choice after analyzing the situation well enough to know that we made the right choice. But there are those moments when we won't have the time and opportunity to think it over and analyze the best course of action to take. That's where real faith comes in. Walking into the unknown is half the battle, but I have the best news ever. If we step into the realm of the unknown with the One who knows and sees all things, when we find ourselves at that same crossroad just like Moses and God's people (were face to face with the Red Sea), our next course of action should be to be still and know that the God who is Almighty is with us, for us, and not against us. We must take that giant leap of faith and believe that if God brought us to this point in time of our lives, it's because He is about to do something far greater than we could have ever imagined. I may be getting ahead of myself in talking about the most spectacular event that took place in Egypt, but I feel from the Holy Spirit, someone needs to know that although you have been freed from your bondage, you are being surrounded by giants on all three sides and the biggest Giant is right in front of your face telling you, "There is no way you will get by me." As Moses and the people were held back by the giant Red Sea that was before their faces, they were also surrounded by Pharaoh and his chariot soldiers. All three sides were closing in on God's people. But here's the thing: God could have destroyed Pharaoh and his army first and then made the decision to open the Red Sea. So why did God open the Red Sea first? When we are in a state of fear and God gives us a way out at that moment, we react quicker than we would if there was no danger ahead. You see, when God's people saw a glimpse of Egypt coming toward them to bring them back to bondage, every one of their hearts was filled with fear. Some knew that if they were caught by Pharaoh's army, as they were once a part of his allegiance, they would be killed for betraying Pharaoh. For others, they knew the punishment would be a thousand times worse than before. Fear will come, but as followers of Christ Jesus, we cannot allow fear to grip us to the point of not moving. On the contrary, when fear does present itself, let it be the motivating factor that pushes us to move in the direction God is telling us to move in. When we end up at a crossroad, remember this, before God destroys His enemies, He will hold the enemy back and show us the way through. So the next time you find yourself in a fearful state of mind, walk out your fear by faith until you get to the other side of your destiny and then turn around and watch as God destroys the enemy right before your very eyes. "'Vengeance is mine,' says the Lord. (Deut. 32:35). When God says it's time to come out of Egypt, although we may have been freed from Egypt's bondage, we will have to face greater challenges on the road that lies up ahead. You and I don't know what lies ahead, but we know that the One who freed us will see us through to the very last step of our lives. And so never think to yourself the unexpected couldn't ever happen to you because God can use the unexpected events in your life to see you through to the promised land.

As we live our lives from day to day, we don't wake up every morning thinking the worst of what could happen. We wake up doing what we normally do, and by the time, we know it, it is time for bed. And we repeat what we have done day by day, week by week, month to month, and year to year. The reason we don't wake up expecting the unexpected to happen is because we tend to think that unexpected things could never happen to us until it does. We all need to grasp one thing: our lives are not exempt from experiencing tragic moments. When those moments come, we need to have a faith-based spiritual survival kit handy so that when those moments come, we will be able to survive the outcome of whatever comes our way. In the same way every household should have a survival kit in case of catastrophic emergency or a fire extinguisher in the case of a fire, we too need to be prepared for the unexpected events that can occur when we least expect them to occur. Real preparation starts when we come to the realization that anything can happen at any given moment that can put our lives in jeopardy. I'm not saying that we must live our lives in fear. However, we need to be on high alert and ready for whatever spiritual warfare from the enemy comes our way. When we fervently study the Word of God and treasure His word in our hearts, we begin to view everything that comes our way differently because we start to believe within our hearts that the Word of God is living and breathing within our very being. Every word spoken over our lives will come to pass despite the unfortunate spiritual or physical catastrophic events that may come our way. When we trust God, He gives us a supernatural peace that surpasses all understanding, and it's in that moment where we need to activate our faith and believe that although it may seem like we are losing, God says, "Be still and know that I Am God." The reason this is all so true is that the peace I am talking about does not come from this world. This peace doesn't come from the external, fulfilling desires that only last you for a moment. What I am talking about is an internal, overflowing, purposeful, genuine peace that only comes through and from Jesus Christ. This peace will allow you to experience rest in God as you've never experienced before.

Like the eye of the storm, the center of it is calm and without rage. So God should be at the center of it all. In all the battles that rage within our minds, God is saying, "Come rest in the eye of my presence and know that I am God who will sustain you in every war that the enemy wages against you. I will be your comfort in every storm that rages against you. If only you will make me the center of your life, I will cause you to inherit my peace, not like the world gives but the peace that I give surpasses all understanding." I don't know who needs to hear those words, but I strongly believe that someone reading this right now is feeling the presence of the Holy Spirit laying upon your heart that everything is going to be okay if you remain in the eye of the storm, who is Jesus Christ.

John 16:33 says, "*These things I have spoken to you, that in me you may have peace, in the world, you will have tribulation, but be of good cheer, I have overcome the world.*" You and I were meant to go through many trials. We are all meant to face many obstacles. Whatever we go through today is our stepping stone to walk on for tomorrow as we journey onward to our God-given destiny. God willing, we shall see tomorrow if we don't give up and give in to the strong currents of this life. Every step represents a footprint of where you've been, not where you are. You may think, *I'm walking this lonely road because no one loves me and have felt rejected more times than I can count.* Every stepping stone that you walk on has a purpose from God Himself, to make and shape something out of you that you couldn't possibly comprehend at that moment. It's not until we have gone through many trials and faced many obstacles that the Holy Spirit causes us to walk into the unimaginable destiny that is waiting for us to arrive so we can experience a life full of healing and spiritual growth in Christ

Jesus. He who began a good work in you is faithful to complete it until the very end. Whatever you and I face in this life and, yes, it may be something horrible and drastic, just remember that when we don't know what to do next, a giant leap of faith can cause us to experience a profound encounter with the one leading us to our destiny. The more we seek Jesus, the closer we will be to Him. We must seek His presence at all costs. It could be in that very moment we are giving Him all the praise, honor, and glory that everything could change and turn in our favor, all because we chose to remain steadfast in our faith and not let what the enemy meant to harm us with keep us down and out for the count but, on the contrary, keep us seeking God's faithful presence.

> *But He knows the way I take; when He has tested me, I shall come forth as gold. My foot has held fast to His steps; I have kept His way and have not turned aside. I have not departed from the commandments of His lips; I have treasured the words from His mouth more than my necessary food. But He is unique, and who can make Him change? And whatever His soul desires, that He does. For He performs what is appointed for me, and many such things are with Him. (Job 23:10–14)*

Believe it or not, this might be a hard concept for some to comprehend, but the fact of the matter is, we are all meant to fail at some point in our lives. Many take failure as a letdown or a setback, but the truth is, God already knows every high and low point of our lives. Before you and I were born, God already saw into our future and has already ordained our Egypt moments that will ultimately lead to our success of one day reaching the promised land, if we can all do one thing: trust in His magnificent plan for our lives. Do you honestly think that when we go through our struggles and hard times God didn't already know how we would react? God knows how many times we cry, God knows how many times we laugh, and God most certainly knows how many times we gave up on ourselves. But that is the point. Before God laid down the foundations of the earth, He already knew what every human being would have to go through and what life would be like for them on earth. I have the evidence to back up what I am about to say. This may come as a shock to many. It sure did come to me as I was one day meditating on God's word, and I heard God say to me as clear as day that every person on this planet was meant to fail including Adam and Eve.

I have heard many people who know the scriptures and those who don't know the word of God say, "If it had not been for Adam and Eve disobeying God, we wouldn't be in this mess right now." But I beg to differ. God knew exactly what He was doing when He laid down the very foundations we walk on to this very day. But before the foundations were laid, God already had a plan to save us from our sins. The Bible says in *1 Peter 1:19* and *20*, "*But with the precious blood of Christ, as of a lamb without blemish and without spot. He indeed was ordained before the foundation of the world but was manifest in these last times for you.*" Adam and Eve were placed in a beautiful garden that God had already created for them to live in as a temporary stay, knowing that the war that had begun in heaven would ultimately continue until the very end on the planet we live on called Earth. When Lucifer rebelled against God and deceived a third of the angels into believing that together they would be able to overthrow God, it caused Jesus in that very moment to rise and tell His Father (and I am just paraphrasing here), "This war is far from over, so I will go to the earth and rescue those who choose to put their faith in you, oh Father." And that's exactly what happened. After Lucifer rebelled against God, God already mastered a plan to save us from our sins. After Adam and Eve ate the fruit, God called out to Adam. He asked Adam a rhetorical question: "Where are you?" God knew exactly where Adam was and what he and his wife had done, but what God was really waiting for was a confession of the wrong they both did. Instead, they tried to justify one another's actions. God will never push Himself on us to do the right thing. That's a choice we all must make. When we truly recognize our wrongdoings, instead of hiding, we will bring them to the light so they can become exposed. God is looking for us to admit our wrongdoings so He can bring healing to our souls. He will wait for us to come to Him with a humble heart and a contrite spirit, and it's in that moment when God says, "*I know the thoughts I think towards you…thoughts of peace and not of evil, to give you a future and a hope*"*(Jer. 29:11)*. Before you and I were thought about by God, He already knew that our failures were going to become a part of us and, through our failures, we would find His only begotten son, Jesus Christ. The story of Adam and Eve is not a story of their disobedience but a foreshadowing of how the human race would fall into the same trap of the enemy sooner or later. And for that reason, God already made way for redemption to take its place in the human heart through the sacrifice of Jesus Christ. I truly believe Adam and Eve were part of God's great plan in getting the human race to acknowledge that although we may have everything God has to offer us, we still chose to walk blind and become deceived by the enemy's lies, ultimately causing us to run and hide from God, which by the way is what Adam and Eve did. The question that runs through most people's minds is, If God knew that Adam and Eve would disobey God by eating the fruit from the tree of good and evil, then why did God put it there in the first place? Most people would say God was testing Adam and Eve to see if they would obey or disobey. But then that leaves us with the question: is God omnipresent? The answer is yes! Very much so. God wasn't sitting back on His throne just hoping that they would make the right decision. God already knew that by putting the tree in the garden and telling Adam He could not eat of this tree, that Adam and his wife, Eve, would do the exact opposite. This is because the tree in the garden wasn't set up for them to be tempted (as it is written in James 1:13, which says, "For God cannot be tempted by evil, nor does He tempt anyone") but to be a mere reflection of how man, no matter how perfect we may seem to be, will always be led away by our own desire and seek after doing our own will and what seems right to do in our own eyes. For that reason, Adam and Eve fell prey to the deception of the enemy's plan to distort God's creation, including the human race.

Take the Ten Commandments for example. When we see the Ten Commandments and really analyze them closely, we find that not one of us living on this earth now or those who lived in biblical times could live up to the Ten Commandments, and so we ask ourselves the very same question: if not one person was able to get to heaven because of our inability to live out the Ten Commandments, then why did God give it to us in the first place? If God knew we would all fall short of His glory and that our works would be as filthy rags, then why would God give us His moral and ethical laws to live by knowing that we would all fail Him and not have the capability to follow all the commands He gave us to live by? Well, in the very same way God placed the tree in the garden as a reflection and not as a temptation, the Ten Commandments were given so as to show us that no matter how perfect we think we are, God's moral and ethical laws will always reflect to us and show us just how unjust and imperfect we truly are. And through our inability to live up to the Ten Commandments, God already made a way through His Son, Jesus Christ, who over two thousand years ago, came to do what Adam and Eve could not do, and that was to kick the serpent out of the garden that belonged to God in the first place. But through Jesus's rightful act of righteousness in living out the Ten Commandments, He has won the victory for all who choose to put their faith in God. In return, Jesus allowed us to come to the Father with every one of our faults and failures, only to be forgiven and redeemed by His precious blood.

Genesis 3:9 says, "*Then the Lord God called to Adam and said to him, 'Where are you?'*" God already knew the outcome of the problem at hand. As I stated before, when God said to Adam, "Where are you?" God was asking a rhetorical question. God wanted Adam to analyze his thoughts and recognize where he should have been as opposed to where he was at that very moment. Now that Adam and Eve knew the wrong they both committed against God, instead of coming to God and admitting their wrongful doings, they did what would soon become in the nature of every human that sins against God would do: run and hide, hoping God didn't hear our conversation with the enemy or see our actions. And then when that didn't work, they tried justifying their sins by throwing one another under the bus, which is exactly what we see happing in today's society. Instead of acknowledging our sins and bringing them to the cross, we choose to play the blame game until eventually some type of judgment is poured out because of our not taking responsibility for the problem. The truth of the matter is, God heard it, God saw it, and God knows it even before we commit it. Even before the very foundations of this earth were laid down by God, God already knew He would have to become the sacrificial Lamb who would pay the ultimate price for us to become sanctified and set aside for God's great works, as I have stated before. *First Peter 1:20* says, *"He indeed was foreordained before the foundation of the world but was manifest in these last times for you. Who through him believe in God, who raised him from the dead and gave him glory so that your faith and hope are in God."* The enemy may always think he is winning by bringing his lies and deceptions to the table, but the truth is, anyone found in Christ Jesus and lives according to the truth is a powerful armor in God's hand. Although Adam and Eve failed, God still made a way for them to remain on the earth by clothing them with tunics of skin, a representation of the fleshly ways all the human race would inherit by an act of disobedience on their behalf. As sure as the enemy's deception worked on Adam and Eve, so the deceptions of the enemy would infiltrate the lives of the many people in this day and age, and they would choose to live a life in the flesh rather than through the Holy Spirit.

Our failures are how the enemy defines us, but our repentance toward God is how the blood of Jesus defines us. Meaning, whatever failure you experience, the blood of Jesus has the power to wash over that failure and make you new. Even though Adam and Eve failed God and the consequences followed, God still chose to stay with them because He is the God who never leaves us or forsakes us despite our faults and failures. God never turns His back on us. On the contrary, we are the ones who stray away from God when we make the wrong choices that ultimately lead us to think God wants nothing to do with us. But it's in those moments when God would come off His throne to find us because He knew this would come to pass and has already made a way for us to be redeemed. God knows we have an enemy that will stop at nothing to destroy the human race, so Satan uses the same lies and deceptions causing us to fail and then puts fear within us so we become paralyzed in our thinking, and instead of coming to God, we stray farther and farther away from His mercy. God is waiting for us to confess our wrongdoing before His presence instead of falling into that cycle of trying to justify our wrongs (like Adam and Eve were trying to do in the garden of Eden). When we confess our sins knowing and acknowledging God already knows all our faults and failures, watch what God will do with your failures, if you don't run and hide but, in prayer, come to God with a broken heart and a contrite spirit and confess to Him all your faults and failures. Let us not try and justify them ourselves, rather let God do the justifying on our behalf by allowing His Son's blood to wash us clean and forgive us and create within us a clean and pure heart so that we will worship the One true living God in spirit and in truth.

The Challenges of Today Make Way for the Successes of Tomorrow

So far, I have come to know that life's challenges and difficulties don't just come to disrupt our lives but to wake us up to a specific calling that God has placed within our hearts. We all dream, and we all hope, but what happens when our dreams become nightmares and our hope turns to despair? This is exactly what happened to Joseph, and it's what will happen to us, because when there is a massive calling on our life, we will have to endure pain and heartache for a while. There is something God has laid upon my heart to share with you and encourage you to keep hope and faith alive because what you think is meant to harm you is God's tool to bring you to that place you never thought you would get to. Your life and my life and the plans God have for us have already been accounted for through the blood of Jesus Christ. God already predestined our lives. Know that in order for us to see the overall picture of God's design, we would have to become like the clay that the potter takes time to mold and shape. Two vital keys to becoming a beautiful vessel in God's hand are water and fire.

I remember as a little girl in art class, probably around fourth or fifth grade, the teacher gave us an end-of-the-year project of making mugs out of clay. There was a process the clay had to pass through before becoming a mug, which would eventually become useful to those who drank out of it. I remember first having to envision how I wanted the mug to look: what colors I wanted for the mug, how thick or thin I should make the mug, and how big or small the mug should be. Then I would measure and cut the clay carefully. So I began the process of molding and sculpting the clay with my own hands and shaping the clay into a mug. An essential part of shaping the mug is taking water from a bowl with your hands and gently smoothing out the rough edges with your hands. In the beginning, it didn't look like much, but as I continued the process of molding and stripping and scraping away unnecessary clay, I began to see the clay shaping into what I knew would become a mug. Next, I began to decorate, carve, design, and really personalize beautiful details into my mug. After the molding and sculpting part came the drying part. The mug would have to sit for a while and dry because you cannot put wet clay in the fire. After the mug dried, it was ready for the final touches before going through the fire. There is a process called glazing the mug. So I began to put the glaze on the mug, and soon after, the clay that was without form began to look more and more like a beautiful mug. Next, before the mug can be put into the fire, it has to go through another waiting period. This can take up to a week before the mug is able to go through the fire and finalize the process. Throughout the entire process of molding and sculpting the mug, it was the fire in the end that makes the mug strong, radiant, and useful for others to behold and take notice of.

The display of God's finished works is for us to behold the mighty works that He has done in everyone and to praise Him for His unfailing touches that cause our gifts and talents to come alive through the heavenly fire of the Holy Spirit and become the display for all to see the light of Christ shining through us. This is what God does in our own lives and is what God was doing in Joseph's life too. Just like the clay had a waiting period before being put through the fire, Joseph couldn't have risen to power and saved his household and those lives around him if he had not been willing to surrender the process and yield to the will of God's plan. God needed to reform Joseph's character. When God created us and formed us in our moth-

131

er's womb, we too were being formed in water and had to go through a period when we had to wait until the time came when we would be born and then be reborn (by confessing our sins and making Jesus Lord and Savior of our lives), and soon after, we become baptized in water when we reach the age when we can fully recognize our sins. Through this process, the fire of the Holy Spirit who comes into us will set our lives on fire for Jesus. As God was forming our internal and external parts, just like the clay needs water in order to remain structured, we need the living water of God's presence in order to remain steadfast and grounded in His aligned will for our lives. As God called Joseph to become someone his brothers never thought he would become, God already saw Joseph in the future before Joseph even arrived at his destination. God has already envisioned all that we would be doing for His kingdom before you and I were even established to be on this earth. From a simple yet complex conception, God already knew how you and I would look like and what we would have to endure just to reach our God-given potential. The challenges Joseph faced were the very success he would inherit. And just like the clay had to go through two waiting periods at two separate times; so Joseph, at two separate times, had to go through a waiting period in His life. As God is molding and shaping our lives, remember that while He is reforming us, He is seeing the outcome of His finished work in us simultaneously. As God is shaping us, He is saying, "It is good!" While we are being reformed in the hands of the Potter, we ought to enjoy the process because after all, God's hand is upon us and moving through us.

Joseph's first waiting period was when he was put in the dry well waiting to be carried to Egypt. When he arrived there, God still needed to chip away and strip down all the unnecessary things that if kept in Joseph's heart would hinder him from arriving at his true destiny. But during Joseph's process, God made sure that Joseph was getting the best care. You see, God doesn't want us to be processed and forgotten about; He wants us in the middle of the process, to know that His hands are still upon us and that He is not finished with us yet. No matter how difficult the process may be, the greatest potter of all is the One making sure we are taken care of despite the fact we are all undone before His presence. Sometimes we must face the facts! Where God wants us to be is where we need to be. We are not meant to understand God; we are meant to trust God. When God is getting ready to put the final touches on your already-predestined future, there will always be that second waiting period before the big moment arrives. Sort of like being in a casting audition, you stand before the directors, you play your part, and then you wait for a callback. In the same way, we all are waiting to hear from God to see what the next step will be, but this is where faith comes in. We must trust that as we are in our waiting period, if you have been obedient in your faith, then all that God has promised you will come to pass. Even if we are in the waiting period longer than expected, continue to trust. The longer the waiting period is, there is something God is trying to show us in the midst of it all. So when we are ready to come out of the waiting period, we will walk right into our calling. Joseph probably thought as he was working under Potiphar, that this was what he would be doing for the rest of his life. But God was just giving Joseph a small reality of what Joseph would be doing later in order to save his family from the famine that was to come. God is molding us and shaping us for a greater purpose. Wherever you are right now, continue to do what God has called you to do— whether that's cleaning the bathroom stalls at church, working that nine-to-five job that causes you to just make ends meet, teaching Sunday school while still having to take care of your own kids, pick up the same toys off the floor for the hundredth time, wake up to the same routine from day to day—because sooner or later you will become promoted to the higher calling God has predestined for you to inherit.

While Joseph came out of his first waiting period (which was when his brothers placed him in the dry dark well, then brought him to Egypt) Joseph was working for Potiphar, God already knew where Joseph's next waiting period would be, and so being falsely accused by Potiphar's wife, Joseph was placed in prison. It was there that God was able to utilize Joseph's gift of interpreting dreams. Even in a place of confinement, God can still use you to glorify His name. The Bible says two men had a dream, and they came to Joseph. The first thing that Joseph said was, "Do not interpretations belong to God? Tell them to me, please." Joseph knew in his heart that, although he was in prison, God Almighty was still with him. Joseph could have had a sour attitude and bitterness toward the fact that he was in prison, but that wasn't the case at all. Joseph didn't know at the moment, but God was preparing Joseph for something more than Joseph could have ever imagined possible. So Joseph interpreted both dreams. Out of the two dreams, only one of the prisoners would be set free from prison, according to its interpretation. The other would perish, according to Joseph's interpretation (from God). Joseph had not still understood fully why God called him to Egypt, because when the cupbearer was set free to go back to Pharaoh, Joseph told him, "Remember me when it is well with you, and please show kindness to me: make mention of me to Pharaoh." Joseph had not yet fully understood that there in the prison he was called to wait until the time came when God would release him, not man. So the Bible says that the chief butler forgot about him and Joseph remained in prison. Our precious moments in life are when we lean on God for support because the only way we are going to come out of the process is when we make God the source of our outcome. When we rely on man to bring us out, the only thing man will do is push us further into the process. Joseph was trying to find a way out through man, but Joseph's waiting period had not ended yet. It appears Joseph's waiting period had an extended period because in chapter 41 verse 1, the Bible says, "At the end of the two full years, Pharaoh had a dream." This means that Joseph's prison time had extended way more than he could have imagined.

Remember when I spoke about the mug I made as a little girl and how there were two separate waiting periods? The first waiting period allowed Joseph to be brought to Egypt when he came out of the dry well. The second waiting period is the longer one because before Joseph can feel the heat of his calling, he must remain in a place where he will be ready to assume the position God had prepared for him and become fireproof to withstand the worst that was to come upon the earth. The second waiting period before the finished work is always the longest, but it is all worth the wait. Joseph was released from prison when God put it in the chief butler's heart to let Pharaoh know of a man in prison who can interpret the dreams that Pharaoh had that no one from his house could interpret. The dreams that Pharaoh had were in fact the very dreams that caused Joseph to come out of prison and rise to his power and fulfill his calling. Never ever underestimate the power of God's plan for your life. What may seem like never-ending is God's way of saying, "What I have in store for you is going to require you to place your entire trust in me regardless of what I permit to come your way or what others say or think about you. I Am the One who holds your future in the palm of my hand, and I will never let you go from my will." Wow! That's a word from the Lord. I don't know who needed to hear that right now, but I pray that you believe and receive it in the name of Jesus Christ.

> *Then it came to pass, at the end of the two*
> *full years, that Pharaoh had a dream. He slept and*
> *dreamed a second time. (Gen. 41:1 and 5)*

Pharaoh dreamed two dreams: the first was with cows, and the second dream was with heads of grain. Apparently, Pharaoh didn't pay mind to the first dream, so God gave him another, slightly different but with the same meaning. This time Pharaoh paid attention and called for those of his household to come and interpret the dream, but there was no one who was able to do what Pharaoh was requesting because the one who was to interpret the dreams was being processed and reserved by God for such a time like never before. Perhaps your waiting season is God preparing you for your greatest victory yet. The spiritual prison (the metaphor of what being in Egypt really looks like) to the one who has no vision looks pointless; and that is why they begin settling for less or relying on their own resources to see them through, which eventually, in the end, amounts to nothing. But to the one who places their faith in Christ, he or she will always look for the hope behind the discouragement and the great outcome to the trial they are facing in that very moment. That is why when we are going through our Egypt moment, it is vital for us to remember the dream that God placed in our hearts and always remember that the reason you are where you are is that you are on a battlefield and the enemy wants you to walk and think like a defeated foe. But God has already established the end to your beginning. From where you are now, God wants to do the impossible in you and through you because there is a nation that is waiting for you to rise and fulfill the calling that is upon your life. You are the voice that God wants to use to bring a historical transformation to this world. I see in the Spirit spiritual doors opening and souls walking through and becoming a new creation in Christ, ready to prophesy, ready to interpret dreams, and watch as they unfold right before our very eyes. If your process is taking longer than you thought, then use the time God is giving you to seek His presence. We must never waste a precious moment of the time God is giving us on this earth because every moment counts for something. We must learn to be productive in every season of our lives. Whether we find ourselves in the pit, the prison, or in the palace, make it known to the enemy that our time is not for the foolish things of this world, but for the challenges we were born and made to face and overcome by the blood of Jesus and to do what we were put on this earth to do: to relay the message of the gospel to all who will hear and accept the truth.

God, at the appointed time, put in the chief butler's heart to remember Joseph. And Pharaoh called for Joseph, and Joseph was quickly brought out of prison. Joseph not only came out of prison, he was also given new garments. When your season of the process comes to an end, God will not only bring you out in victory, but He will also clothe you with honor and integrity. When God is ready for you to go from the prison to the palace, there is no devil that can stop you or no door that can slam shut in your face. This was the moment that would change the course of history for Joseph and his family, along with all those in Egypt, and on earth for that matter. As Joseph stood in front of Pharaoh, Pharaoh said to Joseph, "I heard it said that you can understand a dream, to interpret it." Joseph replied, "It is not in me. God will give Pharaoh an answer of peace." So Pharaoh went on to tell Joseph the two dreams. And Joseph began to give the interpretation soon after, saying to Pharaoh, "The dream of the seven ugly cows coming up out of the river to eat the seven fine-looking cows and the seven thin heads that devoured the seven good heads are one and the same dream." As Joseph made known to Pharaoh the meaning of his dreams, Joseph also let Pharaoh know why God had given him not just one dream, but two dreams, one right after the other. This was because, as sure and established the dreams were by God Himself and as close together the dreams were, God wanted to make a statement that surely He would bring the reality of this dream to shortly come to pass. Joseph also gave wise counsel to Pharaoh by telling him to select a wise and discerning man to lead over Egypt and for the officers of the land to gather one-fifth of the produce in the seven years they will have before the famine occurs.

The one thing that really puzzles me is how much knowledge and capability Joseph had, even being in a country whose people were strangers to him. This is just the purest evidence that God is almighty and all-powerful. Think about it for a minute. Joseph was taken away and sold into slavery, and while his brothers thought he was in a faraway place without any sense of direction, the God of heaven and earth was appointing him to a higher position so he could rise up and save those who later on would have to suffer the same fate Joseph did by becoming slaves of Pharaoh. But by a mighty hand, God would raise up another to go before them and deliver His people. The very same way God brought Joseph to Egypt to save his family from a destructive famine, so God brought you and me forth to go before the world and intervene on their behalf by praying and comforting the lost souls with the hope of salvation that can only come through Jesus Christ, who has gone before us and has won the victory through His death on the cross and resurrection from the grave. If Joseph had not been delivered into the hands of Potiphar, if Joseph made the choice to sin against God by sleeping with Potiphar's wife, if Joseph made the choice not to interpret the chief butler's dream, and if Joseph chose to remain bitter and angry by what his brothers did to him, Joseph would have missed out on the greatest opportunity of his life to stand up and intervene on his family's behalf. You may think you are not important to the kingdom of God and the body of Christ and that people (like family members, coworkers, your peers) may have made you feel unwanted and unloved, but the truth is, God has always seen you as a precious human being who has purpose and meaning in life. Just like Joseph, every single moment of his life was not without God's leading hand; and although Joseph was made to feel less than by his brothers, this was a blessing in disguise that brought Joseph, in the end, to understand that among the many people God could have chosen to become the one who stands in the gap for many to be saved, God had chosen Joseph. But Joseph had to go through a great ordeal just to discover the hidden blessings in becoming the instrument God would use to bring God's people toward a greater future, but not before facing the hardest challenges that lay ahead for Joseph and God's people.

You and I are the ones God has chosen to go through the process of becoming someone great in the hands of God. But the real question at hand is, Are we willing to let God reform us? Are we willing to let go of what we have been holding on to all our lives and step into the unknown where God is? I think just by reading this far into the book, you have already begun to feel God tugging on your heart, calling you to come to His presence, but you are still carrying the guilt, the shame of what others have done to you. Don't continue to carry what you were never meant to carry. Rather let those emotions carry you right into the place God has prepared for you and to remain until he is done molding, reshaping, reforming, and refining you for His purpose. It's in those places where you will really encounter God's presence like never before.

What does becoming successful really look like to you? And if that is success to you, what purpose do you serve in your success? How the world defines success is contrary to what the Bible says true success really is and what it looks like. Success is not something we strive for; it's what we build upon. Who is defined by success has a name. He came to this earth to conquer and redeem and to show us what real success looks like. Success is not the result of what we have accomplished but the very essence of how we define ourselves through the finished works of Christ. Before we can ever see success come to pass in our own lives, we must first come to the realization that our success story is in fact not ours to begin with, but belongs to the One who became our success so we can build upon the solid foundation, who is Christ, and continue building upon His success and not spend the rest of our lives thinking we are successful when in fact we are without success because of not having the One who went before us to show us that success starts with trusting in the only begotten Son of God (Jesus Christ), who freely and humbly came down to the earth He created to show us the way back home through the successor. Not through our successes, but only through Jesus can we become successful. Success is found in God's grace and mercy not through the things of this world. That is why Joseph, despite the rejection, despite the false accusation made against him, despite being thrown in jail and being left and forgotten about for a time, was still able to rise above all those misfortunes. He knew where his success came from, and it was not in material things or people but in God alone. So we all must ask ourselves this question: what or who are we putting our success in? If your success is in someone or something other than Christ, your days of what you call success will eventually come to an end, but if you place your faith and trust in the successor, then half the battle is already won. Once you clearly understand where your success comes from, the other half of the battle is keeping your faith alive in Christ and always trusting that if God has already won the war against Satan and his fallen angels, then nothing in this life will ever separate you from the will of God.

When we have no choice but to enter Egypt, this is none other than God's way of saying, "Just as I appoint the exact time you would have to enter Egypt, so I have an appointed time for you to exit." God has chosen us for such a time as this, to enter into a season where we will have to be brave and put our full trust and confidence in God alone. Where God is taking us through, He has already established for you and me to conquer. He says, "Do not be afraid of them, for they shall rise up against you, but they shall not prevail against you, because I am the Lord your God who has established your steps, and every move you make will be by my leading hand."

When it comes to talking about Egypt, we tend to lean more on the downside of what purpose Egypt serves in our lives, instead of realizing the greater calling God has placed on our lives to remain in

Egypt until the time comes when God, with a mighty hand, raises us up in the midst of Egypt in order to fulfill His purpose. If God called our forefathers to this land and gave them victory. God will also give us victory. It's only when we take our mind off the terror that's before us and make room for the glorious journey that lies ahead that we can still have peace in the midst of adversity. Sure, we will have to encounter moments as Joseph did, but if we keep fighting the good fight of faith, we will reach our God-given potential, just like Joseph did. Joseph wasn't after success. Joseph was after trusting and being faithful to the One who held his success in the palm of His hand. It's time that we begin to rise above the circumstances as Joseph did, and instead of reaching toward success, let us savor the journey as we pass through our Egypt moments, extending our hands toward heaven and declaring that our success story has a name, and His name is Emmanuel (God with us).

CHAPTER 8

•◦●❖━━━━━❖━━━━━❖●◦•

A Long Wait Comes a Long Way When We Trust God through It All

This was a moment in Joseph's life that I do not even think Joseph was expecting. As God had set the appointed time for Joseph to be released from prison, there was a major shift happening in the spiritual realm that would soon be made manifest in the physical realm. Even when the enemy doesn't want to see the power of the Spirit of God rise up within you, Satan has no choice but to surrender to the commands of God's word. That is exactly what took place at the very moment God was promoting Joseph to a higher power of position. When your Egypt moment ends, the enemy will have no other choice but to remain quiet as God promotes you to a higher calling. Even in an unknown place where you least expect something to happen is when God makes the unexpected happen. For Joseph, this was a turning point where everything Joseph had been through pointed to this exact moment that was hidden from Joseph until now. Every single moment of our life points to a hidden purpose designed for us to hold fast to our faith and hope. There is a reason you're going through a crisis right now. There is a reason every time you turn around one door shuts after another. There's a reason every time you take one step forward, you fall three steps back. All the misfortunes in life may be God's way of setting us up for something greater than what we can't see now or comprehend. The hardest part is not waiting but trusting.

141

Waiting is one thing, but trusting is another. Trusting in God's plan is never an easy task, but it's what keeps us in suspense. Not because we don't believe His promises will come to pass but because of the simple fact that while we wait, we also must endure and trust that every word God spoke over us, every dream He has placed within our hearts will eventually come to pass when we trust in the Lord with all our heart and lean not on our own understanding. Oh yes, things will start to fall short of how we thought things would come to pass; and at times, we may get frustrated, upset, and angry, which I'm pretty sure was how Joseph felt when the chief butler forgot about Joseph in prison. But we must remember that God's hand is never too short to save us and position us for victory. It may hurt for the moment, but as we truly study scripture, we will find and realize that it's not the waiting period that gets to us, it's putting our complete trust in God to see His promises come to pass in our lives.

Joseph waited on the Lord, but during his waiting period, Joseph became God's honorable vessel. When he was in Potiphar's house, Joseph was made overseer above all in Potiphar's house. When he was in prison, the keeper of the prison committed all the prisoners under Joseph's authority, and when he stood before Pharaoh to interpret the two dreams, Pharaoh took his signet ring off his hand and put it on Joseph. He clothed him in fine linen and put a gold chain around his neck. So you see, it's not about the waiting period; it's about what you do while you're waiting for the moment when God takes you from your waiting period into a season of victory.

> *And he had him ride in the second chariot which he had, and they cried out before him, bow the knee! So, he set him over all the land of Egypt. Pharaoh also said to Joseph, "I am Pharaoh and without your consent, no man lift his hand or foot in all the land of Egypt." And Pharaoh called Joseph's name Zaphnath-Paaneah. And he gave him as a wife Asenath, the daughter of Poti-Pherah priest of On. So, Joseph went out over all the land of Egypt. (Gen. 41:43–45)*

When we reach a point in our lives when all we have ever known comes face-to-face with the unknown, this is God giving us the opportunity to really zoom in and see what He is about to do with our situation, because only God can alter the effects of our outcome. The only thing left for us to do is not give up or give in to what is trying to hold us back from reaching our highest potential. Joseph stepped into the unknown, not knowing what was waiting for him on the other side, yet knowing the One who knows all things would always have his back. Everything Joseph had to endure was a trial test for the bigger picture at hand. The hardest part of coming to the beginning of your end is standing face-to-face with your opponent. The time had come for Joseph to stand in front of Pharaoh and in front of everyone watching and waiting to hear what Joseph had to say regarding the two dreams of Pharaoh. This couldn't possibly have been easy for Joseph because he had just been released from prison. His release was not because he had finished his time in jail (for a crime he had not committed), but because of an urgent matter that required Joseph's gift from God, of interpreting dreams to be spoken of and interpreted before Pharaoh. Soon there was to come upon the earth a famine that would not only affect Egypt, but the entire earth for that matter. Joseph was the chosen vessel used by God to bring clarity to the dreams and their interpretation and become the one who would change the course of time in many ways. Our existence serves a greater purpose than just occupying a space on the earth. You may not understand it now, but keep walking out your faith in God, regardless of what rises up against you. It will not rise higher than the calling God has placed on your life or your purpose here on earth. What God has already spoken over your life, the enemy heard and knows that it will come to pass because every word that God has spoken never comes back void but full of blessings.

God blessed Joseph in ways Joseph never thought or imagined the Lord would ever have blessed him, and it all happened because of the endurance and integrity Joseph had while enduring his toughest moments before coming to Egypt and while in Egypt. When his back was against the wall, Joseph chose to believe in someone greater than Pharaoh, and that was God Almighty. The reason Joseph was able to withstand the trials that came his way was that, before Joseph was even born, there was a promise from God to Abraham that God would establish a nation through Abraham's seed. Before you and I were born, God had given a promise to His Son that everyone who believes in Him (Jesus Christ) would not perish but have everlasting life. Our very existence on this earth proves that God has not forgotten about us; but through His son, Jesus, He has promised to keep and preserve us until His purpose in our lives is fulfilled.

Joseph was appointed by God to bring his family to a place where, in the latter years, they would have to face hard times like never before in order to come out as an established nation handpicked by God for a greater purpose and to become distinguished as a people sanctified and set aside for God's purpose among all other nations. When God gave Abraham the promise of having his descendants blessed and multiplied, God never said that his descendants would never have to face moments of afflictions. On the contrary, God caused Abraham to fall into a deep sleep and then said to Abraham, "Know that your descendants will be strangers in a land that is not theirs and will serve them, and they will afflict them for four hundred years." Although Abraham knew this, he also knew that as sure as God said it, it would come to pass. God would not fall short of his promises, and so as Abraham continued trusting God, the promises of God were coming to pass, because although Abraham could not see what would happen to his descendants in the future, he believed with all his heart that the generations to come would be blessed through his act of righteousness in believing God's every word. Joseph was a product of Abraham's belief that God would save His people and redeem them to Himself at the appointed time. Our belief that Jesus Christ has broken the chains of curses and evil wickedness for generations to come through His righteous act of becoming the sacrificial lamb who paid the way for us to inherit salvation has enabled the next generation to keep the torch glowing and give way for them to experience all God has in store for their lives simply because we, as parents, teachers, mentors, and pastors, kept on believing God's promises for the generations to come. Although we may not be able to see the glory of what God will do with the generations to come, by faith, we take God at His word and believe by faith just like Abraham did because sooner or later the promises of God will come to pass for generations to come.

When we know whose we are instead of who we are, we will begin to grow in our faith in our daily living. When we purposely place our minds on the celestial thoughts of God, we will begin to knock down and destroy every stronghold that tries to revolt against us. You are not a lost cause but a cause to be used by God for a greater purpose. You are not a mistake but were taken and chosen by God Himself to be sanctified and set aside for a greater destiny. You are not a reject but a projection by God to reflect God's glory and stand up to become the one who stands in the gap for your city, for your family, for your friends, and those who have yet to fully understand what is to come in the latter days. God gave you the dream because He knew that you would be the one to follow through with the calling upon your life no matter the cost and no matter the extreme measures that must be taken to reach the height that only God knows you have the capability of reaching. Every process and trial from God in this life is not to punish us but to prepare us for what lies ahead, and soon Joseph would come to that understanding. Soon we will all come to that realization and understanding of why we have to face our own down south Egypt moments at times, taking heart in God's promises and not folding at the break of Satan's lies and deception.

The Greatest Moment Comes When Souls Are Reunited and Hearts Are Restored

When it comes to the pain that we often face from time to time, more often than not we think about the effects pain has to cause us to fall into the trap of believing the lies and deception that the enemy brings to try and paralyze us and keep us from truly understanding that along with pain comes comfort and along with battles comes victory if we allow ourselves to surrender our pain and battles into the hands of the Comforter, who in turn will give us His peace and strength to see us through whatever we are facing at the moment. The more pain we endure, the more we ought to cry to God for comfort. The bigger the battle is, the greater victory God will cause us to inherit. For Joseph, this was no victory too little, too late, and too short. This was the greatest victory for Joseph. Oh! But this was not just any victory, this was the beginning of Joseph's restitution for all the war the enemy made against Joseph's life. What the enemy stole from Joseph did not compare to the greater blessings God had for Joseph and his family. In all reality, the enemy tried his best to keep the house of Jacob divided by keeping Joseph and his brothers apart from each other and having Jacob mourn the loss of his son. The enemy's plan was to raise mayhem within the house of Jacob and in Joseph's life so Joseph would become discouraged, bitter, and angry; but what the enemy failed to realize was that Joseph was already filled with God's promises. And along with the pain and battles Joseph had to face, he also encountered God's favor and grace that led him straight to his victory. Along with restitution, God opened a door that Joseph waited a long time to see opened, and it wasn't the door to his blessings but the door to restoration. But before God was able to bring this to pass, God would have to bring Joseph through another encounter, but this time Joseph would have to find it in his heart to forgive the past mistakes of his brothers to fully enjoy the rest of his days in a land, where soon after the unfortunate fate of the Israelites would be at the mercy of God's hands.

When Joseph entered Egypt, all the hate and bitterness didn't stay outside of Egypt, and God knew this. That's why God stood with Joseph to strengthen him in the moments when he was betrayed and forgotten about in Egypt by his brothers. God was still doing a work in Joseph's life that would require him to reflect on the reality of why God had placed him in Egypt in the first place. You see, Joseph may have had it in his head that he was brought to Egypt to become Pharaoh's second-in-command, but soon, Joseph would fully understand that what his head thought and what his heart still had not fully understood to be true were too different stories, and this would soon collide with one another and burst forth like a spark to a match that would set the course on fire for forgiveness and love to burn brightly between Joseph and his brothers. God was getting ready to show Joseph that the opportunity for love and forgiveness was right around the corner. This would be the icing on the cake for Joseph's family, to see and fully comprehend that the dreams Joseph had in the beginning were coming to pass right before their very eyes. The message for Joseph concerning the dream may have been clear to Joseph but not to his brothers in the beginning, but the journey leading to the fulfillment of those dreams would have needed to take time so that in the end, every detail of the dream would become clear as day, not only for Joseph's family to see but for God's greater purpose to be fulfilled within every one of their lives. Although Joseph played a major role in becoming the instrument God used to intercede for his family, every one of Joseph's brothers was just as important in the eyes of God as Joseph was because through Joseph's brothers, God established a nation that eventually, from the tribe of Judah, would bring forth the Messiah. But before anyone can inherit salvation, there must be reconciliation from the heart. Joseph knew in his heart that God was calling him to become reconciled to his brothers because verse 8 and 9 of chapter 42 says that Joseph recognized his brothers and remembered the dreams that he had dreamed about them. Joseph also knew that for them to be reconciled, they would eventually have to bring their younger brother with them to Egypt. So Joseph began the process of bringing them back and forth to Egypt until the time came when Joseph would have to reveal himself to them. After so many years, Joseph, along with his brothers and father, had no idea the method and measures God would use to bring back reconciliation and restoration to a family that in the beginning was full of envy, brokenness, strife, and conflict within their hearts. There is not a family problem too big or too hard for God to reestablish and make new. Whatever you and your family are struggling with today, just know that God already has the greatest plan set in motion for your family's restoration. If only you will be the one to surrender your will to the Lord and stand in the gap for your family, you will eventually see God bring restoration forgiveness and transformation to your family, and just like Joseph, it must start with you because God is calling you to be just like Joseph to step out and into the gap for your family to see the salvation of the Lord!

> *Then Joseph could not restrain himself before all those who stood by him, and he cried out, make everyone go out from me! so no one stood with him while Joseph made himself known to his brothers. and he wept aloud, and the Egyptians and the house of Pharaoh heard it. Then Joseph said to his brothers, "I am Joseph; does my father live?" But his brothers could not answer him, for they were dismayed in his presence. And Joseph said to his brothers, "Please come near to me." So, they came near. Then he said: I am Joseph your brother whom you sold into Egypt. But now, do not, therefore, be grieved or angry with yourselves because you sold me here; for God sent me here before you to preserve your life. (Gen. 45:1–5)*

There is just something that moves my soul with such joy and gratification when I read these verses. My heart melts, and my spirit rejoices because there is just something so special and uplifting when it comes to seeing how God restores families that were once broken and torn apart and begin to mend and become whole right before our very eyes. It's like watching the same movie repeatedly and still getting the same reaction when reconciliation takes place in the end. I believe this is because of the simple fact that we were all made to be reconciled to our Heavenly Father in heaven. Just like Joseph stood in the gap for his brothers, Jesus is our brother who stood in the gap for us when we were broken and torn apart. The only way we can see the truth is when we believe in the resurrection of Jesus Christ. The truth is in the One who came to save us all from our sins. Unlike Joseph and unlike you and me, Jesus knew why He had to suffer many things before getting on the cross. Jesus, being human and still equally part of the Trinity, came to this earth to show us the way unto salvation, knowing that many would reject him but later would repent, because Jesus came for the lost sheep, and through His magnificent sacrifice on the cross, his blood calls us back home, to be reconciled to our Heavenly Father. When Jesus's disciples walked with Jesus, they could not understand when Jesus talked about His death on the cross. Many at the time of Jesus's death did not comprehend what Jesus came to the earth to fulfill, because the same Jews who either received a miracle from Jesus or saw the miracle take place were the ones shouting out, "Crucify Him, crucify Him," not knowing that the one they were rejecting would be the one whom they would need to inherit salvation. The point I am trying to make here is, when we are the appointed ones whom God has chosen to walk through various trials of rejection, pain, and heartache, just like Joseph had to, only God will understand the process because only God can bring comforts like no one else and only God can bring us from glory to glory in the process. Those around you were never meant to understand your process. Let us take Job for example. This was a man whom the Bible says was righteous in the eyes of God. Job was a just man and had everything, yet Job experienced every type of loss from his children to his household, his animals, and even his very own health for that matter. I'm pretty sure Job's afflictions caused him much internal pain and heartache. Not even his friends understood the process and soon after began condemning Job and trying to make him think all these things were happening as a result of his sin against God. But although Job felt the physical and emotional pain, no one, not even he, understood the process. Yet in Job 23:10 and 11, Job, in the midst of adversity, says to God, *"But He knows the way that I take; when He has tested me, I shall come forth as gold. My foot has held fast to His steps; I have kept His ways and have not turned aside."* What we do in secret with God will determine the outcome of our process. When God brings us to a place of solitude, it's not for us to wallow in our own sorrows but to begin working in the secret places God has established for us to begin depending on God to see us through in. While you and I are working in the secret places, many will think we are doing nothing; but in reality, if we continue walking despite the darkness surrounding us, remember the light of Christ has already gone ahead to illuminate the areas of our lives that He has already predestined for us to conquer. Don't think of your process as never-ending, rather think of it as a preparation period for the greater season that lies ahead not just for you, but for all those who thought they kept you from reaping a great harvest. But just reaping a harvest is not enough for us to continue walking out our purpose in this life. We all need to and will have to face our down south Egypt moments in order to really value the steps it took to receive all that God has for us to inherit.

There is still one very important detail to fulfilling God's purpose in our lives. As I was meditating one day, the Holy Spirit led me to the scriptures to show me something very fascinating. He brought me to the story of Jacob and Esau. The Bible says Isaac and Rebecca had two sons. From the time that Esau and Jacob were in Rebecca's womb, there was a battle going on that caused Rebecca to inquire of the Lord regarding how she felt. *The Lord said to her, "There are two nations in your womb, two people shall be separated from your body; one people shall be stronger than the other, and the older shall serve the younger.* Scripture says when Rebecca gave birth, Esau came out first, then Jacob; but one day when Jacob was cooking stew, Esau being weary of not being able to catch game that day said to Jacob, "Please feed me because I am weary and hungry." Jacob says to his brother, "Sell me your birthright." Esau was so hungry and tired that he had not fully understood what it meant to give up a birthright that was tied to an inheritance. While Esau was busy trying to satisfy his flesh, Jacob was busy deceiving his brother and swearing him into an oath that later would ultimately cause the two brothers to become separated from one another for a time. Now that Esau becomes the younger brother, Jacob would have the opportunity to inherit the blessing from his father, Isaac, and not Esau. The Bible does not specify if Jacob told his mother what had happened, so it's best to assume that Jacob's mother still had no idea what had happened between the brothers, because, according to Genesis 27:15, Rebecca took Esau's clothes and put them on Jacob. This can only mean that Rebecca still thought her son Jacob was the youngest son. We also know that Rebecca was not pleased with Esau because Esau married women who worshipped other gods, which was unacceptable for one belonging to God's covenant family. I believe in women's intuition.

Although the case may be that Rebecca did not want Esau to have the inheritance due to lack of responsibility and carelessness, Rebecca was only basing on her instinct to make sure her son Jacob obtained the inheritance and not Esau. Rebecca did not know the transition that took place after Esau gave up his birthright, but according to the customs of inheriting the blessings, it was the older brother who got the blessings and not the younger brother. When Rebecca overheard Isaac telling Esau to run and find game because that night Isaac was going to give the blessing to Esau before his death, something inside of her caused her to rise and defend the house of God's covenant. Although rightfully the inheritance in the beginning belonged to Esau, Esau did not value what he possessed. Instead he became careless and lost what had been rightfully his. I just want to pause here for a moment to talk about the value of our inheritance. This life we are living is not about whether we live or die because those two things are appointed for us to encounter, but every one of us has been entrusted with something valuable, and we must seek God and become born again in the Spirit in order to fully understand that what we have inherited through Christ is not to be sold for the things of this world rather protected and valued. I'm talking about our inheritance to the kingdom of God. Jesus came to this earth to bring us salvation and has entrusted us with His word to share the gospel and the message of God to those who will inherit salvation. Jesus is our high brother, and we are his young siblings (to be exact) when Jesus came to this earth. Jesus said, according to Mathew 20:28, that He did not come to be served but to serve. Now that Jacob has become the older brother, he also has become the one who would, later on, have to come back and through his willingness to make things right again and become reconciled to his brother, Esau. What Esau lost because of carelessness, Jacob claimed because it was already predestined by God for Jacob to inherit the blessing, not Esau. Just like in the same way Adam, because of carelessness, lost all rights to the garden of Eden; yet Jesus, who represents the second Adam (according to *1 Corinthians 15:45*, which says, "*And so it is written, the first man Adam became a living being, the last Adam became a life-giving spirit.*" Also, in *1 Corinthians 15:21* and *22*, "*For since by man came death, by man also came the resurrection of the dead. For as in Adam all died, even so in Christ all shall be made alive.*") before the foundation of the world were laid down, God already knew that Jesus would have to come to inherit the victory that was won for us by Him on Calvary's cross and has chosen us as His children to serve with honor and integrity and has held us responsible of entrusting us with the gospel according to *1 Thessalonians 2:4*, which says, "*But as we have been approved by God to be entrusted with the gospel, even so, we speak not as pleasing men, but God who tests our hearts.* With everything that is within us, we all must guard our salvation with fear and trembling." We all must know that our salvation is precious and has been bought at a high price through the precious blood of Christ. Thank God for Jesus who came to take back what the enemy stole from us through Adam and Eve. Even though we all were once doomed to be condemned, Jesus came and chose us to inherit the kingdom of God through His triumphant victory on the cross, and although we all at one point or another felt like we didn't matter, there arose one from the grave who declares over our lives that we are seated in heavenly places with Christ and have been given all the spiritual blessings from heaven. Hallelujah! Thank you, Jesus, for that awesome inheritance. We all must understand that what God has entrusted us with, we all who are in Christ will one day have to be held accountable for how we have taken care of our salvation and what we have done to multiply the gifts and talents as well as being entrusted with the gospel, maintaining integrity, and trustworthiness toward God's word. Let not anyone steal or take away what God has entrusted us with because what God has entrusted us with is far greater than any riches this world has to offer.

The time came when Isaac would have to bless the older brother and give him the blessing, and at this point, Jacob was now the older brother and would soon inherit the blessings of his father. The moment Jacob stood in the presence of his father, Isaac, acting as Esau, Jacob that night received the inherited blessing from his father. Moments later, after Jacob had left, Esau came in looking for his father to bless him; but Isaac had not known what had happened and said to Esau, "Your brother came in with deceit and has taken away your blessing." Although this was an unfortunate situation, God already knew that this was how it needed to be, because from the womb, there was already a tug-of-war going on, but in order for God's will to be fulfilled, there had to be a separation before there could be restoration. So in that very moment, Jacob fled from before his family to his uncle's land, where later God would establish a work in Jacob and cause him to prosper; but in the end, he realize the wrong he had done. Yet God would bring Jacob back to the land of Canaan to become reconciled to his brother through forgiveness. God had a plan this entire time to cause Jacob to prosper and become rich in livestock, not so Jacob can boast of how much he has gained but because, through Jacob's process, there still needed to be fulfilled within his heart: an act of forgiveness toward his brother in order to fully understand the meaning of what it is to truly live in the abundance of God's joy and peace. God is faithful, and therefore, God will always fulfill His promises to His children. But there will always come a time when, although you may have everything your heart could possibly desire, God will tell you, "There is still one thing you lack, despite the fact you are wealthy or have kept my word in your heart. There is still one more step in the process that is the hardest but the most important thing you will have to face, and that is forgiving those who have done you wrong or have done you harm." And sometimes God will have you go back, like He made Jacob do or, in Joseph's case, have his family come to him in Egypt. Either way, no matter how much we gain in this life, all that we have will never measure up to the weight of holding on to unforgiveness. I believe that's why God leaves this part of the process until the final hour because this is where we truly see where our heart is really at. For Joseph, this was not an easy process, and in the end, the only one who stood by Joseph and saw him through was God. And for that reason, God gave Joseph the strength and courage to stand up and forgive his brothers. But the moment when Joseph revealed himself to his brothers was the moment God allowed Joseph to fully understand the process in the journey Joseph had to take in order to bring restoration and salvation to his household.

The time came for Joseph to reveal himself to his brothers, and when he did, the first thing he said was, "I am Joseph. Does my father live?" Now I know that was a question Joseph asked, but I also believe in rhetorical questions. If we look at it from a different perspective, we can see Joseph telling his brothers, "Whom you are looking at is your brother whom you thought was a slave here in Egypt. But through God's mercy, His mighty hand was doing a work in me so that your very lives, along with those back home, would live and not die. As my father lives, is there anything impossible for God?" In the very same way, at the time of Jesus's crucifixion on the cross, the disciples first doubted that Jesus had risen from the grave on the third day, but as the power of the Holy Spirit testifies to the fact that God the Father is indeed alive and well, so Jesus was, is, and will always be the pure evidence that our Heavenly Father is alive and well. As I began looking at scripture and really dug deeper into Joseph's life, I found something very interesting that really caused my faith to grow in knowing that every story and scripture in the Bible points to Jesus's salvation for all his creation. As I mentioned before at the beginning of my book, every part of Joseph's life, along with his brothers and the Egyptians, was a pure description of Jesus, the Jews, and the Gentile's life and what Jesus had to endure in order to bring forth a supernatural salvation that would cause those whom God ordained to be saved to inherit eternal life, to live and not die. But as Joseph revealed himself to his brothers, there was an instant pause and epiphany, and in a blink of an eye, what Joseph told to them also became a reality that the One whom they had rejected before was the one who stood in the gap for them to bring them through the trials they were facing. *Luke 24:35–40* says,

> *And they told about the things that had hap-pened on the road, and how He was known to them in the breaking of bread. Now as they said these things, Jesus Himself stood in the midst of them, "Peace to you." But they were terrified and fright-ened, and supposed they had seen a spirit. And He said to them, "Why are you troubled? And why do*

doubts arise in your hearts? Behold my hands and my feet, that it is I myself, handle Me and see, for a spirit does not have flesh and bones as you see I have." When He had said this, He showed them His hands and feet.

God has preserved our lives through His only begotten Son, Jesus Christ, for such a time as this, to become the one who, with the spirit of Christ, rise and stands in the gap to declare that our families will not die but live again in the kingdom of God.

Joseph could have never fulfilled God's calling on his life if he had not forgiven his brothers for the way they treated him. When Joseph finally revealed himself to his brothers, everything God had been working in Joseph's heart had been fulfilled. Joseph made known to his brothers the true reason he was brought down to Egypt (after he had revealed himself to them). The Bible says Joseph made everyone go out of the room (except his brothers) to cry aloud before them and to let them know that he was still alive and well. The one whom they could never in a million years fathom to be the one who would save their very lives was standing right in front of them, saying, "You sold me here to Egypt, but it was already established by God for me to go ahead of you all to save you all from a famine that would have brought destruction if I had not intervened on your behalf. But now don't be grieved or angry because you sold me here, but rejoice because God has sent me here to preserve your life." Truly, this was a priceless moment in time for Joseph and his brothers. I mean, think about it, before we all can come to the thought and reality of inheriting salvation, we must first be reconciled through Jesus. In the very same way, Joseph's brothers had to ask for Joseph's forgiveness in order for salvation, restoration, and transformation to take place. There may be deep wounded scars from what others have done to you in the past; but it's clear, according to the scriptures, that when we release our hurt and pain to the Father, He always makes a way for us to see that what had been causing our pain was God allowing us to encounter those moments so that in the end, after we have completely put our trust in Him, we would see the greater picture of God's design for our lives, instead of holding on to unforgiveness that will ultimately cause our heart and soul to drown away all the inner joy and happiness that God wants for us to truly experience through forgiveness.

A Healed Heart Will Seek to Forgive Others

I remember this one moment as a teenager I was jumped by these two girls in the streets of Huntington. I was coming back from Wyandanch after drinking about twelve beers. As I was approaching my friend's house, which was two houses over from where I lived, I heard a voice call out to me and say in a friendly voice, "Hey, do you want to come to hang with us?" I knew who this person was, but what I didn't know was they were setting me up to get jumped. It was getting dark, and as we approached one of the back streets and got out of the car, there was a bunch of girls surrounding me. Then two girls began to throw me down to the ground and kick and punch me repeatedly. Next thing I knew I was being lifted off the ground by my ex-boyfriend and put into the bushes. He told me he had nothing to do with this and that he was calling my mother to come pick me up. I remember my face hurting and my ex shining his lighter to see what was causing me my pain. When he looked, the expression on his face frightened me, and that's when I heard him say, "They slashed your face." At this point, I was in shock because it all happened so fast. So why am I telling you this story? Well, after this incident occurred, I had so much anger and trust issues that my life got so much worse. I began drinking and smoking more. I was driving without a license and getting locked up for having warrants because of not appearing in court. At this point, I was just a huge mess. One day, years later, I was walking into a Spanish deli when I saw one of the girls who had jumped me. All those emotions quickly ran through me, and I told her to stay there. I went back home and got a kitchen knife with the intention of stabbing her, but when I got there, I asked the clerk where the girl had went. He said she just left. Looking back now, I truly believe that God had purposely allowed her to leave to spare my life as well as her life. Now, fast-forward to who I am now. There came a time in my life, as a new creature in Christ, that I began praying for her and asking God to put her in my path so I could talk to her about Jesus. I had already forgiven her in my heart, but I just felt this need to see her and let her know that Jesus loves her. About three weeks later, I needed to return something at the local Walmart I always go to. I was waiting in line to return my item, and as I approached the counter, there she was. I just knew in my heart this was God answering my prayers. I looked at her and said her name, but the look on her face told me that she didn't recognize me, so I told her, "It is me, Melissa." When she heard my name, she quickly remembered me and thought that I would probably react in the same way. But I leaned over to her and said, "I have found Jesus, and I want you to know that Jesus loves you very much." I also told her that I was praying for her as well. When she heard those words, I saw her countenance change. I wanted to talk more, but the return line was so long, so I said to her, "Have a blessed day." I have not spoken to her since, but I pray that she has come to know Jesus as I have come to know Him. Forgiveness is not a key element, but *the* key element to moving on with your life. Whether that other person chooses to forgive you or not, our job is not to make the other person forgive us but to set ourselves free from unforgiveness. But when someone asks us for forgiveness, we need to continue to forgive no matter what. The most important thing in this life is forgiving those who have done you wrong or have done harm to you. This is because we are not the justifiers or the judge. No matter what has been done to you, always remember that God has a perfect plan to see us through any and every tragic moment we encounter. The process may not look perfect to us because of the pain and suffering that comes along with being processed, but to God, every puzzle piece fits within the masterpiece of God's greatest work in us. We are all designed by God to face and conquer our greatest challenges through Christ Jesus. When we learned to lean upon God's understanding, we will begin to live a life full of forgiveness toward those who thought they had done us harm but were actually pushing us further into the will of God's purpose. It's when we begin to realize (just like Joseph did) that everything God permitted to happen was to save the lives of those who caused you to be where you are right now in the hand of God's will. Don't think for one moment or doubt that where you are right now God isn't working it out for you. Wherever you may find yourself, just know that God sees you and is waiting for you to speak, because it's in our lowest moments that God reveals himself to us. And however He chooses to reveal Himself, it will always be in a way where you'll know beyond a shadow of a doubt that this was none other than God's presence flowing through you and letting you know that He is on your side. When God shows up, so does reconciliation and restoration, but before this can happen, we all must trust in His plan to bring us all back together, and when He does this, it will be a moment in time that no one can take away from us. When Joseph revealed himself to his brothers, their brothers were at the lowest point in their lives. They had experienced a moment in time when they thought they were being punished for what they had done to their brother; but this was the exact opposite, because instead of being punished and condemned for what they had done, grace was making its way into their hearts. We all deserve to be punished and condemned for our sins against God; but just like God sent Joseph ahead and showed them grace instead of punishment and condemnation, Jesus too went ahead of us as the sacrificial lamb, to die a harsh punishment that was meant for us, to forgive us and show us mercy and grace. When Jesus said, "It is finished," on the cross, this meant that everything that was spoken of about Jesus in the Old Testament and the New Testament had been fulfilled through His crucifixion on the cross. Today that same grace and mercy that was poured out on Calvary's cross for our sins are still offered to everyone who comes to Christ and asks for forgiveness.

Sought by God, Led by God, Freed by God

After God had established and brought Joseph's family from Canaan down to Egypt, on the way down, God gave a vision to Jacob (Joseph's father). This was not the first time God had spoken of what God's people would have to endure later in order to become a mighty nation under God's authority. If we look back into the scriptures, we are going to find that when God speaks a word, He will confirm it through the generations to come until that prophecy comes to pass. We may never fully understand why God does what He does, but seeing all that God has done in His faithfulness to keep us in His perfect will is enough for me to fully trust him with my life. The seas will have to roar when a storm takes place, and the mountains will have to shake when an earthquake takes place; but if we are standing on the solid foundation of who Christ Jesus is, whatever needs to be washed away, removed, and reestablished, only God knows how to bring it to pass. Don't let the weight of this world bring you to a place of confusion but rather trust in the promises God has spoken over your life. God gave a prophecy to Abraham concerning the latter days of what His people would go through in the land of Egypt. This passage is found in Genesis 15:13 and 14, which says, "*Then He said to Abraham: 'Know certainly that your descendants will be strangers in a land that is not theirs and will serve them, and they will afflict them four hundred years.*" But on that nation with whom your descendants will serve, I will bring judgment, and afterward, they will come out (of the land) with great possessions. This was the first time God had spoken to Abraham concerning this. That those under God are going to face the ultimate test of trials. This is because before we can testify of God's greatness, we must believe within our hearts that if God is permitting us to see these horrible events come to pass, then He will surely allow us to see the victory that comes from these tragic moments. After God gave Abraham this vision, God says to him, "You shall surely go from this earth in peace." In other words, "Don't worry about your descendants because, just as I have brought you through Egypt, I too will bring up your descendants from Egypt." As we pray for the generations to come, we must also believe in God for the victories they will see, despite the tragic moments they will have to encounter in order to see those victories come to pass.

About three years ago, I am not quite sure if what I saw was in my dream or a vision, but I remember having an out-of-body experience. I was in a library, and I remember going upstairs and coming to a room where I saw a hole in the wall that led to the universe. As I was staring in astonishment, I was lifted off the ground and brought into the universe. I then heard a voice say, "Look all around, for the times are changing." When I looked, I began to see the planets align themselves one after the other as they were orbiting in space. I saw planets that were shiny and had been formed with diamonds. Others sparkled with dazzling colors. I can't explain this part clearly, but the planets began marching around the stars. Then I heard a voice say, "Now it's time to go back." Suddenly, an angel came and took me back to the earth, and when I arrived, I saw cars everywhere on the road, but no one was in them. I then looked up and saw young boys and girls sleeping on clouds that were suspended in the air. They were all in a sound sleep. Nothing could wake them. It was then that I saw a bridge high and lifted up, and before I knew it, I was transported to the bottom of the bridge. I then began to see the clouds that the youth were sleeping on begin to move toward the top of the bridge. And to my amazement, as the clouds suspended in the air began to float over the bridge, I saw the youth walking up, and fire were coming out of their mouths. Instantly, I was transported up to the bridge, and I asked the angel who was by my side what this meant. And he told me this was the great revival of the youth that was taking place. I saw young men and women speaking in tongues I had never seen or heard of before. But then I looked and saw a girl who looked disturbed by what she was seeing. She became angry and said, "This is not for me," and left. I tried to stop her, but she said to me, "Leave me alone. I want nothing to do with this. I'm going to find a party to go to and drink." As I saw her leave, that's when I woke up and realized that this was a message God was giving me to warn the youth that there is coming a time when, instead of seeking God's face, they will be in a spiritual sleep due to the distractions of this world. But before the Lord comes, there will be a great revival, and the youth will rise, and God will give them the victory as He did with His people in Egypt. I am believing God for that great revival, and even if I don't see it in my time, I am confident that God will surely bring it to pass.

When God allows us to see into the future (whether in a dream, vision, or having an out-of-body experience), this is a call from God for us to begin praying and interceding for the generations to come and declare them blessed in the holy name of Jesus Christ. Although we may not specifically be able to pray for a particular person we don't know, we must (at times) generalize our prayer to a degree where we no longer pray for just a revival but for the Holy Spirit to spread quickly through a generation called by God to speak the truth even when it becomes difficult or those who oppose what we stand for have no choice but to hear the message, because a heart set on fire by God will cause many to see the truth and draw near, not only to be touched by God but to become transformed and made new by God through the blood of Jesus Christ by the renewing of the Holy Spirit. I believe the dream I had represented the great revival that is getting ready to take place soon. The universe I saw along with the planets aligning themselves and marching around the stars, I believe, represents heaven getting ready for the coming of the Lord. And as spectacular as this event was in the universe, so it will be in the day Jesus returns. The angel who brought me back to the earth said to me, "It's time to go back to the earth." I believe this was a metaphor of how God the Father is going to tell His Son when the time comes for Jesus to return to the earth. The cars I saw on the road, I believe, represents movement, travel, or how we get around; but in this case, there was no one in the cars. This was because those who were supposed to be in their cars were suspended in the air on the clouds sleeping. The Lord, later on, revealed to me, "The reason the cars were still and the youth was sleeping in the clouds is because the advancement of technology has slowed them down from spending time with me in my presence, and so as time went on and hearts began to turn away from seeking my will, their spiritual desires started to fade away, which in turn caused them to fall into a deep spiritual coma." The cars that stood still on the road represented their means of transportation, which eventually ran out of gas, and with no gas, there is no way of getting around. In the same sense, without the Holy Spirit, we will eventually burn out and fall into a spiritual coma. But as God is merciful, gracious, slow to anger, and abounding in steadfast love and faithfulness, God already knows the appointed time of when this revival will take place. Although the youth had been in this conditional state of mind, God was already heading them toward the bridge, which I believe represents Jesus Christ, and aligning them to an awakening that would become the greatest event that will happen moments before the coming of the Lord would occur. There is coming for the youth the greatest revival ever heard of, because although the youth may be asleep, the only one who has the power to awaken them is God Almighty through the power of the Holy Spirit. When God speaks a word, it will come to pass. No matter what we face in this life or how far down we have to travel to see that revival come to pass, as sure as God delivered time and time again His people from Egypt, so God will give us the victory and cause an awakening to rise up within us as He moves us toward that bridge (who is Christ) so we can see a mighty spiritual revival take place, just as it says in *Zephaniah 3:9*, "*For then I will restore to the peoples a pure language, that they all may call upon the name of the Lord to serve him with one accord.*" I truly believe the fire I saw coming out of the youth's mouth represented none other than the Holy Spirit reviving and restoring the youth back to their supernatural state of mind, and although there was one who did not want to receive the impartation of the Holy Spirit. Unfortunately, there will always be that one who would be led away by Satan's lies and deceptions, and despite the fact that the truth is staring them in the face, they will continue to live in their old ways and not partake of the truth that can set them free. As God has called us to pray over every city, every nation, and over every need that God places in our hearts to pray over, we also must remember that only God knows who will come to Him with repentance and who will turn away from the truth. As God has called us to intercede for the generations to come, we also must keep in mind that what we do today for the kingdom of God will set the scene for those to play their part for generations to come. If we are having to face Egypt today, this could be God's way of setting our generation up to walk by faith (despite the harsh things we must see and encounter) in order for the next generation to reap the promises that the former generations sowed with tears, pain, and suffering. This is because what we sow into to the next generations to come depends on our faith in God's plan to bring us through Egypt, knowing that we may never really fully get to experience the fullness of God's promises but that we, as the former generation, had paved the way for the next generation to inherit what we have sown in them. And that is a harvest of faith, to walk out their calling with love, power, and sound mind, knowing and believing that if God was with us, God will surely be with the generations to come.

Abraham was the first to encounter Egypt, but he wouldn't be the last. Along with having to experience going through Egypt, Abraham also knew that Egypt was a place of transition and restitution. He knew that if God said his descendants would have to remain in Egypt for a time, Abraham also knew in his heart that God would bring them back up with transition and restitution. This is what having a personal relationship with God looks like. As our children get older, we all must know that they will have to face their own process, but even though they will have to go through their own Egypt or down south moments, just like God promised Abraham that although they would have to remain in Egypt for some time, they would come out with great possession when their process was over. This can only mean one thing: God has already established their coming in and going out. So no matter how fierce the battle gets, just remember the promise God made to us concerning our children and our children's children, our children's children's children, all the way to the thousands and ten thousands generations to come, it will certainly come to pass as long as we continue passing the torch of God's word on to the next generation and praying for God to deliver them from every affliction that tries to keep them in bondage.

As I was reading further into the scriptures, I found something very interesting that the Holy Spirit pointed out to me that I had not noticed before. I have read the book of Genesis repeatedly, but this time it was as though God highlighted the exact verses he wanted me to gain revelation from: *Genesis 46:2–4.*

> *Then God spoke to Israel (meaning Jacob), in the visions of the night, and said, "Jacob, Jacob!" And he said, "Here I am," So He said, "I Am God, the God of your father; do not fear to go down to Egypt, for I will make you a great nation there. I*

163

will go down with you to Egypt, and I will surely
bring you up again, and Joseph will put his hand
on your eyes."

God didn't only give this prophecy to Abraham, but He gave it to Abraham's grandson (Jacob) as well. God is so faithful to His promises that although we don't deserve God's confirmation, He still gives it to us. When God spoke to Abraham, Abraham had not yet received the promised son but believed God for that promise. Imagine being told that years from now, after you are long gone, your descendants will become strangers in a land they don't know and will become afflicted for four hundred years. I believe when we die in faith, we pass on a greater example than if we just give in to the fear of the unknown. Abraham knew that when God spoke a word, that word would come to pass. Just having faith allows you to believe in what you know God has the capability of fulfilling in your life, but having supernatural faith goes beyond our own comprehension. And this was what Abraham had within him and why he was able to communicate with God on a higher level. Learning to hear God's voice is the key to having a healthy relationship with the Father. When we begin to hear His voice more and more, we begin to grow spiritually. God doesn't just want to talk to us when things are going well; He also wants us to be attentive to His voice because there are times when God has us travel through Egypt or gives us a vision in the night of our children or family member who will soon enter a season of affliction. But if we do not heed the warning signs God is giving to us or the instructions that He has laid before us to follow, we won't be able to lead the coming generation to a higher level of faith. As for us, we will be in a constant battle of confusion, and this does not come from God but from the enemy.

God told Abraham in chapter 17 verse 4 of Genesis: *"As for Me, behold my covenant is with you, and you shall be a father of many nations."* God spoke to Abraham, and Abraham continued to walk in great faith. This passed on to his son (Isaac) and continued with his grandson (Jacob), whom God once again revealed that God would permit His people to go down to Egypt. But this time, God mentions why, and it's to make a great nation out of Israel. This is the purest evidence that we are never left alone no matter how much we may feel like we are. God is always giving us confirmation, whether through his word, person, or prophecy, letting us know that although we may have to walk through the valleys of the shadows of death, we are to fear no evil because the rod and staff that God holds in His hand will lead us to our greatest victory yet. And even when we become afflicted by the enemy, God is ready to fight on our behalf as we call upon His name in faith, knowing that just as God allowed us to enter in with mercy, He will also give us a way out by grace. God is getting ready to demonstrate to all those who have thus far placed their faith in him His mighty powers over all the earth. The enemy has been afflicting God's people for far too long, and I believe that we have just entered a time where supernatural events are going to take place. Where the enemy brought affliction, God is bringing supernatural healing. Where the enemy brought chaos, God is bringing backorder. Where the enemy placed his hand, God is coming back to take the enemy's hands off what belongs to God. And soon, there will be a great revival that will shake the nations, and all who were afflicted shall be set free by the Spirit of God's mighty powers and wonders. God is doing a work in you that you at this moment can't possibly imagine. Just know that among billions of souls on this earth, God chose you and me to stand in the gap for the nations and has promised that He would never leave us nor forsake us. The moment you and I chose to put our faith in Christ Jesus, our very lives were placed in the hands of the One who stands over us day and night, declaring us to be more than conquerors through Christ Jesus. His name is Jehovah Nissi, and He never ever loses a battle. No, not one!

A Final Confirmation Yet to Be Heard of a Prophecy Yet to Be Fulfilled

By this time, Joseph's father was already aware that his son was alive and well. As Jacob was making his way toward Egypt, Joseph was on his way to be reunited with his father, whom he had been separated from. And so, when Joseph saw his father, the Bible says Joseph presented himself to Jacob and fell and wept on his father's neck a good while. Wow! What a beautiful picture to see and behold. A son reuniting with his father after having been away for so long on a journey that, in the end, brought salvation through a life-changing experience, which could have been done only through an extraordinary act of love. The Bible says that Joseph went up to meet his father in Goshen. As Joseph represents Jesus, we can see that Jacob represents our Heavenly Father, and the picture we see clearly represents Jesus reuniting with His Father after enduring every trial and tribulation but, in the end, had won the victory for us all and now has ascended to the Father to present Himself as the sacrificial Lamb who has gone before us to save us from eternal condemnation. I believe the tears shed by Joseph and his father represents the joy and gladness Jesus and His Father felt when Jesus presented Himself unto the Father whom He had been separated from because of the weight of the world's sin that was poured upon Jesus when he took our place on the cross and became the sacrificial Lamb who would cause many to inherit eternal salvation. You and I are here because there was One who went before us and conquered the grave. We all have the opportunity to inherit salvation, although we have all fallen short of the glory of God, through Jesus's act of love on the cross. Despite our faults and failures in life, despite the fact that we have all rejected and despised Jesus at one point in time or another, Jesus still chose to faithfully walk down the lonely road of rejection, being despised by many, and constantly having to face heartache, knowing that through it all, He would be the One to bring forth a new beginning to all those who choose to put their complete trust in Him. As Jesus conquered the grave, He declares over us that we have been made more than conquerors through his triumphant sacrifice on the cross.

Just as Joseph conquered every challenge that came his way because God stood by him every step of the way, so God says to us today, "Do not fear or become dismayed because I the Lord Am with you wherever you go." The Bible says in chapter 50 verses 24 and 25:

> *Joseph said to his brothers, "I am dying, but God will surely visit you and bring you out of this*

land to the land of which He swore to Abraham, to
Isaac, and to Jacob." Then Joseph took an oath from
the children of Israel, saying, "God will surely visit
you, and you shall carry up my bones from here."

In various times Jesus told His disciples that He would have to go away but that God would send a Helper to be with them and lead them through every situation. In the very same way, whenever we are going through our Egypt moments, we can always count on the Holy Spirit to see us through. Just as sure as Joseph's bones did not remain in Egypt and Jesus did not remain in the tomb but was taken up and out by the Holy Spirit, so those found in Christ Jesus living out the will of the Father will not remain in Egypt for long, because just as Joseph took an oath and said to his brothers, "God will surely visit you," the same promise that was prophesied then has come to pass now. God has allowed us to receive His Son through his redemption on the cross. But this doesn't mean that everything from here on out will become a walk in the park. On the contrary, our biggest battle is yet to come! Just as God's people had made it to Egypt because Joseph chose to stand in the gap for his family, this was only the beginning of what God was about to do in the lives of the Israelites and what they would have to endure in order to come out as a strong nation. Everyone who chooses to place their faith in Jesus will have to endure many afflictions, but as the Bible says in *Psalm 34:19*, *"Many are the afflictions of the righteous, but the Lord delivers him out of them all."* So now we begin to see before our very eyes that every Egypt moment led to this moment that was first given to Abraham by God while in a deep sleep and to Jacob in the visions of the night, which was confirmed through Joseph's mouth and which eventually became a reality because God's people were about to enter into a season that would change the course of time and become the most memorable event to ever take place in the Old Testament. Every Egypt moment has led to this very moment when God would fulfill His promise to Abraham through Moses. But before this promise could come to pass, the Israelites would have to face their greatest challenge yet. This was not going to be easy or a walk in the park for God's people;

but the same way God sent Abraham's wife to pass through Egypt, they all came out blessed. God sent Joseph to Egypt to go ahead of his family to rescue them from perishing in the famine and brought restoration to Joseph's house. God has predestined a baby who would travel to Egypt, remain in Egypt until he finds his identity, and ultimately becomes a born leader who will lead God's people into a victorious exit out of Egypt. But before I get ahead of myself, I want to share my testimony on how God (in the year 2021) brought me through my own Egypt moment that I thought would have been the end of me had it not been for the Lord's grace and mercy pursuing me the whole time.

For a while, I had suffered depression in the dark. No one knew about it because I chose to find ways to hide it, instead of seeking proper medical help. I self-medicated myself hoping things would get better. Although I was going to church and at times participating in worship services and speaking about the love of God, I was drowning in my own sorrows. And as much as I tried so hard to not let how others treated me get to me, it became my biggest battle yet. Every voice that the enemy placed in my head became thoughts of unworthiness, thoughts of doubting of me being here and having a purpose was even worth living for. The enemy just kept feeding me these lies because I kept believing and keeping them within me; and just like eating something that is poison, eventually, it caused me to become sick internally. At this point, I had fallen so deep that I started to feel as if anything I tried to do or say didn't matter. At random times, I would begin to cry and not know why. I started to shut people out of my life, but I was able to fake it well when I would go to church. I would go to church and act as if the issues I was facing had disappeared, but the reality of it all was that I was doing more harm to myself than I thought because at church, I would put on a clown face, trying to mask the root of bitterness of what was really going on inside my heart. As I stated before, I had been criticized and rejected my whole life; and so being in church, looking for that comfort in my brothers and sisters, only led me to find that not everyone in the church is the church. There are those who see your dreams and visions but do not have the capability to comprehend that God has called you to fulfill that dream and vision and not them. So what you begin to see are people that have become envious and have subliminally begun to start despising you and making you out to be someone you are not, which in turn causes more harm to that person than it does to the dreamer. Boy, I wish I had discovered that then, but instead, I chose to believe in the lies of the enemy instead of believing what God had spoken over me as a child. But then again, God gave Joseph the dreams, and Joseph had to go to Egypt. From those dreams, the reality caused Joseph to rise up and become who God always intended for him to become, as those around him were permitted by God to envy and despise Joseph until the appointed time would come when Joseph would rise up to deliver his family. And know beyond a shadow of a doubt that God had handpicked Joseph among billions to go ahead and be the change their family needed in order to see salvation. Looking back now at what I had to face and go through just so God could have all my attention was all worth it, and if I had to do it again, I know that God would remain with me through it all, just like He is with me now as I am writing this book.

CHAPTER 9

Every Operation Led Me Closer to the Great Physician

Through the years I have been married, I have struggled with my identity of who I was in Christ. Although my husband saw me for the woman of God I am, I still struggled with believing that he saw me that way, and so bringing insecurities to a marriage caused us to have a lot of friction in the beginning. And when we had our children, I began to feel the attacks of the enemy, not just emotionally but physically. I had altogether, including my oldest daughter from a previous relationship, four C-sections; so you can just imagine the physical pain I suffered. As time went on, I began having back problems from a previous accident I had while working and ended up having back surgery. Then over the course of three to four years, I ended up having my gallbladder removed and an abdominal hernia mesh implant, which was supposed to be a simple operation that turned into a complicated surgery that left me days in the hospital to recover. At this point, I was physically and emotionally run-down to the point that I started believing that I deserved everything that was happening to me and that this was going to be the condition of my life I would remain in. Even though those thoughts crossed my mind, I still somehow got the courage to praise the name of Jesus and call out to him in desperation, and it was in those moments where I would feel His tangible touch hold me and tell me that everything is working for the good to those who love God and are called according to His purpose. All I could do was cry, weep, and hold on to my faith. The worst pain for me at that moment was knowing that I had to pull it together for my children because they were still way too small to even attempt to understand what I was going through.

Where we were living at the time had been infested with mice, and although maintenance tried to take care of the problem, every night, we would hear them in the walls and most nights, I would stay up crying in terror. When I opened the closet door to the pantry in the morning to look for my kids' snack, the bags would be chewed up, and there would be bite marks on the food. I was so terribly disturbed by all of this that I would begin to cry out to the Lord for help and strength just to survive another day without having to see these rodents.

As I mentioned earlier in my book, I have an older daughter from a previous relationship. For any mother going through a tough time with your child, never give up on them because although they may walk a path you had not intended for them to walk, ultimately the choice is theirs and the consequences of their actions will also be theirs to bear as well. We love our children, but we must remember that God loves them a whole lot more. And because God loves them, He will not give them more than they can handle. Most of the time when we as parents find ourselves constantly fighting the same battles with our kids, this is God's way of saying that unless you release the battle to me, the battle will continue until one of you gets hurt. When we bring our petition to the Lord through prayer and supplication, trust and believe that God has already made way in the supernatural realm, and if we faint not, we will eventually see it come to pass in the natural or physical realm. God will hear from His throne room and cause His angels to guard us and our household until His purpose is fulfilled in and through us.

From the age of twelve to sixteen, I faced one of the hardest challenges of my life. My daughter and I would never see eye to eye because so many things have happened from having her at such a young age. As she entered her teenage years, my husband and I decided to enroll her in a private Christian school. The payments were very high, but my mother and her grandmother on her father's side were willing to help with the payments each month. We all thought this was the best thing for her because as born-again believers, we truly believed that my daughter would benefit from learning more about Jesus and focusing on her studies, but for the first year, I started to notice that when my daughter got home from school each day, she would not speak to me and would go straight to her room and shut the door (typical teenage stuff). There would be days when I would receive phone calls from her teacher saying, "Your daughter today was constantly at her locker looking at herself in the mirror and not focusing on her work." One day I received a phone call from her teacher with a concerned voice, and we talked for about a half an hour on the phone. I was a little shocked by what the teacher told me but a part of me knew this was coming. The teacher said to me, "Your daughter is a beautiful young girl and has a lot of potential, but I see in the future destruction coming her way if she does not heed the voice of God because the enemy has a target on her life to destroy her before she discovers her true God-given potential." The teacher told me, "She is in class, but it's as if her mind is not here, and when we are doing work, she doesn't focus enough to complete the work that's before her." As a mother, I remember having the feeling of worry come over me like never before, because when the teacher said the word *destruction*, it brought me back to a dream I had years ago with my daughter. I was climbing up a bridge trying to catch up to my daughter. The bridge though was rising and getting taller and taller. As I reached the top and went to grab her, she turned around, and when she looked at me, her body was her own, but her face was the face of a demonic spirit who told me, "Your daughter is mine, and I will do everything in my power to see you in hell." After we talked, the teacher prayed with me. After the conversation, I began to ask God for help because I knew this was bigger than just a little girl going through a season in her life. This was the enemy waging war against my child. Throughout the years, it got harder and harder. It felt as if the more we sought the Lord, the bigger the battles got in our home. My daughter had allowed a demonic spirit to enter her two times, and we had to call the members of our church to quickly pray and rebuke those spirits. It got to the point when, because I was physically weak from having so many surgeries and not being able to fully recover from them properly, it caused me to fall victim to the enemy's lies and believed that I would never see victory. But what the enemy failed to realize was that the victory had already been won for me through Christ, and although I was in the condition I was in, the enemy made it clear to me that he would do everything possible to block me from truly believing that God would get me through this.

I am not going to sugarcoat anything I write but tell you the truth because I believe with all my heart that we are set free by the truth. I started to lose hope in everything and in everyone. My daughter was growing worse and worse every day, and I just couldn't take it anymore. I began self-medicating myself with opioids that I had from my previous surgeries just to make the mental and emotional pain go away. But all that did was cause another problem on top of the problems I was facing. I had caught an addiction to them, and I felt as if I couldn't live without them. Instead of seeking God, I began taking the pills as my saving grace. And so, as I continued taking these pills, trying to numb the reality of my pain, I grew worse and began looking at life as just an empty space I was occupying for the moment. All I could think about was not being here any longer and how life would be better off without me here. When we begin to self-medicate ourselves (whether it's using drugs, alcohol, having an addiction to watching pornography, etc.) and try to avoid the root of the problem, what begins to spring up from those roots are bitterness, anger, resentment, judgment toward ourselves, hate, regret, envy, jealousy, and the negative list goes on. When these things take their full place in our lives, it begins choking us until we eventually give in to them and begin acting in irrational ways. I became so angry with everything that was happening that I started to believe that everyone around me was out to get me, and so I began looking at everyone as if they were the root of my problem. I began losing my passion for music, and I did not want to face the reality of my problems head-on. And so, slowly but surely, I was becoming depressed and full of anxiety, not wanting to go to church fellowship gatherings, and if I did go, I wanted to quickly leave the moment I got there.

I remember one day I was in my room, and I was watching a Christian program on TV of a woman giving her testimony of how God delivered her from depression and everything she had to go through just to find deliverance. Instead of wanting to be delivered from my own depression just like that woman, I began having these thoughts of suicide (that the enemy already had planted in my mind), and I remember being angry at God because in reality, I wanted what that woman received, but the truth was, I wasn't giving all my pain and hurt to God. I was self-medicating my pain with pills and keeping my pain at a distance to where I knew all I had to do in order to numb the pain was pop a pill, which only took my pain away for a couple of hours, only to have the pain come crashing down on me like a ton of bricks. At that moment, I shut the TV off went and told my oldest daughter to call my mom and my husband and tell them to come and take care of her because I couldn't do this anymore. I quickly shut my door, pulled the blinds down, and remained in the dark until my husband and my mother came. I told them life would be better off without me. My husband stood by my side the entire time, encouraging me and by letting me know how much he and the kids love me. My husband fervently prayed over me, and I remember feeling a sense of peace come over me that I had not felt in a while. From that moment, I began seeking God and asking the Holy Spirit for guidance. Although the worst of what happened to me had passed, there was still yet another encounter I had yet to come across, but this would be the encounter that changed the course of not just my life, but my very own family as well. This would be the moment that led to my true transformation and restoration.

Soon after, I began to seek God again and ask Him for the forgiveness of my sins and to see me through every trial I would have to face in this season. It wasn't easy coming off the opioids; but with the help of the Holy Spirit, my husband's support, and my mother helping me with my kids, I began to slowly experience life without having the urge to pop a pill. I enrolled in school for the medical assistant program and began seeing life in a whole new way. I felt as if I had purpose and meaning. Although things didn't get better with my daughter, my mother and I came to a mutual agreement that, through the courts, my daughter would remain with my mother. She was placed in a much better school district. After two years of her not being compliant in private school and us not being able to keep up with the payments, she was placed back in public school, where she constantly got in trouble. Eventually, she got into a fight, and that's when I knew she needed to get out of that school district. So my daughter went to live with my mother. It was a little rough, but as the years went on, my daughter got the proper help and began pulling her grades up. Soon after, my husband and I found a place close to where my daughter and mother lived, and my kids were placed in a much better school district. Things started looking up, and I began working in the morning and going to school at night. Little did I know I was setting myself up for the perfect storm that would come and shake my entire world to the ground.

There are always those moments in life when everything is going well and just when we think things can't turn for the worse, we find ourselves in a storm, and we try to figure out how we got there in the first place. This is exactly how I felt when life began to get the best of me, and I tried to take on more than I could handle. I wanted so much to prove to myself that I could do it all on my own, so I continued to work and go to school. By the time I got home from night school, I was so exhausted, and all I wanted to do was sleep. This became a daily routine that eventually caused me to neglect my husband and my family duties. I kept every emotion bottled up inside and continued to study and work hard. I didn't realize it at that time, but I was heading down a road of destruction. But I didn't bother to heed the warning signs because I was too caught up in wanting to be the best wife and mother I could be for my husband and children. Although my intentions were good, my action plan was all wrong. When we don't consult and bring our plan of action to the Lord, we begin to call our own shots and walk according to our own agenda. Now I'm not saying that my working and going to school was a bad thing, but when we don't prioritize our goals and ask the Lord to lead and guide us, we start to become frustrated in trying to complete something that is not within our season to complete. And in trying to go ahead of God, we become confused in our thoughts, and we become disappointed when we don't see the results we were expecting to see. I found myself going into a cycle of wanting my husband to be proud of me, but instead, all I got from him was, "You are taking on too much," and we would constantly argue over this matter. I remember nights when I would just cry and hope that one day this would all be over and I could show my husband and my children how all the hard work I put in finally paid off, but that day never came, or at least not in the time I thought it would come to pass. I began having those thoughts of drinking wine to help relax and stay calm. In the beginning, they were just thoughts, but eventually, I started pondering on it, and one night after school, I went to an Applebee's around the corner from my school. I had some studying to do for a test that was coming up, and so I sat down and looked at the menu. There was the wine selection, and I gave in to that temptation and drank a glass. After I went home, I remember having the feeling of, "This isn't so bad," and so I continued to drink a glass of wine, telling myself that a glass of wine a day is not bad. But one turned into two and two turned into three until I began using wine as a way of trying to cope with all the stress that was in me about work and school and then having to deal with my responsibilities at home. Not to mention I was physically neglecting my husband as well, which really caused friction to grow fast within our marriage. This became an ongoing thing. I slowly stopped going to church and began viewing everyone in the church as hypocrites because along with the stress, the feelings of rejection came running back to my heart like a wave crashing down on me, with the enemy whispering in my ear (as I watched on the church Facebook live page), "Look they rejected you and criticized you for your voice and look how they are standing on the pulpit preaching what they don't practice." Even though I let myself believe these lies from the enemy, it still did not negate the fact that God was permitting these things to rise in my life so that in the end, I would come out fireproof and be able to stand against the wiles of the enemy's deceptions. Because my war wasn't and isn't against flesh and blood but against principalities and rulers of darkness, against Satan himself, at the moment all these things are happening, as humans, we begin to look at it from a fleshly point of view as opposed to a spiritual point of view. These were the lies I was allowing the enemy to infiltrate my mind with. And it didn't take long until I began having feelings of resentment toward them and despising them for the things that had happened to me in the church.

When the enemy has something to hold on to, he will make sure he grips us to the point where we begin to believe every lie he speaks. If we are not rooted in the word of God, we will have no other choice but to give in to the enemy's lies and eventually start acting upon those lies until we become what we think in our hearts to be true. For me, it was the belief that no matter how much I did, it didn't matter, or at least that's how I began viewing life. I continued drinking more and more until one night I was in my truck and those suicidal thoughts began crossing my mind once again, but this time I saw myself on top of the Robert Moses bridge ready to jump off and end my life. I had already finished an entire bottle of wine. I pulled into a parking lot, and in front of me was a giant rock. At that moment, I had not realized that that giant rock that I was looking at was Jesus telling me I didn't have to take this route that leads to destruction. But because I was filled with so much hurt and pain, I blocked it out and began writing a suicide text to my mother telling her that she was the greatest mother in the world and that I would never be able to measure up to the good mother she was to us and how I was very sorry but I made the decision to take my own life by jumping off the bridge. My mom called, and all I said to her was, "Please forgive me, but I can't live anymore. I must jump off the bridge. Please take care of my kids." That's all the enemy needed to hear because after that I felt a strong force telling me that nobody was going to miss me and that it would be in everyone's best interest if I wasn't around. I went to the 7-Eleven and bought NyQuil and another bottle of wine because my thoughts were when I jump, I don't want to feel a thing. I wanted to have the feeling of just wanting to sleep, so I took four pills, and as I was driving on the parkway, I remember having a half a bottle of wine left, which I threw out the window as I was approaching the Robert Moses bridge. I had put my phone on Facebook live. I don't remember at that moment the words I was speaking because at that point I felt the NyQuil running through me. I left my car on the bridge, and as I approached the bars of the bridge and climbed up and looked down, I said to God, "I'm sorry but I can't do this anymore." That was when I heard a still, small voice say to me "If you jump, you will be eternally separated from me. Step down, I am not finished with you yet." When I heard those words, immediately the sensation of feeling under the influence left my body, and I felt the love of God's grace and mercy come over me like nothing I had ever felt before. I managed to get down and get in my truck. I began driving. Anyone who has visited Robert Moses beach knows that there is one way to enter, and to exit, you must go all the way down until you can't anymore and make a U-turn and go on the other bridge that leads back toward the parkway. The enemy knew that God had spoken to me, but that didn't stop him from still trying to take my life that night. I thought that I had made the U-turn all the way down, but apparently, I only turned around midway and was now driving on the opposite side of the road. At this point, it became dangerous since I could have been in a head-on collision accident and died or, worse, I could have killed someone. There was a blessing in disguise as I was stopped by the sheriff. I remember, after getting out of my truck, the sheriff asking me a bunch of questions, having me walk in a straight line, and reciting the alphabet backward. I got into the sheriff's police car and told the sheriff, "I know what I have done was wrong, and I completely take responsibility for my actions, but I also know that God can take a bad situation and turn it around for good when we repent of our sins and turn to Him." That's when I told the sheriff, "Jesus loves you more than you know, and God has a plan for your life." How ironic, right? Here I am the one in hand-cuffs bound by the police officer going to jail, yet I was still able to relay the message God had put in my heart to tell the officer. You'd think the officer would have ignored me completely, but he did just the opposite. He said to me, "Thank you for that." I then asked him if he could put on K-Love, and to my surprise, he did. He left it on the whole time. To this day, I wonder if he kept it on and continued listening to K-Love. Only God knows and one can only hope. I was taken to the second precinct, where I was going to be released to go home instead of staying the night and waiting for the judge the next day, but because my mother had called in and said I had attempted to commit suicide, they sent me to the hospital for an evaluation. When I got there, the police officer told me she was going to take the cuff off me because she didn't view me as a threat. Before getting to the hospital, I had explained to her that I am a mother of four kids married, working, and going to school but I just let life get the very best of me and allowed myself to become overwhelmed with life's storms. But the reality is, I have recognized that this isn't the way out. She looked at me and said, "I understand where you are coming from, but I want you to know, in life, no matter how hard it gets, never stop doing what you're doing because eventually, you will get there someday." I felt that even though I deserved to be condemned for what I did, God was showing me grace and mercy through the sheriff and police officer. When I was brought into the back waiting to be evaluated, I remember the cop telling me before she left, "Everything is going to work out." I was evaluated by the psychologist and was released about an hour later. I spoke to my mother and my husband and later found out that my pastor, along with her son, was on their way to the bridge to talk me out of jumping. My husband also said when my pastor saw the Facebook live, she called the congregation to begin interceding on my behalf. She told my husband, "Don't just pray but cry out and intercede for your wife because the enemy is trying to take her out at this point."

I believe prayer is the most powerful tool we as believers in Christ have because it is our greatest measure of communicating with God. *Jeremiah 33:3* says, "*Call to me, and I will answer you, and show you great and mighty works, which you have not known.*" Every time we call out to God, he hears us and answers us because He is waiting for us to talk to Him so He can demonstrate to us his awesome powers—and not just any power. When God says He wants to show us something, that something God wants us to see will never be small but great and mighty, immeasurable, and out of this world. As I was saved by God's mighty hand through the prayers of everyone interceding for me that night, I also saw grace and mercy as I had never seen before. What was meant to completely destroy me that night

God was already turning it around for the good even though at that moment I could not see it. God already saw me writing this book and sharing with the world how important it is to always continue walking in hope and faith despite our Egypt moments and despite your having to go down south at times, just to see God's hand raise us up right before our enemy.

After that night I knew that things would have to get worse before they got better. And from that moment, God continued working within me. I continued working and going to school until one day I received a phone call from my daughter's school saying that they needed to bring my oldest daughter to the hospital youth psychiatric ward because she had attempted suicide and told the social worker at school what she had done. I ended up picking her up and taking her to Mather Hospital, where she was held there for a couple of hours; and to my surprise, when they had done urinalyses test, they not only found drugs in her urine but massive amounts of opioids in her system as well. At that point, I knew that whatever I was facing, the enemy was trying to destroy my own seed as well. This caused me to realize that the enemy was using the same tactics to try and take out my daughter. So they had to commit her to the psychiatric ward for the youth that same day. She stayed there for a week. She was so angry at me. I almost signed a release form to have her released into my custody so she wouldn't have to stay there, but a woman came up to me and said, "I know this is hard for you, but your daughter is in the right place, and we will take very good care of her." Everyone there was super nice and friendly, but I couldn't help but feel like I wasn't making the best decision at that moment. As I turned to walk away after I said I love you to my daughter, I heard her say, "I hate you and will never forgive you for what you've done." I left with tears streaming down my face and felt so broken inside and beat up emotionally that at this point I was a wreck.

School got harder, and I had to face court appointments. Lawyer fees needed to be paid, and I had to get my truck out of the impound shop. I felt like the weight of my wrong decision-making was weighing so heavily upon me that it got harder and harder for me to focus at times, so I ended up leaving my job and just going to school at night. I was given a court date, and when I arrived and was sitting in the courtroom, I overheard the DA say regarding my case that I would easily get three years of probation, psychiatric evaluation, and so many other charges. All I could do at that point was leave the courtroom and cry because I could not bear the weight of what was happening to me. It was like I was trapped in a nightmare, and all I wanted to do was wake up and tell myself it was just a dream, but in reality, this was the start of my Egypt moment after years of holding in the pain of rejection from my physical and spiritual family, not reaching out for help, and also not heeding the warning signs God was giving me to discern the dangers of giving in to rejection and allowing others to define who we are. I lost my identity in Christ because I allowed the enemy to creep on in and slowly but surely making me feel like a victim to my own feelings. I should have brought down those strongholds with the word of God. Like I mentioned before, God already knows our failing moments, and he uses our failing moments not to point out who we are but to give us a reflection of who He is (merciful and gracious); and although we fail sometimes or make the wrong decisions, when we come to full repentance (meaning, you undoubtedly recognize the sin you have committed against God and are ready and willing to wholeheartedly turn away from your sin), God is right there, willing and ready to forgive you and wash you with His precious blood and make you a new creature in Christ Jesus. When we go through a dark season, this does not always mean it's because of something you allowed to occur in your life. Being processed is a part of life, and many times we all must face the fact that in order for us to truly step into our God-given calling, we must learn to endure the process. Yes, God has forgiven us, but along with forgiveness comes preparation for what is to come, because let's face it, we all have fallen short of the glory of God, and all need the Holy Spirit to lead us through this life. It's only through our failing moments that we all can learn to appreciate the journey. I want you to know here and now that no matter how difficult your season is or how dark your nights are, just know that God is light and has already illuminated your path. So when those moments of affliction come your way, you can look within your heart where

Jesus is and find Him there every time. No matter the time of day or night, Jesus will always see us through to the other side.

The way man defines the process, and God's definition of it is totally different. The process we all must go through is not determined by endurance but by our ability and will to surrender to the One who has given us the opportunity to be processed. When we surrender to the process, we will truly come out refined and ready for what lies ahead. But if we are in the process and think that just by enduring the process we will see a great outcome or victory, boy, are we greatly mistaken.

For example, there were two students in college. Both must study for a big exam to receive their doctor's degree. The one student endured the process of studying by just memorizing the answers but not fully understanding the material. On the other hand, the other student put in long hours to study the material and understood that this test will determine how he leads his practice later when he becomes a doctor. Who do you think will have the greater outcome? The one who endured the process by memorizing and passing the exam but didn't learn or understand a thing, or the one who not only endured the process but understood the material and by utilizing the time given to him he would eventually pass and commit his life to helping others, all because he chose to surrender to the process? I'll let you decide that one.

The process for me was far from over. So I waited for my lawyer to come out of the courtroom and speak to me. He came out and explained everything to me just as I had heard from the DA. He told me that they adjourned the case and had given the lawyer some time to gather information about my life and to show the court that I am not a criminal but that I am a mother and wife as well as a hardworking medical assistant student that has never had charges like this before and to lower the charges to a less offense. Isn't that just like a DA? Their job is to look at us like a criminal and charge us with the most severe punishment. This is exactly what Satan's job is: to act as a DA, willing and ready to accuse us before the Father and prosecute us to the most severe capital punishment. But thanks be to our Lord and Savior, Jesus Christ, who is our defense attorney, He goes before us and steps in to defend our rights as children of God. No matter what accusation the enemy tries to make against us, when we allow God to step in and fully take over, Satan can try and condemn us all he wants, but the reality of the matter remains that God has the final say in the course of action. In the end, it will work out for the good of God's glory. I was soon to discover this in my very own life.

As time went on and the pandemic began, they kept adjourning the cases due to the courts having to shut down. Finally, after so many times of having to reschedule the court date (about one and a half years later), I went to my lawyer's office and he gave me the good news, which I knew was God showing me grace. He said, "The district attorney and I came up with a bargain plea. Instead of three years' probation, you would only have one year, and your charges would go from a DWI to a DUI." I would also have to do community service of 105 hours, plus take a course on alcohol and drug, have a breathalyzer devise installed in my truck for a year, and a psychiatric evaluation. It seems like a lot, right? But for me, this was the best thing that could have happened to me on account of what the DA first wanted to place on me in the first place. So I pled guilty and accepted all the responsibilities, not knowing that after this court process, God would not only touch the judge's heart to lower the charges but, to my surprise, when I had finished my year, the judge dismissed all the charges and released me on a conditional discharge, wiping my charges clean as if I never had a charge in the first place. As I am sitting here right now, the verse that comes to mind comes from Zechariah 10:6, which says, "I will strengthen the house of Judah, and I will save the house of Joseph, I will bring them back because I have mercy on them, they shall be as though I had not cast them aside; for I Am the Lord their God and I will hear."

The first couple of months of starting probation, I had to remain in my own down south season, yet even in my season of hardship, I still saw the hand of God's mercy and grace working for me and not against me. Before I knew it, I had graduated as a medical assistant and received my certificate. I quickly got a job right out of extern and began working as a medical assistant. I was assigned to a probation officer, who monitored me and referred me to the YMCA alcohol treatment and for a psychiatric evaluation. When I signed up for the YMCA, I attended one-on-one sessions and group sessions. Because of the pandemic, every session was virtual. During the first couple of sessions, the counselor was getting to know me, and so I held nothing back and told her who I was and what had happened to me and how I ended up needing to be here. The first couple of weeks, I had no idea that it would lead me to become the powerful woman of God that I am now. The entire time I was in the program, I saw God's hand moving in ways I had never seen before. I began motivating other women and talking about my faith in the Lord. I remember this one lady in the group who spoke about a dream she had, and the moment I heard it, I also heard God say to me, "I want you to interpret the dream for this woman and tell her that I love her and all these things that have happened to her were because I have a purpose for her life." When I told her what the dream meant, I first let everyone know that interpretations of dreams come only from God. The woman after said to me, "Wow! That's amazing." About a week later in the group session, the same woman talked about how she found God and how she wanted to pursue the things of God. This brought so much joy to my life because for once in my life things started to make sense and scripture started to become real to me. I knew that it's not in our strongest moments but in our weakest moments that we see God's undeniable strength manifest in our own lives. What the enemy meant for evil, I watched God turn it around for good. Sometimes in life, we think our situation is the worst until we encounter other men and women who have it so much worse. I encountered women who talked about their addictions to cocaine, crack, and even crystal meth; and through hearing their story, God gave me the opportunity to share my faith in Christ and saw how many women and men were encouraged after a session. One Monday night, at my one-on-one counseling session, the woman at Wednesday's group meeting (when I missed a session the week before) told my counselor, who then told me, that I have had a powerful influence over them. My counselor told me (remaining anonymous) one of the women testified that the night I was encouraging the women in the group, one of the women had thoughts of going back to smoking but remembered the words I spoke and was able to overcome that temptation. I told my counselor that I only speak what God puts in my heart to speak and that I was so happy to hear that she did not go back to smoking. I felt at that exact moment God telling me, "You are exactly where you are meant to be in life." I truly believe that even when we are in Egypt, God can still use us in ways we never thought He could. Remember, God used Joseph in the prison, and God will use us right where we are as long as we make ourselves available to Him.

As time went on, I developed a good relationship with my probation officer, and one day she called me down to the station to be evaluated by a psychologist. I remember I sat down and spoke with the psychologist and told her my story of how I am a born-again Christian who allowed herself to become overwhelmed with life's problems, and instead of reaching out for help, I just allowed myself to think I can do it all on my own, but eventually, I have come to know and believe that reaching out for help is not a sign of weakness but the ability to find strength through our unstable moments in life. Let's face it, we all need help, and we all fall short of God's glory, but just like I told my counselor before, I believe all this needs to happen to me because there is a greater picture I can't see right now but God has already put together, and all I can do is trust Him and have faith that all things will work out for the good to those who love God and those who are called according to His purpose. Within forty-five minutes, the psychologist shut her book and said to me, "I am telling the court you do not need any psychiatric help." She told me she would clear me of this matter to the court. As I was leaving the office, my probation officer came and said to me, "I want to let you know something. The light of the Holy Spirit shines so brightly all around you." I began to tear up and said, "Thank you so much for those words, because sometimes we doubt the possibility of influencing people's lives because of the condition we are in." She said, "Oh yes, you have more of an effect than you'll ever know."

Although I knew God was still near and working through me, the process was anything but far from over. My greatest challenge had not come yet, but I was learning so much about the process that year. I still needed to fulfill 105 hours of community service. At the time I was working at Excel Urgent care as a medical assistant, and everything was going well. I felt as if I was finding myself again and coming back to the identity of Christ's unfailing presence until one day as I was getting out of my truck to go into work early in the morning. The parking lot was covered in snow and ice, and before I knew it, I slipped and fell down on the ice, fracturing and dislocating my tailbone and injuring lower and midback and needed medical attention. I went to my primary doctor. From there, they called an ambulance, and I was taken to the hospital. From there, I began to seek other medical attention from specialists. Through X-rays, I was told my tailbone from the fall had curved inward badly and I had to have injections into the coccyx area. After multiple failing attempts of injections, I finally saw a coccyx surgeon who reviewed the MRI images and immediately told me that my tailbone was not only broken but dislocated and the only way to fix it was by having it removed. About two weeks after my surgery, I went back to the hospital (due to a lot of pain) and had an MRI done, and there they found that I not only had fluid buildup but I also had tested positive for a wound culture infection and within a couple of days I was brought back to the OR for repeat surgery to clean out the infected site. I wasn't able to work and was denied worker's compensation because although it was in the parking lot where I worked, they felt it wasn't work related, and so I received no compensation from my employer, but all of that changed, because when God is in the midst of it all, the enemy would try to cancel out what God has already predestined for us to inherit. But the truth is he cannot discredit the faith that we have in God Almighty, and for that reason, after many appeals, the third judge found me in favor of receiving the wages for my injuries that occurred in the parking lot of my employer. When I tell you God fights, He not only fights, He makes it known to the kingdom of darkness that they messed with the wrong child because whoever belongs to God, He defends to the T.

I saw a miracle happen right before my very eyes. But before things got that far, a few months after, I was denied worker's compensation. I was also let go from my employer, and life got hard after that. I felt the physical attacks wrap around me like a wall that was built around me with nowhere to go. I was constantly in and out of doctors' offices, getting treated for the injuries I sustained from the slip and fall. I was frustrated, confused, and mad at the same time because I thought working as a medical assistant was what God wanted me to do. After all, I went to school. and soon after began working in the field I always dreamed of working in. So how does this happen? These were my questions, along with tears, as I prayed to God, "Why God? Why is this happening to me?" I found myself at times screaming in my heart, and at times, I had to put my face into the pillow and scream and cry just so my kids wouldn't hear me. I was just so wounded. But it was in those exact moments when I was able to feel the tangible presence of God wrap His arms around me and whisper to me, "I know the plans I have for your life." I would just sit and hear His voice say to me, "Everything is going to be all right." One day I heard the Lord say to me loud and clear, "Why have you stopped writing the book I put in your heart to write?" It was in that moment that I began to reflect back on this very book that I had started to write but had put it on the back burner and thought nothing of it until God spoke about it. He said, "You took your hands off what I had placed my hands on for you to complete to search, for what I had not placed my hands on for you to prosper you in." I understood at that very moment that God was calling me to stay home and finish this very book because He had promised me that His anointing would be all over this book and many who read this book would become transformed and find their purpose in this life. So I finally surrendered everything to the Lord and began sitting at my computer every chance I got to hear from the Lord and write what He put in my heart to write about. At times it felt like my fingers were typing all by themselves, but it was the leading power of the Holy Spirit guiding me through.

In the beginning, what I thought was getting ready to destroy me was God setting me up and preparing me to weather the storm and become the chosen vessel to stand up and intercede for my family and to stand in the gap to proclaim God's word even in the midst of the storm. When all chaos breaks loose, whether in your home, in your job, or even in your church, just know that God has chosen you to stand in the gap for your family, your coworkers, and your brothers and sisters in Christ. What you are facing right now does not determine or dictate where God is going to bring you to after all is said and done. But how you perceive your process will determine your outcome. It's okay to come to God with your emotions and be transparent, but we must also always come back to what the truth says about God, that He is loving, merciful, and true. And when we come to the knowledge of the cross and truly humble ourselves and repent of our sins and confess and believe with our whole heart that Jesus is Lord and Savior, trust that we will experience a life-changing moment that will lead us back into the arms of the Father, who has been waiting for us to come to His presence. It's when we come to realize that if God is for us, no one can come against us. We will find our God-given destiny and help others find theirs through our choice of not giving up during the process but surrendering the process into the hands of God Almighty.

After everything that I had gone through, I myself knew that I needed to come back to the cross and cry out to the Lord in repentance, and when I did, I knew by faith that the Creator of the universe had forgiven me of all my wrongdoings and made me a new creature in Christ Jesus. But this certainly didn't stop the enemy from trying to come in and infiltrate my mind and take me away from my God-given calling on this earth. I wanted more than ever to serve God, but I just didn't know where to start. So as the months went by, I felt empowered by God to continue writing this book, and throughout this process, I have felt God more now than I ever have then when I first started writing this book. I will explain why in just a moment. But first I want to continue talking about the assignments I had to complete while on probation that will ultimately lead to where I am now and how I stand with God in this very moment.

Around April of 2021, I started my community service, and I was supposed to work outside, cleaning up garbage from the parks, but God had other plans for me. I received a phone call from a woman who told me that I would be working in an office for an organization and that I would be answering calls and filing paperwork and taking down messages. When I got there the first day, I was given the privilege of being placed at the front desk of the office the entire time I was there while others were stuck in the backroom stuffing envelopes. I didn't think about it until I started reading about Joseph, and I remembered the privileges God gave to Joseph despite the situation he was in. Doing community service didn't feel like an obligation but rather something I looked forward to doing every Monday, Tuesday, and Thursday. I got along great with the two women in charge of the organization to the point where I felt like I knew them forever. They would tell me things like, "I am so grateful that you are here with us. You're a lifesaver. I'm going to miss you when you finish your hours here." I felt so good about coming in to help because despite the fact I developed a great relationship with these women, I also gained a little knowledge regarding criminal law. I believe everything happens for a reason and that it's not just about leaving a footprint in the sand; it's about where we leave our footprints. I believe where we are is where we are supposed to be leaving our footprint, with the gospel of Jesus's signature engraved at the bottom.

Although it may seem like at times we are not doing anything for the kingdom of God, the reality is, God knows what He is doing in our lives more than we know. Life may often throw us a curveball, and just because we didn't see it coming, it doesn't mean God didn't either. On the contrary, God already knew what was going to happen, and instead of letting us in on what was happening, He chose to allow us to try and swing, knowing that we would miss the ball. I believe this is because God knows that at the very precise moment the right pitch will come that will cause us to hit one out of the ballpark, and at that moment, we will reap an amazing feeling, all because we chose to wait until the appointed time to hit what we have been missing all this time. In the very same way, God will allow us to encounter moments of failure because he knows that through our failures, we will continue to seek His face and humble ourselves in His presence. God cares and is very much interested in our failures. In fact, the very reason Jesus had to come to this fallen, broken, and evil world is due to our failure to fully obey God and His word. And although we failed to understand God's plan, He still chose to come down and show us the way back home through His Son, Jesus

Christ. Before Jesus could finish the works of His Father on the cross, there was a process that needed to be fulfilled, and although Jesus (being the Son of God) knew what He had to do in order to bring forth salvation, this did not stop the enemy from trying to stop the plans of God from being fulfilled. Every single struggle Jesus faced while here on this earth was a part of God's plan to bring redemption, not through pleasure but through pain. Pain is a major part of the process we all must go through in order to see that during our pain, the only One who can help us through is God Himself. He is always willing to hear us and see us through our pain and frustration. When all else fails and everyone abandons us, we know beyond a shadow of a doubt that God, who allowed all this to happen, has also made way for us to endure, trust, and surrender to the process by faith. I know because before I was able to sit and write this book. I too had to face the most difficult time of my life; but the hardest, most difficult, and most defining life-changing moment of my life occurred on July 26, 2021. This would be the day I would never forget because on this day I came face-to-face with the unknown, and in the blink of an eye, I saw my life flash before me, and at that moment, I began to realize how much life itself has purpose and meaning but was slowly slipping away from me. It was an experience I never thought I would have to go through, but God permitted me to experience this life-and-death moment so I would truly understand the importance of life and why I was called here for such a time as this.

It was an early Monday morning on July 26 when I went in for scheduled gastric sleeve surgery. But I want to backtrack about a week prior to the surgery date. Three things happened to me that at that moment I wouldn't be able to understand as well as I do now. My daughter, who at the time was pregnant and had a high-risk pregnancy, had an appointment with her ob-gyn; and I was on my way to her appointment. My head was clouded with so many thoughts about the pregnancy, the baby, and my daughter that I was not fully paying attention to the signs on the road. There were two lanes on the left and two lanes on the right, and turning left, there was a bridge. The lane to the far left allowed the cars to either turn left or continue straight; however, the other left lane was only to go straight.

I was on that lane thinking I was able to turn left and go under the bridge when suddenly, a massive dump truck going straight hit right into the side, more toward the back, of my truck. At that moment, I thought, *If that truck would have hit me on the driver's side I would have been seriously injured or possibly dead.* Thank God there were no injuries, but the point I am trying to make is, the enemy will put tons of distractions in our minds to derail us from getting to where we need to go to. Our mind is a battlefield, and we must protect it daily with the helmet of salvation in order to know beyond a shadow of a doubt that no matter what lie or destruction the enemy comes with, we are well guarded with the protection of God's saving grace. What could have ended my life was God shielding me from the enemy's destruction. I just want you to know something before I go on. When God shields you from a tragic moment, don't think for one moment the enemy walks away with his head down. No, not at all. In fact, this makes the enemy angry and gives him the motive to try and strike again and again, but the word of God says in *Isaiah 54:17,* "*No weapon formed against you shall prosper, and every tongue which rises against you in judgment you shall condemn. This is the inheritance of the servants of the Lord, and their righteousness is from me says the Lord.*" Every time the enemy tries to form a weapon, he may form it, and he may try to use it, but he will never fully activate it because God has already gone before us to deactivate what the enemy secretly devised to take us out with.

About three days prior to my surgery, I was given a very intense dream from the Lord. I dreamed that I was outside with my family and we were all about to go into a building. When we were in the building, I looked down and realized I had two different shoes on. I told my husband and children I would be right back, and I went to find the other pair in the back of the trunk of my car when all of a sudden there arose a strong wind, and when I looked up, I was caught in a tornado. I was being tossed every which way, and the scary part was I was all alone with no one to physically save or rescue me from this tornado. At that very moment, I felt hopeless and helpless. Then suddenly, I was in a building that was not stable and had no stability at all. I felt the rocking back and forth, and I could

191

hear my children but could not see them. I finally caught up with my husband and my girls, but my son was nowhere to be found. I looked outside and began to see the scenery moving, and I thought, *Why is the scenery moving?* But to my surprise, it was the building coming down, and when we crashed to the foundation of the building, I heard my son's voice. To my amazement, I found him. After that, I woke up and knew deep down in the core of my spirit that this was a prophetic dream, yet I was not able to interpret the dream just yet. Not knowing this dream would be tied to another dream the night prior to the surgery, the Lord gave me another prophetic dream. In the second dream, I was in a room on a table surrounded by a body of water, and swimming around the table were many sharks. I was paralyzed and unable to move. Then suddenly, I was brought to an upright position and standing staring out the front door. Standing and staring at the front door, I saw a very tall man staring back at me with a sad look on his face. To my surprise, I saw a massive shark leap out of nowhere from behind the man and devour him whole. When I turned my head away and looked again, he was right beside me as if he was not eaten by the shark. I woke up and, again, knew this was a prophetic dream; but still, I had no knowledge of its interpretation. I had no idea that the next day would be the day that these two dreams would be the prophetic prophecy that would come to pass right before my very eyes.

It was a normal start to my day. I woke up prayed and began to get ready to make my way over to the hospital. Originally, my husband was supposed to go with me, but he got a phone call about a job he needed to do, so I told him not to worry because my mother would be able to take me, and after work, he could come and see me. He felt bad because he wanted to be there with me, but for some reason, I just kept insisting he go to work instead of coming with me. So my mother and I made our way to the Mather Hospital. There I was brought in and admitted. All was going well so far. The nurse and staff came into prep me for the surgery, and I saw my doctor, who reassured me that everything would be fine and that after the surgery I would stay about one to two days in the hospital to be monitored. The nurse came back into the room to put the IV and got me ready to go into the operating room. As I was waiting, suddenly out of nowhere, I began to feel this high alert of anxiety run all through my body. I became overly nervous and overwhelmed to the point that it felt like ants were crawling all over on the inside of me, and I couldn't help but feel scared. My mother quickly went and got the nurse. She came in and tried to calm me down. She lowered down the lights and began talking to me, and within about two to three minutes, the anxiety went away, and it was as if I never had it in the first place. The nurse told me it was time for me to head into the operating room, so we made our way over. I remember my mother giving me a hug and telling me, "Don't worry, Jesus is with you, and everything will be fine." I looked at her and said, "Amen." So like any other surgery, I went in and sat down at the operating room table. Then they began putting the medication through the IV, and before I knew it, I was out. I woke up in recovery with massive chest pain. I tried to tell the nurse about it, but she said it was just gas pain and that later, when I start walking around, it would ease up. I have had seven surgeries in the past, and I knew what gas pain felt like, but this was different. After about an hour or two, they brought me up to my room and propped me up in a chair, and all I remember was the pain kept getting stronger and stronger, but I couldn't move. I kept coming in and out, almost as if I was fading in and fading out. This is the only real way to describe the feeling. I remember the nurse aide coming in and saying I needed to walk around to try and release some of the gas, but I tried to explain to them that this pain is very intense and is in my chest, but they insisted that I get up and walk, so that's what I did. I was only able to do a half lap before I told the nurse aide to put me back to the room in my bed. I was brought back and placed into my bed, where I just didn't want to move. The pain got sharper and more painful to bear, but because I felt like no one was listening to me, I just tried to block out the pain by sleeping. The next thing I remember was opening my eyes and seeing my husband walk in. I told him how much pain I was in. I said to him, "Please get me up so I can walk." (At this point, I believed the nurses that it was just gas pain). My husband managed to get me up, and as we took a few steps toward the door, the room started spinning and my body went weak. The nurse aide and my husband brought me back to the bed and called the nurse. At this point, my words were slurred, and I couldn't think straight. The nurse came in, and the next thing I knew, the entire rapid response team was in the room. They started asking me all these questions to see if I was responsive or able to identify with what they were asking me. When the nurse took my blood pressure, she had a very hard time getting a diastolic reading because my blood pressure went low. I began going into hypothermic shock, and soon after, I began shaking intensely. At this point, I started to fade in and out, and every time the doctors saw me fading out, they would begin to ask me some more questions to try and keep me awake. They started putting more IVs in me and sending for a massive blood transfusion because the doctor said I was losing too much blood too quickly and that I would need to go back to the operating room due to perfuse internal bleeding. I remember them sticking me several times trying to get an arterial vein but not being able to. I was in so much pain, yet I couldn't move one bit. At this point, I was barely able to breathe. I remember just gasping for air and thinking, *Is this it? Is this where it all ends for me?* I was in a state of shock that anyone who asked me a question, I would give them a blank stare and then, seconds later, answer. Soon after, they rushed me down to ICU, where I waited for the doctor who performed the surgery to arrive. When my doctor arrived, I remember the ICU doctor saying to my doctor, "There needs to be a better protocol. This patient has lost too much blood already." When I heard those words, my heart sank in me, and all I could do was look up at the ceiling and, in my heart, cry out, "Lord, please do not let me die here in this hospital. I beg you please for my children's sake." The two biggest things running through my mind at that very moment were, I haven't even begun to fulfill all that God has predestined for me to do, and I still have so much to teach my children about the Lord. I remember that soon after I prayed to God with the little strength I had left in my body, my doctor came in and took one look at me and looked up as if he was looking up at God. The next thing I knew, a big sigh of sorrow came out of him. He then looked at me and said to me, "You are bleeding profusely internally, and we must get you back into the operating room as soon as possible. But before we can do that, we need to bring you in for a CT scan to identify exactly where the bleeding is coming from." The response team came in once again because at times I was becoming nonresponsive, and they had to resuscitate me due to loss of blood. By this time, I had about five IVs in my arm. I was becoming nonresponsive at times, and they almost had to put another IV in my thigh, but by a miracle, I became responsive enough for them to bring me down to finally get the CT scan. The moment I was in the machine, I heard them say immediately, "Here is where the bleeding is coming from, and the hemorrhage is quite moderate." While I was in the CT machine, I began to cry and beg the Lord to free me from this, because at the point, the pain was too much for me to bear. I said to the Lord, "Please make this stop, God. I don't know how much more pain I can tolerate before I give in and let go." That's when I felt them pulling me out of the machine and taking me to the operating room. Before they had brought me into the operating room, the ICU doctor came in and said that there is a strong possibility that while in the operating room, I may become unresponsive, and for that reason, I may wake up with a few breathing tubes down my throat. I was brought into the operating room, and all I can do at this point was try and gasp for air and hope that everything would be fine. I also remember thinking that the pain was so severe that all I wanted to do to make the pain go away was sleep. Next thing I knew, I was in ICU in the morning with three tubes down my throat. This was the scariest moment of my life. I literally felt like I was paralyzed not being able to move a muscle, being bound by cuffs and not being able to breathe on my own. So about twenty minutes later, the ICU doctor came in and explained to me what went on in the operating room. He said I became unresponsive about three times and had to resuscitate me, and that is why I woke up with these breathing tubes. It was at that moment when I prayed within my heart and ask the Lord to cause me to breathe on my own again, and suddenly, I felt within my lungs—and the only way to describe it really—a wind of fresh air. Then for the first time, I was able to breathe in and breathe out without depending on the machine. I still wasn't able to talk due to the breathing tubes, and my wrists were still bound to the bed, but I remember asking God to please touch one of the doctors or nurses so they would come back into the room, and to my surprise, the cleaning lady came in, and I began to hint to her that I needed to tell the doctor something. In the beginning, it was frustrating because she did not understand what I was trying to say, but after a while, she left, and I saw her talking to the doctor. Soon after, the doctor walked in and I was able to signal to him that I was able to breathe on my own, and about thirty minutes later, they released me from the cuffs and took the breathing tubes out. The doctors were amazed at how well I was breathing, but I knew that God had done something new in me, and although the enemy meant all this for evil, God still had His hands on me. Although this was an unfortunate moment in my life, God knew that from this, I would come to know him as my Redeemer. It's like *Job* said in *19:25* and *26,* "*For I know that my redeemer lives, and He shall stand at last on the earth; after my skin is destroyed, this I know, that in my flesh I shall see God.*"

I ended up staying in ICU for about a week, and I still needed to be monitored, but I knew that the worst was over and that I would continue to see my husband and my kids again. Most of all, I would see life in a whole new way after having gone through what I went through. The recovery was very hard in the beginning, but I knew that if the Lord permitted me to go through this Egypt moment never having abandoned me, then the God of Abraham, Isaac, and Jacob would allow me to come forth one day and testify to how big our God truly is and how Jesus has the power to make all things new.

CHAPTER 10

• • • • —————— • —————— • • • •

Still Not Out of the Wilderness Just Yet but I See the Promised Land

Focusing on what is real is so much more than just focusing on what is important, because we can focus on what is important and not think of it as something real enough to accomplish, but when we focus on what is real, we will make what we are seeking after important, and in doing so, we will begin to see that, that which is real becomes the most important thing we need to focus on, and that is our salvation. We all have entered this world at an appointed time, and we all have an appointed time to exit this world, but we should not focus so much on the life expectancies rather on the reality of what we are putting our beliefs in because not everything (although it may seem good or important) may be of God. But when we place all our focus on God (being that He is the reality of our focus), everything that matters to God and is of great importance will come to pass in our lives—that is, if we hold fast to our faith and focus in on the reality of who God was, is, and will always be.

In the year 2021, this became a reality to me. This was the most life-changing year for me. I learned that when we tried to put our important expectancies before or above the will of God, we only set ourselves up to become someone we are not. In 2020, I thought by going back to school and getting a job would be the right thing to do. After all, I was putting the important things before me, telling myself

I can do this, but the reality was that I was digging a deeper hole for myself. Instead of focusing on who God is, I was stuck in a pattern of how this was all going to come to pass. And although it seemed like I was making progress in school and work, the reality was, I was neglecting the very important things in life, and that was my family.

When we don't learn to put up boundaries, the boundaries will come looking for us. Unfortunately, as much as I wanted the important things in life to come to pass, I wasn't giving all my focus and attention to the Lord, and for that reason, I was being pulled and led astray by my own expectations. But God, in His never-ending mercy, had to put up a boundary that came to me at the precise moment I was heading down toward my destruction. God allowed the storm to bring destructive wind forces to my life, not to harm me but to remove everything that needed to be removed out of my way so in Him, everything that was left standing could be rebuilt again. And as a result, my family watched as God made a way despite the afflictions and despite the oppression. God made His way toward Egypt, toward my darkest down south moment, a place I never thought I would have to go through, let alone face in order for me to see what true deliverance looks like in my own life.

Today I find myself walking a totally different path than I was walking on before. Not to say that I never had to go through another crisis, because while we are still living here on this earth and in this fallen and broken world, we will always have to encounter an Egypt moment. However, having been miraculously delivered by God's sovereign hand caused me to fully understand that every single moment of our lives serves as a purpose in God's eyes and is being recorded by heaven, so when we do encounter those moments, we can look to God for deliverance and know that if God brought you this far, it's because every Egypt or down south moment led you to become the man or women of God you either are today or whom God has already ordained you to be. As we embrace the journey of life, always consider that trials and tribulation are bound to come and we must hold fast to the word of God. Knowing what God has done in the past should motivate us to know and rejoice in this: that God is getting ready to do it again. The only difference is, it's not what He does but with who He is about to do it for, and that person is you! Get ready because God is about to deliver you out of your Egypt moment, and if you still do not believe, just keep on reading, and I guarantee you that by the end of this book, you will not only believe but you also will see the hand of God moving in your life as you have never experienced before. You are next in line to encounter the greatest moment of your life because God is not finished with you yet!

Great Possessions + Great Seed x Great Nation = Great Deliverance

There was a road paved for us long before we all were formed in our mother's womb. A purpose that was predestined for us by God Himself, to bring us hope for tomorrow. We all have seen and felt the crushing weight of this world at times fall upon us; but the great news is that when we come to know the One who came to show us the way unto salvation, we also come to the reality that although we have been given the gift of salvation by believing in the crucifixion and resurrection of Jesus Christ, we who are in Christ are being built up from the foundation, who is Christ Jesus, to become a city on a hill, the light of the world, and the salt of the earth. But before this can happen, there has to be a plan set in motion in order to proceed with a blueprint and make that blueprint come to life.

In order for the building to stand firm, there has to be a solid foundation and people who are experienced to know where every material needs to go. There are measurements that need to be taken; beams that need to be set up in place in order to hold the structure of the building; and not to mention all the hammering, wilting, banging, and heavy noise that must take place for the building to stand firm. When we look at the finished work of a building, we only see its beauty from the outside. We don't really look at the building from the inside, ground up. This is because we often don't take the time to realize what is really holding up the building. We become paralyzed at the amazing structural view of something that would never have existed if it weren't for the firm foundation beneath, holding and bearing the weight of its glory. Why am I telling you all of this? Well, because, in the very same way, before the Israelites became a strong nation, before the world would see them as God's precious people and the apple of His eye, they too had to go through a time of affliction and tribulation. There was a blueprint God brought into existence through various men of God. They became the ones God used to bring about His awesome message of redemption; and although the chief cornerstone wasn't laid down in the days of Abraham, Isaac, and Jacob, they were the blueprint, along with Joseph and Moses and the twelve tribes of Israel, who would at various times represent the Messiah, who is Christ Jesus. Jesus Christ, at the appropriate time, would then establish His kingdom upon the earth and cause many to become free to build upon the solid foundation and watch as many gaze upon the beauty of the Lord, who in turn will come and build their house upon the solid foundation, all because our lives should always reflect the foundation, who is Jesus Christ. He came to bear the weight of the world upon His shoulders so we as God's children can continue to build upon that solid foundation until God calls us home.

There will always be a beginning and an end with man; but the greatest part of all is that, with God, there was and will always have an eternity. But in order for us to see that eternity here on this earth, God has established a way for us to inherit eternal life. But before you and I could have ever been given the opportunity to become saved and delivered, someone had to walk that lonely road for us, and His name is Jesus Christ. We could never become a city on a hill if the One who came to make a way didn't die for us on a hill. Just like Jesus paved the way for us to pick up our cross and walk, Jesus already knew what it would feel like to carry the cross because He carried it all the way down the Via Dolorosa as a way of showing us that we too will have to go through difficult seasons but that we too can stand strong, all because Jesus went before us and conquered death so we can be delivered and live again in the kingdom of God for eternity.

After reading Genesis many times, I have concluded that before God does something great in someone's life, He first brings them to a place of solitude. Where you are right now you are not meant to stay.

God wants to show you a place where your faith can grow in ways you never thought possible. After you have paved the way for your family to see the glory of God, they too can come to see the greatness of our Lord. In leaving your comfort zone and entering into a season of growth and development, knowing that your family may think you're crazy and out of your mind and knowing beyond a shadow of a doubt that God had called you to pave the way for your family to one day (as they face trials and adversity) come to know Jesus as their deliverer, it will have been worth all the pain, hurt, and rejection you have received, just to see your family saved, delivered, and in heaven one day. Abraham had to leave his father's home to pave the way for God's people to one day become a strong and fortified nation. When Abraham left his father's house to lead his family to one day see the promised land, we see once again Abraham representing Jesus's role of Him having to leave His Father's house to lead all those who would inherit salvation back home to the eternal promised land, which is in heaven and is heaven.

I believe Abraham, Isaac, and Jacob represent the Father, the Son, and the Holy Spirit. The reason being, although they all had different names, they all formed the same purpose in mind: to establish the covenant and fulfill that covenant all the way through till the very end. And that is just what they did. The Bible says in Romans 4 that Abraham is the father of all righteousness. Here we see the trinity of the Father. In Genesis 22:1 and 2, we find God telling Abraham to bring his promised son, Isaac, whom Abraham loved to the land of Moriah to be sacrificed (although God did not permit Isaac to be sacrificed). Here we see the trinity of the Son. And in Genesis 28:13–15, God speaks to Jacob through a dream and tells Jacob that his descendants will be as the dust of the earth and they shall spread abroad to the west and the east to the north and to the south. Through Jacob's seed, all the families of the earth shall be blessed. He goes on to say thereafter, "Behold I am with you wherever you go." This is no other than the trinity of the Holy Spirit as it says in *John 1:1–4,*

> *In the beginning, was the word, and the word*
> *was with God. He was at the beginning with God.*

All things were made through Him, and without
Him, nothing was made that was made. In Him
was life, and the life was the light of men.

As we read these verses, we find the light of the Father shining through Abraham, the light of the Son shining through Isaac, and the light of the Holy Spirit shining through Jacob, as each one of them represented the Word.

At the beginning of my book, I had mentioned that before we can investigate the miraculous event that took place in Egypt, we had to come back to the beginning of where it all started and who it first started with to fully understand why and how God's people ended up in a place called Egypt and why God chose to establish a nation in Egypt and for such a long period of time. There are times when we need to go back before we can go forward. If we do not know our history, we may be doomed to repeat it again and again. I believe this book has given me the insight I truly needed to not only write but to also thank God for the long hours I put in to hearing God's voice and receive deep revelation from heaven. Yes! As I wrote this book, at times I cried and laughed, but most of the time, I was struck with awe as I watched the Holy Spirit take over at times and speak life into this book. I heard the Holy Spirit tell me one day when I was meditating on His Word, "My breath is all over this book, and those who read it will be touched by my presence." That's when I knew that this book was no longer mine but the Holy Spirits to do what He wills with it.

The word of God says that after the death of Joseph, his brothers and all that generation, the children of Israel, were fruitful and they increased abundantly. The impact of Joseph's surrendered life to God really paid off in the end. For one man's obedience, an entire generation and those thereafter would be called blessed, all due to God's promise to Abraham and his descendants. The children of God grew in numbers so fast and so rapidly after Joseph's death, which caused the land of Egypt to overflow with God's chosen people, although they hadn't yet understood that the season they were about to enter into would be just as big as their miraculous deliverance would need to be. Have you ever been outside on a sunny day and everything just seemed to be going well, when all of a sudden you look up and see from a distance dark clouds rolling in and it makes your heart tremble within your chest? This is exactly what happened to the Israelites in Egypt. They were all enjoying their time in Egypt, becoming fruitful and multiplying, when all of a sudden, there arose a new king over Egypt who did not know Joseph or any of his people. The only thing he knew was that they were a threat to him and his people. The enemy doesn't care about who your ancestors were in the past because they are no longer around, but you and I are, and he knows that those who have the light of Christ shining within them automatically become a threat to the kingdom of darkness, and Satan hates that with all his being. God's people were not ready to comprehend the vicious turmoil that laid ahead for them, but the enemy sure did confess something so intriguing that caught my undivided attention. In verse 9 of chapter 1 in Exodus, the new Pharaoh stated something that the enemy will always have to confess when it comes to God's people. He goes on to say, "Look, the people of the children of Israel are more and mightier than we." Will you look at that! No matter how our lives may look like to us, and, yes, even to the enemy, our lives are within the strength of God's will and so the enemy must confess our victory in Christ even though he tries to keep us in bondage. "*Where the Spirit of the Lord is there is freedom*" (*2 Cor. 3:17*). The only tactic the enemy knows how to use to try and keep us in bondage is fear, but as long as we know whose we are, we will not be led away by the deceptive tactics of the enemy. Satan's biggest fear is when we know how to take up God's armor and fight with the weapons of our warfare. Pharaoh wasn't concerned with them becoming fruitful; it was the multiplying that put him in a state of panic, for fear that they would rise up against him and his people to make war and align themselves with their enemies to fight against the Egyptians.

Why do you think it's hard for a nonbeliever to become a believer? Do you honestly think that the enemy is going to make it easy for a nonbeliever to come and align themselves with Christ just so the enemy can become a defeated foe in that person's life?

Absolutely not! The Israelites had no idea the havoc Pharaoh was about to bestow on them because they had not yet had that supernatural encounter with God. And so, out of fear, Pharaoh begins to place them in bondage and causes them to become enslaved under his power and tyranny. When we don't know the One who possesses all the power (God Almighty), we will become slaves of fear rather than followers of faith, and this is exactly what was happening with God's people. We know from previous scriptures that mention various times regarding God's people one day becoming an oppressed nation in the hands of Pharaoh, but scripture is not clear as to whether or not the generation before the enslavement of God's people was warned or aware of what was to come in the near future. If this was the case, then we can be certain that Pharaoh's jealousy was the motivating factor in rising up against God's people. In the criminal law, the detectives always say that in a murder case, jealousy is a huge motivating factor for a lot of the hate crimes that take place. When the enemy knows you are multiplying and becoming strong and mighty in the Lord, he will always try and find a way to weaken you through fear of the unknown. This could be something or someone that comes into your life to wreak havoc or rain on your parade in order to keep you from going forward and walking into the destiny God has prepared for you. I have news for you. What is meant to happen will happen, no matter the cost, season, or price that must be paid. God has a plan, and although we all have a destiny by God to live life abundantly, this does not mean that we will "row, row, row our boat gently down the stream" because life isn't always merry and but a dream. The bigger the establishment is in your life, the greater the process will be. Life can become devastating and cruel at times due to the sins of mankind. We now live in a fallen and broken world, but God can piece together the brokenness of this world and cause a miraculous turnaround. But we must first understand something very vital if we want to continue walking forward in life: what we are encountering now may hurt and seem like God has forgotten about us. But God is not mad at us for thinking this way because He knows it's in our human nature to sometimes think this way, but the key to being persistent (and you may think I am crazy for saying this) is in remaining weak within yourself. If there is one thing that gets the enemy angry is a spirit that is poor and a heart that is humble because Satan knows that when these two things take place, multiplication occurs. I have been in situations where I have been physically weak, yet I have seen the hand of God move in a tangible and supernatural way. Paul states in 2 Corinthians 12:9 that God's strength is made perfect in man's weakness. The more Satan afflicts us, the more we ought to remain weak before God. This is easier said than done, but remember that our actions come from words, and our words come from our thoughts, and our thoughts come from our circumstances. So when we find ourselves being attacked by the enemy, especially when all is going well and we are at the peak of our greatest season, don't dismiss the idea that nothing can go wrong or that God can't alter the course of man's desires to fulfill His promises that surpass all human comprehension. For the Israelites, this was a moment where everything would change. They would have to now become accustomed to a totally different lifestyle than they were used to and embark on the longest journey that would set the course for God to raise up the one who would deliver God's people out of bondage. Abraham, Isaac, and Jacob, along with Joseph and his brothers, all fulfilled their role on this earth in bringing forth God's prophecies, and now the time of the prophecy was about to be revealed.

So now what? Pharaoh, through tyranny and dictatorship, has come in and placed God's people under slavery. How do we begin to fathom such cruelty on Egypt's behalf? Well, although this may seem like a tactic from the enemy to stop God's people from becoming a victorious nation, this was only the beginning of the great and mighty wonders that were about to shake the land of Egypt like never before. While God's people were becoming slaves in Egypt, God already ordained and established a work in the one who would first have to walk a mile in Egypt's shoes to fully understand that the calling that is upon his life is not just any little old calling but the most incredible calling that he would have to encounter in order to see God's people delivered from the evil hands of Pharaoh himself. The word of God tells us in verse 11, that Pharaoh set taskmasters over them to afflict them with their burdens and caused them to build supply cities. The more they afflicted them, the more they multiplied and grew. Here we see a painted portrait of God's people being afflicted, yet they were still able to multiply and grow. When we are in the perfect will of God's purpose, no matter where we are or where we find ourselves, as the body of Christ and as the church of God above our afflictions and above all the heavy burdens that the enemy tries to place on the church of God, we will continue to grow and multiply simply because the gates of hell shall not prevail against the church of God. This is what made Pharaoh (as scripture says in verse 12) dread the children of Israel. That word *dread* found in the *Webster's* dictionary means "great fear." Pharaoh was in great fear not because they were multiplying, but through and above their afflictions, they were still able to multiply beyond measure. Satan does not only fear a church that multiplies in stature, but greatly fears a church that, despite the afflictions, despite the persecution, and despite the opposition the kingdom of darkness tries to surround the church with, continues to stand strong, multiply, and grow, because it's only through adversity can we see the hand of God moving strongly within the body of Christ. As we can see, the children of Israel were now becoming a nation that was held down by slavery and harsh bondage. The afflictions seemed to be spreading more rapidly and more fiercely because now even as they were forced to work as slaves, they were also mandated by Pharaoh to work under any condition or illness they may have, and we're not just talking about a minor cold or cough, the Bible says that the taskmasters made them work with rigor, which meant shivering and high fever or harsh and strict treatment. This was quickly becoming a nightmare for the Israelites, but on the other hand, the strong and vigorous God of heaven and earth was not about to leave His people in the valley of the shadows of death. On the contrary, God was setting the stage for the miraculous events that were about to take place, but before this could happen, God had to raise the one who would commit his very own life into the hands of the Great I Am.

Perhaps for such a time as this, God is calling us to rise up and commit our very own lives into the hands of the Great I Am, to do whatever is necessary to save a generation who is in bondage by the enemy. Do not resist God's voice but rather let His voice draw you near to His presence so He can reveal his plan for your life and you can begin your Egypt process in fulfilling the awesome purpose that through you God wants to accomplish. Yes, even in Egypt, God can show you who He is. He sure did with a man named Moses, and He is about to do it again, only this time it's with you because God has had His eyes on you, and even though you couldn't see Him, His eyes have always been fixed on you. Just like Moses would embark on an interesting yet complex moments in Egypt, you too are about to experience and embark on a new journey, because the reason God is taking you through this season in your life is to shape you into the born leader you were always meant to be.

CHAPTER 11

You Were Called and Chosen to Go before
Dignitaries and Declare the Wonders of God

In the kingdom of heaven, there are ranks of angels and each have their own specific roles given by God to fulfill, but all the angels were created by God to minister forth to those who will inherit salvation according to *Hebrews 1:14*, which says, *"Are not all angels ministering spirits sent forth to serve those who will inherit salvation?"* There is a huge commission from the Lord above, and He has called us as individuals to form the body of Christ through love power and sound mind. Although we are not angels (but saints), we have the capability of ministering to those who are called to inherit salvation. As the angels come forth to minister to us who have received salvation, we, as saints, called by God to do extraordinary works through Christ must also minister to all nations and declare to the enemy that God has already led captivity captive and has already (through the Holy Spirit) distributed the many different gifts that we as saints have been given. As we have been given different gifts and talents to minister forthwith, so we shall minister forth to those who will inherit salvation. Just as the angels hold different positions in the kingdom of God and the gifts we have been given may differ one from another, we all have been commissioned by God to minister forth in the body of Christ to a generation that has been held in captivity for far too long and needs the Spirit of the Living God who resides within us to break those chains and set them free from bondage. I just want us all to understand something very important here. When we look at the people of God, we think that they were only physically in bondage, but that isn't entirely true. When Pharaoh began placing them under bondage, they began to fear Pharaoh; and through fear, they became paralyzed in their thought process, which in turn caused them to surrender their lives into the hands of Pharaoh. That is the overview of what happened. I am not taking away from the prophecies that needed to be fulfilled for God's people to later on see the hand of God displaying His wonders in Egypt. What I am saying however that this is how it had to be because, in this fallen and broken world we live in, for every perverse society, there will be a Noah and his family who will build an ark; for every perverse city, there will always be an Abraham who will intercede; for every famine, there will always be a Joseph who will rise up to go forth with integrity to save nations from a deadly famine; for every Midianite, there will be a Gideon who will come out of the threshing floor to trust God to defeat an army that outweighs God's people by the thousands; for every Goliath, there will always be a David who will rise up and slay a giant and declare victory for God's people even before God's people can see the victory before them; and for every Haman who tries to annihilate God's people, there will always be an Esther who will go before the king and defend God's people from becoming destroyed.

Speaking of women, I want to talk about something very important that the Lord has lain upon my heart to speak about, and that's the empowerment of womanhood and how being in Egypt relates to empowered women and God's purpose. God doesn't just use men to fulfill his purpose. On the contrary, women have played a major role in fulfilling God's plan throughout history. Women have been empowered by God with a great multipurpose to carry out extraordinary measures of faith, to go above and beyond measure, and to be a helping hand to those who God puts in their pathway to help.

If we look at scripture, we will find that the women in the Bible were used by God to bring forth those who would become saved through God's grace. In Exodus 1:15–21, we see the king of Egypt calling two women by the names of Shiphrah and Puah.

These two women mentioned by their names were summoned by the king of Egypt to kill all the male babies born at birth. These women could have easily fulfilled their duties and killed all the male babies, but they knew that above this injurious cruel act, the fear of God was in their hearts. The Bible says in *Proverbs 9:10*, "*The fear of the Lord is the beginning of all wisdom.*" These two women acted out of fear (reverence), and in doing so, they could not carry out this unethical command the king of Egypt required them to fulfill. An empowered woman is not a woman who carries out their duties no matter the cost or consequence; an empowered woman is one who with dignity and integrity fears the Lord above all else and is willing to stand for the truth to preserve lives instead of taking lives. When we fear the Lord and stand in the truth of God's word, we will see victory. I commend these women for standing up for the truth because there is no question when it comes to killing babies in/outside the womb. It's altogether wrong and unjust, and because these women stood up for the righteousness of these little innocent babies, God made sure these women were not harmed for their just act of obeying God. Although later the king of Egypt commanded his people to kill every male child and cast them into the river, Pharaoh had no idea that through a wise woman, he would not carry out his plan successfully. Through a woman, God would cause Moses to be put in a basket; and through a young female child (Moses's sister), Moses would be watched over; and through a female servant (of Pharaoh's daughter), Moses would be drawn out of the waters; and through Pharaoh's daughter, Moses would be spared, only to be raised for a time by a woman named Jochebed (who was Moses's biological mother). You may not believe this, but every single one of these women was empowered by God to be a part of God's great plan in delivering His people from Egypt. God has a special place for women, and it's clear throughout this entire journey. God would use a woman to spare the one who would rise and become the mediator between Pharaoh and God's people. God empowered women to carry out His plan of redemption. God has called men to conquer and overcome, but He has also called and empowered women to be the vessel that helps carry out God's plan.

There is another woman in the Bible whom God not only empowered but used to carry out a plan that would change the course of time. Her name was Rahab. Most know her as a prostitute, and some by what she did to save the spies who came in to spy out the city of Jericho, but very few know that Rahab was a heroine not because she helped the spies escape Jericho or spared their lives from being killed. Rahab was an empowered woman of God because she feared the Lord and proclaimed the Lord God to be above heaven and earth. When a woman knows that God is the Almighty One and that besides Him, there is no other, the enemy cannot stand against her because the Lord is on her side and fighting a fight that can only be won by God Himself. Rahab succeeded tremendously in carrying out God's plan to bring in His people (the Israelites) to go in and destroy the city of Jericho. And in turn, Rahab and her family were not only spared, but by a man named Salmon, Rahab had a son named Boaz, who had married Ruth and conceived Obed, who begot Jesse, and Jesse begot King David, who became the father of Solomon, all the way to the Messiah, Jesus Christ, and, through the Holy Spirit, Mary, the mother of Jesus. Mary, a virgin who never knew a man before Jesus was born, was empowered by the Holy Spirit to carry the promised child who would save the world through a selfless act on the cross. God gave the privilege to Mary Magdalene, a woman who was formerly known as a prostitute and had seven demons yet was set free by Jesus Christ to give witness and testimony to His resurrection from the grave. Mary Magdalen was the first woman empowered by God to preach the gospel of Jesus Christ crucified, placed in a tomb, and resurrected on the third day by the power of the Holy Spirit. Not only did she preach it, but she believed it with her whole heart. Women have been empowered and destined to do great and mighty works in the Lord for so many years. Since the beginning of time, Satan has had a target on women and has tried to derail us from fulfilling our true calling on this earth. We as women were always meant to be the helper and not the head. That's why God created Eve in the first place, to be a companion to her husband and a helping hand. So why the need for women to dominate their husband or feel independent at times? The answer is simple yet complex for some to comprehend or understand at times. I'll try my best to explain.

In the garden of Eden, when Eve gave the fruit to her husband, we see that the serpent approached Eve with the intention of causing division within the marriage by sweet-talking Eve into doing something the serpent knew would be inevitable. If you read the beginning of Genesis, when the serpent began talking to Eve, the main topic here wasn't about getting Eve to disobey but to allow Eve to dominate her husband by wanting to become like God, ruling and reigning. You see, Eve was never meant to rule over her own husband or think more highly of herself. But the serpent's number one aim was to get Eve to make her own decision based on how she felt, and for that reason, Eve took it upon herself to make a decision that would lead her to help her husband join in, and both would have to suffer the ultimate consequence of being banished from a place they were always meant to live and be fruitful in. Since then, women have had the tendency to step outside the box and claim to be an empowered woman yet using their empowerment for all the wrong reasons. Take Jezebel for example. This is a woman in the Bible who ruled over her husband, Ahab, and caused him to defile the children of Israel in such a way that her death became the very reflection of who she was. Eve gave the fruit to her husband and caused him to sin also. This is what we have seen happen long before our time and in our own society today. God created women to live with the empowerment that complements a man's being. But Eve allowed herself to become the dominant one; and having done so, she went from partnership to supremacy, just like the enemy wanted. When we as women know how to use and not abuse our role given by God as the helper, we will become a powerful instrument in the hands of God, to be used as a vessel for God's honor and glory in fulfilling great and mighty works through Christ Jesus. In this life, whether men or women, we all have a specific assignment to complete; and through the process, every good standard and moral action being fought for, there will always be those who will rise to bring controversy and adversity, just because this is the world Satan uses to try and accomplish his mission in contaminating and tainting the truth of God's word and trying to take the human race away from following after God's purpose. But for every Pharaoh who rises up against the people of God to place them in bondage, there will always be a Moses who will stand before dignitaries with a strong voice and declare freedom for God's people in Jesus's name. We as the church should not back down but raise our voices and proclaim to the nations that there is still power in the name of Jesus. We must choose to embrace our Egypt moments and fully understand that without knowing our way around Egypt, we won't be able to stand firm against principalities and the rulers of darkness. If we do not know who we are in Jesus Christ and the magnitude of what He has done for us on the cross, we won't have the courage to step foot into our God-given destiny and to spiritually fight and intercede on behalf of those who need deliverance. I can stand here today and say beyond a shadow of a doubt that if it hadn't been for my Egypt moments, I would have never been able to write this book. It's not because I faced hard challenges, or had to go through life's rejecting moments, or even because I have a story to tell. All of this is contrary to the reality that none of us deserve to have our story told because the story is not about us to begin with. I am able to speak freely because I have come to realize that everything that happens to us on this earth has everything to do with God's restoration between himself and man through what Jesus has done for us on the cross. And because of this, I chose to surrender my story of bitterness, resentment, and anger and chose to lay it all down at His feet so He can pick back up the pieces of my life and turn it around to glorify His name. I have absolutely no doubt in my mind that God is the One moving through me as I speak and encourage others to embrace their Egypt moment. So the next time we think about trying to tell someone about our own story, take a hard look into your Egypt process and remember who has always been with you through it all so you would come to surrender your story into the hands of the Potter who has the capacity to bring about something new that we never thought existed until now.

Moses was called by God, chosen by God, and led by God to do the impossible and the never-before-seen miracles of God. Only, before Moses could do this, he too would have to remain in Egypt for a time and encounter moments that most are not willing to go through in order to be used by God in such a miraculous way. Many people want the promised land without crossing the desert; and few are willing to go through Egypt (figuratively speaking) and raise a voice for the captives because in order to do that, you have to have gone through the fire and learn that even in the fire, God still prevails. God has a massive plan for each one of our lives, but before we can discover all that God has for us, we must be willing to do whatever the Holy Spirit calls us to do, and this will require us to surrender our all, yes, our all—all our time, our entire life, and every fiber of our being. We are living in times where many, just like God's people in Egypt, are becoming more and more enslaved from the sins in this world. This is because they fear more of the governmental power on earth than the established work of Christ Jesus, who came over two thousand years ago to set us free. Think of your voice as a well-oiled machine. If that machine is left sitting for a while, it will lose its functions. That machine will need to go through a process of lubrication and reconstruction in order to be used once again. You and I all have gone through a dry season where we have fallen off the bandwagon and have felt useless. I can imagine this is how Moses must have felt while he was being raised in Egypt by Pharaoh's daughter, an Israelite living in the great pleasures of Egypt yet seeing his descendants enslaved by the very people he claimed to be like. This must have made him feel useless at times. But there in the land of Egypt, God had already established Moses's return to Egypt because the God of heaven and earth who holds our tomorrow is already in our tomorrow today with an established work in His hand for the future. While God's people were becoming devastatingly abused and beaten as slaves in Egypt, God was doing a mighty work that was yet to be seen by Moses and His people. With God, there is always an appointed time for His will to be fulfilled, and that time had not come just yet because the one who would come back to free God's people had not yet had his private and profound encounter with the Great I Am. You and I cannot begin to fulfill our great destiny if we first do not have that profound encounter with the Creator of heaven and earth. The enemy knows this. That's why he spends all of his time trying to derail us before we come to truly understand our calling. The enemy knows that what God has established, no man can discredit, and God Himself will see his people through it all. Whatever you're facing now will not determine your outcome but will determine your stamina of endurance. God called you, and you have the responsibility to seek the Lord in private so He can show Himself through you as the mighty and powerful God that He is. Don't you think for one moment that just because you disqualify yourself from thinking you can't possibly do what God is asking of you, He has given up on you. On the contrary, you are the perfect person to be used by God. I will explain why in just a moment, but before I do, I want to talk about a couple of people who quickly tried to disqualify themselves from fulfilling their destiny and had a defeated mindset from the enemy, but in the end, they became a powerful instrument in the hands of God to display God's power and mercy.

In Judges 6:11, the Bible says that Gideon was threshing wheat in the winepress while an angel of the Lord came and sat under a terebinth tree. As we can see here, Gideon was hiding from the Midianites, because at that time, God's people were hidden in caves and strongholds, trying to stay away from their enemies. Although the Midianites were more numerous than God's people, that didn't stop God from calling a man named Gideon to display His mighty powers through him. So the angel of the Lord (Jesus) calls Gideon (while Gideon is scared for his life) a mighty man of valor. Listen to what Gideon says to the angel of the Lord. He replies, *"Oh Lord, if the Lord is with us, why has all this happened to us? And where are all His miracles which our fathers told us about, saying, did not the Lord bring us up from Egypt? But now the Lord has forsaken us and delivered us into the hands of the Midianites."* What really fascinates me is what the angel of the Lord says to Gideon after Gideon dismisses what the angel of the Lord spoke and begins complaining that "if only God would have been here to save us, none of this would be happening right now." While Gideon was thinking that God had forsaken them, God was trying to show and tell Gideon that not only was God there, but He was going to do a great work through Gideon, only Gideon couldn't perceive what the angel of the Lord was saying because

Gideon was too busy believing that he and God's people were already defeated by the enemy. This type of thinking is what the enemy feeds off of because he can only channel through what you give him access to. God could have stopped right there and said "Nope, this is not the one who I thought would say yes and walk out his destiny with courage," but God didn't do that. This is because God doesn't look at our potential status; He looks at our established status through who He already created for us to be. That's why despite Gideon's reply, the angel of the Lord spoke once again to Gideon and said, "*Go in this might of yours, and you shall save Israel from the hands of the Midianites. Have I not sent you?*" If there is one thing, we all must understand, it's that when God chooses someone to go and fulfill his purpose, *it's because that person has already been* marked by God to do what God has already empowered he or she to do. It's natural for us as humans to feel afraid and think that it is impossible. In reality, all that is true, but when we are speaking of God's infinite power and authority, this surpasses every intellectual thought of man's perspective or outcome to any situation at hand. We tend to think that, and I have heard many times in preaching that if that person God has chosen doesn't move, God will use another. I beg to differ though, because despite Gideon's fear, God still chose Gideon to fulfill his purpose through Gideon in the end. What God has established in you, He will move through you and bring you to a place of victory through the power of the Holy Spirit. God will not change His mind or back down from what he has already established to accomplish in fulfilling His will. In reference to what the angel of the Lord said to Gideon, it was, and is, relevant to us in every way. Gideon wasn't yet able to comprehend what the angel of the Lord was trying to tell Gideon, but that didn't stop God from pursuing Gideon. While Gideon was stuck on thinking that God had forgotten about them (meaning the Israelites), God was letting Gideon know that He was with Gideon, and because God was with Gideon, God had every right to declare over Gideon a man of valor. God will never call us what we are if His presence doesn't go before us, because God is the only reason we can claim victory and declare that we are more than conquerors through what Jesus Christ has already accomplished on the cross. God was, is, and will always see us as more than conquerors, because through His Spirit, God has accomplished more than we could ever imagine. But just like Gideon, most of us can't see the full picture of what it looks like when God fights our battles simply because we fear those who are in the world more than we declare that He who lives within us is far greater. Despite all that may stand in our way, whether it is our fear of the unknown, the anxiety of letting go and letting God, or the feelings of insecurities, God has chosen us to go out into the battlefield; and with His armor, He has called us to fight the good fight of faith. It doesn't matter how we view the outcome of what God is doing, all that matters is that the God of heaven and earth called us to be a part of something massive and great and has given us the privilege to be chosen for such a time as this. Think about it, among billions of human beings walking this earth, God chose us to make a difference within our generation. Wow! That's huge and maybe something far complex to imagine right now, but that is the point why "*God has chosen us to be a royal priesthood, a holy nation, His own special people, that we may proclaim the praises of Him who called us out of darkness into His marvelous light,*" according to *1 Peter 2:9.* This is how much God truly cares, not just about us as believers but the entire world. God has chosen us to stand in the gap for those whom He has already predestined to redeem as His very own and lead them toward deliverance through His own Son, Jesus Christ. What God has chosen for you to do, He will not relent to fulfill it through you. It's up to us to say, "Yes, Lord, here I am. Sanctify me and set me aside for your great honor and glory." It doesn't matter how long it takes for you to realize that God specifically handpicked you for a specific assignment because His purpose one way or another will be fulfilled, but just remember that the more you and I resist the calling, the more others who are suffering out there are waiting to hear a specific word from God and will continue in their affliction until you rise up and make that determination to walk out your God-given destiny. Eventually, Gideon did, after God had narrowed his army from 32,000 soldiers to only 300, only to have them stand still and know that God was, is, and will always fight for His people. We do not have to be confused when it comes to trusting God. Just trust that in the end, just like

God did with Gideon's enemies (the Midianites), He will put your enemies to scatter in confusion and cause you to see the full picture of why you were chosen in the first place because He already knew that you would give Him all the honor and all the glory.

Before Gideon understood God's plan, he was filled with doubt and fear, but in the end, God gave Gideon the greatest privilege of seeing God go before them and confuse their enemies. Like most of us are when it comes to fulfilling God's will, before we can see what God is doing, we allow the thoughts of the enemy to enter and paralyze us from walking right into the finished works of God's established victory. And in turn, many who are at the break of entering into something great remains in a period of waiting until we realize that the whole time we were trying to figure it all out, God has been saying to us, "Be still and know that I am God." And that's when we must make that determination to remain where we are or begin walking despite our fears and anxieties. The greatest battles won were the ones that were fought by God Himself.

But what happens when we deliberately say no way to God and try to flee from God's presence altogether? This sounds like a road map we all have tried to travel on at one point or another in our lives. Jonah, a man in the Bible who fled when he heard the voice of God say, "Arise, go to Nineveh, that great city, and cry out against it; for their wickedness has come up before me." Instead of Jonah talking to God about his true feelings, Jonah decides to try and run away from God. How funny is it to think that we can just run away from God and think that God will move on to the next. The Bible says that not only did Jonah flee from God's calling, but he also went down to Joppa, and there found a ship to get on, and so that is what Jonah did. He went down to Joppa, got on a boat, and went down to the bottom of the ship, all because he was trying to avoid the greater calling that was on his life. From the looks of things, you'd say that Jonah looks as if he is going to escape his calling after all. Or is he? While Jonah and the crew are rowing merrily down the stream, God already predestined a storm to come and change the trajectory of Jonah's initial way of thinking. Let's make one thing clear here: we cannot change our own course of action and think that it is the will of God, because what God has established and accomplished from the beginning is who and what He will use to demonstrate His mighty powers. For example, God created the light in the beginning, and the light is what He uses to let the darkness know that over evil, He has the power to overcome darkness. Another example is water. God made the waters; and to this day, He uses water as a metaphor to proclaim sanctification through purification, like the washing of the feet. Everything God has established and accomplished must be used for His honor and glory. That is why when we try to run away from God, we will eventually find ourselves coming back to the same scenario, because God will not give up on us even though we give up on ourselves. He is not drawn back by our insecurities. In fact, when we try and escape our God-given destiny, He takes our incredibility and shows us through various trials that we need Him to show us just how flawed we really are; so in the end, when He shows up to save us, we can proclaim His wonders to those who are all around us and give Him all the credit. God didn't form us and then say, "There's no way I could ever use this one." When God formed us in our mother's womb, we were all made in His very own image, which means that when we truly identify ourselves with our perfect heavenly Creator, there is no way that we could ever think or imagine a perfect God messing up what he has taken the time to form with His precious hands, a perfect God messing up what He made. Jonah was never the problem because Jonah was a man of God. What made Jonah try and run away from God was his way of thinking. God told him to go to a city where wickedness had reached its all-time high. But Jonah couldn't bear the thought of standing up in front of a city and declaring to the people all the wickedness that has gone up before God. God said for Jonah to cry out against the city, but instead, Jonah began crying out for his own life to be saved. If you read the beginning of the book of Jonah, you will realize that God never told Jonah that He had intentions of saving the city but only to go and cry out against it. Could this be the reason God all along had to send the storm? Was there a lesson to be learned for Jonah before God could have used him to cry out against Nineveh? Or perhaps God needed Jonah to realize that he too needed to understand that disobedience is wickedness, and just like Jonah had to cry out to the Lord against his own wicked act of disobedience, God was showing Jonah a reflection of what Nineveh needed from God as well as what Jonah did at that moment.

Repentance for their wickedness and deliverance from God: these two men of God (Gideon and Jonah, made in the image of God just like you and I) could not escape the great calling that was upon their lives just because fear and insecurity set in. Rest assured that when we continue to hide like Gideon or run like Jonah, no matter how deep or how wide we go, God still sees us. God is still pursuing us, and God has never taken His eyes off us. The measure we use to run and hide from our purpose is the same measure God will use to bring us back. Gideon hid in the threshing floor out of fear from the Midianites, and God approached the situation by narrowing down the army Gideon was so confident in to win the battle against his enemies, but God had to show Gideon that through the same measure of fear that led him to the threshing floor would also be the same measure of fear (when God narrowed down Gideon's army to only three hundred soldiers) that would bring Gideon back to a place of faith in the end. The same with Jonah. In the beginning, Jonah ran from God because he didn't or couldn't comprehend the thought of God even looking upon an evil, wicked, and disobedient city like Nineveh, let alone send someone to cry out against it. So with the same measure of disobedience, God had to bring Jonah to a place where he would have to reflect on his very own action of resistance that would eventually lead him back to God, in the same way Jonah tried to flee from God in the first place. So you see, in the end, God's will for our lives is not to harm us but to give us the greatest opportunity to be used by the greatest most wonderful and all-powerful God of heaven and earth. God loves us so much that he can't stand the thought of us not stepping into our God-given destiny that He preordained for us to walk out even before we were born. We were chosen by the Creator Himself to go out and be the change this world needs. You may feel unqualified at times, but that just means God is positioning you like a joint that has been out of place and needs to be rehabilitated so it can gain its use and function properly for what it was intended to be used for. In the very same way, God is doing a work in you that will cause you to feel uncomfortable at times, but is very necessary because without being renewed in the word of God, we cannot function properly in the body of Christ. Every member may make up the body of Christ, but every member is also made to function differently. God is calling us to step out of our comfort zone and operate in the gifts and talents He has given us. In order to do that though, we must be willing to let God bend and shape us, even to the point of us having to go down south and visit Egypt's toughest moments in our lives. When this opportunity to press into God and seek direction from the Holy Spirit comes our way, instead of looking at it as a tribulation period, we ought to look at it as a combination of our weakness and God's strength coming together to bring forth and birth something great through what God has already established in us so we can continue to fulfill our calling till the very end. I believe the reason these men became such powerful instruments in the hand of God is not that they eventually came to fulfill their God-given destiny, but because they were transparent with God from the beginning and both showed it in different ways. Take Gideon for example. He showed his insecurity by hiding from the Midianites while threshing wheat in the winepress and then telling the angel of the Lord that he is the least of them in his father's house. Jonah's idea of showing his insecurity was by disregarding the calling on his life and thinking that by running away, his problems would be far behind him. This is what we all battle with every day when it comes to fulfilling the will of God, simply because the enemy knows that even when we try to hide or runaway, God is sovereign and will move heaven and earth just to get through to us, and that makes the enemy angry. Yes! Angry enough to make war against God's chosen ones. The blueprint of our lives is within our reach to grab, gaze upon, and take hold of; but the one who constructs our lives and builds us up is God Himself.

Moses saw the blueprint of his life through the Egyptian and the Hebrew man who were fighting. There was an internal battle that rose up from within the core of Moses's spirit. The very moment Moses saw an Egyptian fighting with a Hebrew man, this became a reflection of what was really going on within Moses's life. Moses was raised and lived in Egypt by adoption. Taking the role of an Egyptian prince was eating him up inside because, on the other hand, Moses was a Hebrew from the Levi descendant. Moses's calling was not to become a prince of Egypt but a deliverer sent by the Most High God, but Moses had not discovered this just yet because he had not had that profound encounter with God. In order for Moses to fully understand his calling and purpose, he had no other choice but to flee from Egypt. How ironic is it that Joseph had to travel toward Egypt and stay there until the time came to save His people in the end and Moses had to flee from Egypt until the time came when Moses would return to save his people in the end. Both men had to go to Egypt and remain in Egypt, and out of Egypt, God caused them to become Israel's saving grace. This is another picture of Jesus Christ as Lord and Savior. *Matthew 2:14* and *15* says,

> *When he arose, he took the young child and his mother by night and departed for Egypt, and was there until the death of Herod, that it might be fulfilled which was spoken by the Lord through the prophet saying, "Out of Egypt I called my son."*

God called Joseph and Moses to Egypt to mark an era that would cause many to look upon Egypt and say the great events that took place were out of Egypt. This may seem ludicrous to many, but we all have to remember that God's way of thinking is higher than our own and His plans are higher than our own plans. Take Moses for example. Who would have thought that Moses killing the Egyptian man and stopping him from beating the Hebrew man was a foreshadow of what Moses would come back to Egypt to do? Save the lives of God's people from the hand of Pharaoh. Although this was an unjust act on Moses's part, it was the wake-up call that he needed to cause him to flee from where he was to a place God needed him to get to in order to find God's presence.

Now Moses was tending the flock of Jethro his father-in-law, the priest of Midian. And he led the flock to the back of the desert and came to Horeb, the mountain of God. The Angel of the Lord appeared to him in a flame of fire from the midst of the bush. So, he looked, and behold the bush was burning with fire, but the bush was not consumed. Moses said, "I will now turn aside and see this great sight, why the bush does not burn." So when the Lord saw that he turned aside to look, God called to him from the midst of the bush and said, "Moses, Moses!" (Exod. 3:1–4)

God's people had been in slavery for quite some time now, and as we see, Moses is no longer in Egypt but has fled for his own life since he was a wanted man in Egypt for killing an Egyptian soldier. By this time, Moses had been living in the land of Midian with Jethro and Jethro's seven daughters of which one of them became Moses's wife, and together, they had two sons, one of whose name was called Gershom, which means "stranger in a foreign land" or "a stranger there." Moses had been removed from his land twice, and his people (the Israelites) were strangers in Egypt, and now Moses was estranged from his people, living in a land far from home. In the process of Moses transitioning from Egypt to the land of Midian, God had not forgotten about His people. On the contrary, with Moses being where he was and Pharaoh coming near to his death, for all intents and purposes, the plan of God was moving right along and on schedule.

After Pharaoh's death, the Bible says that God's people groaned because of their bondage. They cried out, and God heard them and remembered His covenant with Abraham, with Isaac, and with Jacob. God looked upon the children of Israel and acknowledged them. As I began to really scrutinize the scriptures, the word *remember* used in the context of this verse stuck out to me like *rhema*, and after carefully analyzing this word, I discovered something interesting. When we think of the word *remember*, we often tend to lean more on the forgetting side and regaining from memory what we forgot about.

That doesn't sound like something our God would do, right? Of course not! So I began looking up similar words and found the word *recall*, which means to officially order (someone or something) to return to its former place. I began to realize then that in this verse, God wasn't saying that He had forgotten about His people and then has remembered His people but rather now, it was time for God's plan to be put into action. And soon, Moses would have to return to Egypt and fulfill his destiny in becoming the deliverer the Israelites would need to free them from their bondage. But before this could take place, Moses would have to go to that secret place, a place God has already established for Moses to walk into, a place where Moses would encounter the One who would set all of Egypt on a journey no one on this earth would ever forget. God is saying to you today, "I have a plan for your life, and I have already established the place you will go to find my presence. I have led you this far and have preserved your life for such a time as this. Come now, for I will show you great and mighty works which you have not seen." Do you think your coming into this world was by accident? Do you really think that God took the time to carefully piece you together and breathe the breath of life in you just to forget about you? Absolutely not! Everything we must go through in this life always serves as a platform for you to get that much closer to your destiny. It may look like you are not making much progress because of delays or rejections; but I can guarantee this much: if God allows us to walk through troubled waters, He will sustain us until we accomplish, through His Spirit, all that is to be fulfilled in us. Moses found himself fighting and battling with his identity and complacency. Although Moses was born a Hebrew, he was placed in Egypt and raised by Pharaoh's daughter with the intention of one day becoming a ruler in Egypt. But God already knew this was how it had to be, because even in the detail of our lives, God is the one who is taking those flawed details that we think are meant to hurt us or set us back and use them to glorify His unforgettable name. Life is not about our greatest achievements but in the details of our lives, because it's when we look back at the smallest of details that allows us to piece together the little moments that may be small but never overlooked. For Moses, this was a turning point for him, simply because he began to realize that Egypt was not his home. This world is not our home either. Just as Moses was born from the descendants of the tribe of Levi (which means united or joined together in harmony) and then was forced to live for a time in a place where he would eventually have to go away from and one day return, so are we united with our High Priest, Jesus Christ, through His sacrifice and intercession, to live in a foreign land that is not our own and one day leave this earth only to come back and rule and reign with Christ until the time comes when Jesus puts an end to all injustice.

Moses, unaware of what was about to occur, would soon step into a season of transition, only this required Moses to first have led a flock to the back of Mount Horeb to a secret place where God had predestined only Moses to walk into. You may be unaware of what God is doing in you and through you at this very moment, but God has specifically chosen you for this assignment, and those who are with you are meant to go with you to the place where you are headed. God has given you the privilege of walking into a place where He will speak to you, and you will hear His voice.

There is a supernatural event that took place as Moses went to the back of Mount Horeb. God knew that Moses would lead the flock to the back of the mountain and that Moses would be in a place where he would turn aside to see such a sight that would cause him to draw near to the presence of the Lord. I must ask this question: what is it you have or who are you leading with you to a place of holiness? Whatever you are doing or whomever you are leading, whether it be a group of men or women in a campaign, a sports team, coworkers at your job, or a congregation at a church, lead them to that secret place because while you are leading them, God is leading you to have a profound encounter that will set the course of your destiny to be fulfilled in due season. God can use anything and anyone to lead you into that secret place. In this case, Moses was tending the flocks of Jethro (his father-in-law) and leading them straight to the back of Mount Horeb, where Moses had no intentions of seeking such a profound encounter with God. Yet for all intents and purposes, God used the flocks to bring Moses to a holy place where Moses would become curious, and that is just what Moses did unintentionally. I must stop here for a brief moment because something has just occurred to me regarding unintentional moments. They are actually God's ways of setting us up to have a profound encounter, which in turn will launch us into the next season of our lives.

In 1 Samuel 9, Saul's father, Kish, sent his son, Saul, to go with his servant to go find the lost donkeys. Saul and his servant passed through towns, trying to find the lost donkeys until they arrived at a specific location (named Zuph), where a man of God named Samuel (the prophet) would be. Although the donkeys were supposedly lost, this current situation is what brought Saul and Samuel together. Saul was about to give up and go back home when his servant said to him, "Look now, there is in this city a man of God, and he is an honorable man. All that he says surely comes to pass. So let us go there; perhaps he can show us the way that we should go." We see that God used Saul's servant to compel Saul to enter the city and seek Samuel, the prophet, unaware that God was using Saul's servant to intentionally bring Saul face-to-face with Samuel so that he could anoint Saul, king of God's people. Even though Saul was unaware that his season of transition was drawing near, God already prepared Samuel to receive Saul and anoint him king and lead God's people through a brief season of victory.

God will cause the circumstances of those around you to bring you to a place where they will have to watch as God takes you from where you are to where you were destined to go, only the one leading the way is the one who will have to endure more than the others following, because the one leading has the capability (through the wisdom of God) to understand the assignment without fully knowing the assignment, which in turn is led by the One who holds the assignment and has the power to manifest the assignment in and out of season.

Moses led the flock to the back of the mountain unaware that the assignment that had been marked upon his life to fulfill was about to become manifest to him in such a supernatural powerful way. Moses leading the flock on an ordinary day would come to realize that the God who took him from his mother's home to live in

Egypt and then caused him to flee from the land of Egypt was about to lead him into an epiphany that would result in Moses going from the prince of Egypt to the deliverer of the Israelites. God used the flock to move Moses in the right direction. God is using the circumstances of others to lead you in the right direction. You may think you are in that place just because it's your daily routine, but God is setting you up to have a profound encounter with him, and soon you will be standing on holy ground watching as God reveals Himself in such a way you will know beyond a shadow of a doubt that God is in your midst. God used lost donkeys to bring Saul to his place of destiny, and God used a herd of the flock to bring Moses to a place where He would discover his true calling and begin His journey back to Egypt. But before Moses could leave the mountain of Horeb, he would have to get well acquainted with God and fully understand the assignment in order to carry out God's plan of deliverance.

> *Then He said, "Do not draw near this place. take your sandals off your feet. For the place you stand is Holy ground." Moreover He said, "I am the God of your father, Abraham, the God of Isaac, and the God of Jacob." And Moses hid his face, for he was afraid to look upon God. (Exod. 3:5 and 6)*

One thing we must understand as believers in Christ or as nonbelievers, when God shows up, His presence alone is enough for us to draw near even though we may not understand what is happening at that moment. When we are standing on holy ground, we become bare in the sight of God's presence. God told Moses to take the sandals off his feet as a symbol of uncovering the very part that God would use to sanctify his mission in going to Egypt and departing from Egypt. God needed Moses to understand first and foremost that sanctification starts with uncovering the truth. The truth is that Moses, by nature, was a murderer because he had killed an Egyptian soldier of Pharaoh. Moses, for the first time, was standing in the presence of God and was given a command to take off his sandals, simply because, in God's sight, we are all sinners and need to be stripped and uncovered before the Lord. Moses was no saint, and neither are we. Our feet, just like the feet of Moses, have also run to things that were not pleasing to the Lord; yet the Lord still calls us to his presence. But for us to come into his presence, we must be undone and uncovered before the Lord. Sanctification is a process, and Moses was about to enter a sanctification process, but it first started with Moses coming before the Lord with bare feet and standing before the Almighty God with reverence. When God called Moses, Moses thought that by just turning aside to see the burning bush (that was not consumed), he would be able to capture a sight unseen by any-one; but the reality is that, without holiness, no one can see the Holy One. We cannot come to stand before God just because we see from afar something that catches our attention. What catches our atten-tion doesn't necessarily mean that we are in its presence, but rather, we are close to entering holy ground. Before we can fully come to entering the holy place (where God is), we must become sanctified and made holy before God. God told Moses (the moment Moses even tried to step into a place of holiness), "Do not draw near to this place." God was strictly and specifically letting Moses know that who he was about to have an encounter with was the One who makes all things pure and holy. Holiness begins with obedience to the voice of God. Any time God wants to use us to bring glory to His name, there always must be a sanctification process, and the first step toward sanctification is acknowledgment of God's presence. Anytime we are in the presence of God, there is a sensible feeling of being undone in His presence. When we are touched by God, we quickly begin to realize just how much of a sinner we really are and just how holy God truly is. When Moses turned aside to see why the bush did not burn, God quickly told Moses to take off his sandals because the place where he was standing was holy ground. The moment Moses was fully aware that he was in the presence of God was when (as the Bible says) Moses hid his face from God and was afraid to look upon the Great I Am. This is the pure evidence that being in God's presence is not only something we desire but must be something we all need to be fully aware of, because the truth is, as God is holy, we who come to His presence must be made holy (separated) and sanctified (set aside) in order to remain in His presence. And this happens when we surrender our will to the will of God's purpose. This is not always an easy process. It sure wasn't easy for Moses because God lets Moses know the reason for His visit and that Moses was the chosen one to go back to Egypt and speak to Pharaoh regarding the freeing of God's people, but before Moses could even think about returning to Egypt, Moses would have to spend time in God's presence. God has chosen us to come to His presence simply because God has a plan for each one of our lives, and our lives were designed by God to surrender to His will. This, however, for many people is not an easy task because although there is a hurting and enslaved generation, there is also a growing number of people who know the word of God yet choose to run away, disobey the word of God, and turn to their own pleasures and self-will, instead of coming to know their true assignment on this earth. For that very reason, many are called, but few are chosen, as it says in Mathew 22:14. This means God has appointed a specific assignment to each of us, but only those who choose to fulfill God's purpose will come to understand the assignment. Moses, in the beginning, did not and could not understand his assignment because this was no little task for Moses. Moses knew that Egypt was no place for anyone to play games. Moses saw firsthand all the misery and agony the children of God was in because Moses was in Egypt and encountered the harsh things that took place with him not being able to do anything about it, but now has come the time when God would tell Moses that the assignment that God has placed of Moses's life would require him to return to Egypt, and before Pharaoh, Moses would become like a god who would stand in the midst of his people and perform all kinds of signs and wonders. Not only would Moses stand before Pharaoh with boldness, but God also told Moses that in the end, God would give His people the ultimate victory because for this reason, God has shown up to make His name great throughout the earth and for all generations to come and know that the Great I Am is the one true living God and there is none beside him. But hearing this, Moses was quickly disturbed in his heart and could not fathom the very thought of God taking a person like him and performing all that God said He would do. I know what you are thinking. Moses is crazy for not believing in God and taking God at His word, right? But believe it or not, this happens to even the best of us. It's sort of like when we watched cartoons as kids. Do you remember when the cartoon character stopped for a moment to stare into space and then a cloud would appear, and he/she would imagine themselves doing the unthinkable, only to come back to reality and say, "There's no way." That is what we do when we think about the supernatural works God wants to do through us. We become doubtful and begin disqualifying ourselves because we think the task is far over our heads to complete. This is exactly what was happening with Moses. God had told Moses that He was going to go down and bring His people up from Egypt to a good large land that was flowing with milk and honey. People were already inhabiting the land, but God would allow His chosen people to go up to conquer and possess it. God also told Moses that He would be with him and that this would be the very sign that God's people would see victory. This was the ultimate encounter that God's people would have with the Great I Am in the land of Egypt. This was going to be a process like never before seen by anyone. Every Egypt moment that the previous generations encounter all led up to this one huge miraculous event, which would set the staging ground for everyone in the world to see and know that when God establishes a plan, that plan will follow through. You may not realize it right in this very moment, but God has called you to rise up and begin the journey of redemption for your family to come and see the glory of God. Perhaps that is why you have gone through so much in your life? Maybe the turmoil in your life was God's way of saying, "I have a greater plan for your life, and everything you have done thus far hasn't worked because I am the solution to your struggles." Or perhaps you were just meant by God to walk through Egypt like Moses did, only to find out that the high life wasn't meant for you to get caught up in, but to understand that in this life, we must become the change in order to see the change that this world so desperately needs. Moses had no choice but to live in a place where he in reality did not belong, but because there was a hidden design in God's plan for Moses, Moses had to remain in Egypt until the time came when God would reveal Himself to Moses.

There was, is, and will always be an appointed time when God will show up; and when He does, He will not show up just to show up, no! When God shows up, it's because the assignment that He has placed upon our lives has come to pass, and whether we want to understand it or not, God will make it known to us that He has already appointed us to an assignment that he chose for us to fulfill. Moses, on the other hand, could not quite get what God was telling him because although Moses heard God, Moses wasn't listening to God but rather focusing on the trouble at hand instead of the solution that was in his very hand. I will further explain what I mean in the chapter to follow this one right now, but before I do, I want to touch base on something interesting that the Holy Spirit laid upon my heart one day as I was on my way to a women's conference in Allentown, Pennsylvania.

After reading Exodus 3:8, I began meditating on this verse. Suddenly, I heard the voice of the Holy Spirit say to me, "Those who are in Egypt right now are being called out to conquer nations that are stronger and mightier than them." At that moment I couldn't decipher exactly what the Holy Spirit meant until He said the word *technology*. God is calling us out of Egypt to conquer nations that are stronger and mightier than us, but by the Spirit of God, we will be able to overcome. Then the Holy Spirit said to me, "I sent out Joshua and my people to first go and spy out the lands of those whom I would overthrow with a mighty hand." We are living in a generation where technology has become so advanced that it has taken control of most of the population and its use has risen to its all-time high. There are so many nations that have placed technology as their stronghold and saving grace and, in turn, have manipulated so many into thinking that through this advancement of technology, we have progressed to the point of not needing anything but technology to keep us going and staying stronger than we have ever been. Yet behind this hidden agenda from the kingdom of darkness, there is a replica of what Satan is trying to establish as the all-seeing eye of God (through technology) who we know that the only sovereign, supreme, omnipresent God is Yahweh. This agenda from the enemy has already begun to infiltrate the world's industry through the advancement of technology. Although this is what the world is coming to, in the end, it will not prosper against God's plan of redemption because there is still a remnant out there who will not back down and give in to the lies and deceptions of the kingdom of darkness's agenda but will rise up and speak out against these things with a supernatural boldness, which can only come from the kingdom of God. Everything you and I have gone through this far has been to build endurance for what is to come in the near future. If you're in a season of growth, you should embrace it because after growth comes a season of preparation and thereafter comes favor to fulfill God's will over your life. Not just yours but your entire household as well. Keep in mind that our Egypt and down south moments aren't just for our benefit but for those who are around us. The only difference is, God chose you and me to be the instruments that would draw our family, friends, and those around us toward Christ's redemption.

Growth Preparation and Favor

One morning as I was studying the book of Exodus, the Holy Spirit said to me, "There are three reasons why I allow those whom I have chosen to pass through the south and go through Egypt." I ask the Lord what the three main reasons are, and He replied in analogies:

Growth

Anytime something needs growth, it also needs to be isolated and unseen for a time. For example, when we are sleeping, there is something called the pituitary gland. This gland releases a growth hormone that helps our body grow and repair itself. This growth takes place when we are in our still or relaxed state of mind (dreaming). We are unaware of the growth process and cannot feel it happening, but the evidence of this occurring is when we continue living our daily lives. Without fully taking knowledge of the growth process, we begin to see change happening. It has been said that the deeper sleep you are in, the body also releases an increased production of proteins. This also helps cell growth and repairing of anything that is damaged.

Another analogy are the seeds that are planted in the ground cannot sprout up unless it breaks forth through the dirt, soil, or even concrete. Under the surface, there is an isolation process, along with a breakthrough process, that is taking place at that moment; but anything above the surface cannot see this happening until the time of manifestation arrives. What had to be in darkness and in its isolation process eventually becomes the very thing that is made manifested to bring glory and honor to God's name. This does not mean that the process is over, but rather the isolation process has been successfully carried out, and on the surface, the manifestation of what was hidden for such a time becomes known to all that this is what was bound to occur all along. In the very same way, in order for us to really grow and flourish in what God has sought out for us to fulfill in this life, it is a must that we for a time remain in a dark, isolated period process and become broken before the Lord. The isolation process isn't the easiest process, but in order for us to get to the other processes that will come along in the future, we must first overcome the isolation process. Just like there is a time when that young girl/boy stops growing yet will still have to encounter other levels of growth and maturity, so we too in our spiritual walk after overcoming the isolation process will have to press on and grow in other spiritual levels of our lives to maintain stability and integrity. This is what God was doing in and through His people. God was building character through their isolation period, and in order for the Israelites to fully understand their growth process, they also needed to trust God to see them through to the other side. Moses was that growth hormone they needed in order to continue growing as a people chosen by God to come out of their isolation period. If there is a reality we all must face in this life, it's that, without an isolation period, we won't understand the calling that is before us. Just like the body needs adequate sleep so accurate growth takes place accordingly, if we don't learn to rest in God's word daily, we will stunt the very process that was meant to bring growth and launch us into the very next phase of our process, which is the preparation process.

Preparation

Before we can come to see the finished work come to pass in our lives, we must first allow God to place before us the preparation of instructions that will lead us into a season of trust and movement. The preparation process enables us to really press into God's presence and find the right resources we need to bring us up and out to the place of the unknown where God has prepared our hearts to receive instructions according to His perfect will. This process isn't the easiest one also because for us to keep our faith alive, we must always keep our focus on what is in front of us and not around us. As God prepares our hearts to receive instructions, the enemy is also lying in wait like a lion seeking whom he may devour. Remember the enemy comes to kill, steal, and destroy anything that has to do with God's children entering a new level or season of God's glory. We need to keep our eyes always fixed on Jesus and our hearts pure so the enemy cannot taint or distort the plans of God for our lives. Our preparation process and how we perceive God's instructions to move into a new season depends on how much time we spend in God's presence. Every strategic move of God will never go without God's voice being heard first. Whether it's through His word, in the stillness of His voice whispering into your ear, a servant of God coming to you with a word from the Lord, or a message from an angelic being (like an angel in a dream, vision, or in a physical impartation of God's glory), God will always make mention of His presence before we proceed to go forth with what He has commanded for us to do. Preparation is the key to living out our God-given potential. There are so many verses in the Bible that give us a good view and understanding of why we need to step into a season of preparation and why it is vital that we continue to seek God in His word. God's word is the detailed road map and goes hand in hand with our prayer life. Just to name a few of the many verses in the Bible, we will see just how important it is to take heed to God's word while in our season of preparation.

Prepare your work outside; get everything ready for yourself in the field, and after that build your house. (Prov. 24:27)

A voice cries: "In the wilderness prepare the way of the Lord; make straight in the desert a highway for our God. (Isa. 40:3)

By faith, Noah, being warned by God concerning events as yet unseen, in reverent fear prepared an ark for the saving of his household. By this he condemned the world and became an heir of the righteousness that comes by faith. (Heb. 11:7)

As we can see from these few verses just how preparation is vital for our souls to prosper, we cannot continue to grow and step into our God-given calling without proper care, instructions, and preparation. If we look at God's nature, we see a majority of His nature is full of God's beauty; but unfortunately, there are places on this earth that, although they are a part of nature, have grown alongside the beautiful creation of God. There's no root; and so they look dead, dry, and trampled on. This is because although these particular plants, trees, etc. grow, they have no stability to continue in the process of preparation. They become lifeless, and eventually, they wither with time. When we have no stability, we have no foundation. Without a stable foundation, we have no guidance, and without guidance, there's no need for instructions. And without instructions, there's no preparation, and with no preparation, there's no life. Before we were brought into this world, we were already thought about by God, and God prepared within each and every one of us a foundation (who is Christ Jesus) to become our stability and guide us with all preparation to give us the instructions He has laid upon our hearts to fulfill. As God predestined our lives to go forth and prepare the way for others who don't know the Lord to receive Him into their hearts, God has given us a strategic floor plan that will lead us to a greater destiny. But first, we must fully understand that without preparation, there is no way we will ever get to where God wants us to go. A family cannot arrive at their vacation destination unless they first sit down and plan ahead, and this involves preparation. A pilot cannot fly a plane nor can a captain direct a ship unless they have gone through the process of preparation in knowing how to operate these heavy machineries. When we learn to prepare our hearts (in God's word), our time in Egypt or down south will cause us to continue relying on the One who will continue to supply our needs in preparation for what is to come. After God has allowed us to accomplish the preparation stage and we have fully obeyed God, we will step into a destiny full of favor from the Lord. I believe this is where we see the glory of God rest upon our lives in the most supernatural way possible. Yes, there will come a season in our lives, if we hold fast to our faith, even when the enemy tries to come against you and attack the assignment God has placed on your life, God Himself will give you rest and favor above your enemies. This means that every time the enemy tries to raise a weapon over us, that weapon will hit the ground, and you will trample over it and keep walking in the fullness of God's great and abundant grace; and the last phase, without a doubt, will be the most amazing seasons to live through, which is the season of favor!

Favor

There is an abundant favor of overflow God wants each one of His children to inherit. When we come to understand who God is, we will understand that God gives us the desires of our hearts when we delight in Him. Favor comes when we seek ye first the kingdom of God, and not just His kingdom, but His righteousness as well, because through His righteousness, we can obtain favor from walking upright with integrity. Let's take for example a young girl who is turning sixteen years old. Her parents decide to celebrate her turning sixteen by throwing her the most amazing celebration. As she transitions from a girl to a young lady, we see here that because of her just becoming sixteen and having obeyed thus far her parents and sought to do what was right in their eyes, her parents have showered her with favor and blessings to honor her growth and maturity. She is given all of this because of the love and care her parents have for her. In reality, God doesn't have to give us or owe us anything. We inherit favor simply because God declares it over our lives, not because He has to but because He wants to. God's main objective here is that He does as He pleases, but everything that God does is never to hurt us or serve us with evil intentions. Everything God has planned for our lives is full of abundant favor, blessing, and hope. Favor comes when we submit ourselves to the One who holds our future in His hands.

Another example of favor is a baby in the womb of a woman who is close to giving birth. In honor of that woman carrying a child close to the end of the third trimester, a baby shower is thrown. The baby is the one getting all the gifts and blessings, yet the baby is unaware of this because although the baby is hidden away and unseen, there is an abundant overflow of blessings awaiting his or her arrival. In the very same way, although it may seem like we are hidden and tucked away from God's favor, God is already celebrating your shower as you get ready to come out of the birthing process and encounter the abundant overflow of God's favor and blessings that awaits your arrival into the next season of your life. I have proof (in the scriptures) that backs up that what I am saying is true. You are about to come out of your preparation stage and into your season of favor because the word of God is truth, and anyone who believes in God's word will see abundant overflow occur in your life, and it's closer than you are more aware of!

> *May the Lord give you increase, you and your children, may you be blessed in the Lord, who made the heavens and the earth. (Ps. 115:14)*

> *Surely goodness and mercy shall follow me all the days of my life. (Ps. 23:6)*

> *Let the favor of the Lord our God be upon us, and establish the work of our hands for us; yes, establish the work of our hands. (Ps. 90:17)*

Moses after having spent some time in the land of Midian and having a profound encounter with the Great I Am has now been ordered back to Egypt, not by Pharaoh but by God Almighty. You may not want to believe this, but Moses was actually entering into a season of favor with God. If you have ever read the story of Moses, you'd say, "How is it possible when Moses went to Egypt on a rough assignment and everything that occurred in Egypt devastatingly left many dead or at some points in denial about God coming to rescue them from the hands of Pharaoh and his people?" The truth is that, the only way Moses could ever have gone back to Egypt was with God's favor because should Moses have gone with just God's command and had not realized the favor he possessed from God to speak out and proclaim liberty for the captives, the events that took place would have been of no benefit to Moses whatsoever. But scripture tells us that God Himself told Moses that He would be with Moses's and Aaron's mouth and teach them what they shall say. Not only would God be with their mouth, but Moses would be as God. On top of all of this, God tells Moses, "I also command you to take what you have with you," which was the rod, because with this, Moses was going to perform the signs that would later on cause great turmoil in Egypt but also a great deliverance for God's people as they walk out of Egypt in victory. I don't know about you, but this sounds a lot to me like favor from the Lord over Moses's life. I believe that God is calling us to go down into the enemy's territory and invade and interrupt the enemy's assignment. The enemy at this very moment thinks that just because the world is in chaos, he is winning; but truth be told, everything that is happening is preparing those whom God has chosen to rise up and walk with favor and integrity to disarm every single weapon of warfare and attack from the kingdom of darkness, to proclaim with boldness and favor from the Lord the gospel of Jesus Christ. This, in fact, may bring conflict and turmoil; but in the end, it will bring about a great deliverance like never seen before. I believe it is the great awakening that is soon to come upon the earth like never before seen. Moses came back to Egypt. This time he would not come to rule and reign over Egypt but to become the greatest and most powerful instrument in the hands of God to do the impossible and unheard-of works that no man has ever seen before. God is doing a work in you that the kingdom of darkness cannot stop.

> Go and gather the elders of Israel together, and say to them, "The Lord God of your fathers, the God of Abraham, of Isaac, and the God of Jacob, appeared to me, saying, I have surely visited you and seen what is done to you in Egypt; and I have said I will bring you up out of the affliction of Egypt to the land of the Canaanites and the Hittites and the Amorites and the Perizzites and the Hivites and the Jebusites, to a land flowing with milk and honey." (Exod. 3:16 and 17)

> But I am sure that the king of Egypt will not let you go, not even by a mighty hand. so I will stretch out my hand and strike Egypt with all my wonders which I will do in its midst, and after that, he will let you go. And I will give this people favor in the sight of the Egyptians; and it shall be when you go, that you shall not go empty-handed. (Exod. 3:19–21)

As we walk out this journey called life, we must understand something important, God knows and sees the affliction of the people living in this fallen broken and cruel world. God has called us to visit Egypt and remain there until the time comes for God's will to be fulfilled in our lives. The time came when God spoke to Moses and let him know that the place where he is sending Moses back to has already been visited by God and that every cruel act that was taking place in Egypt was already sought out by God Himself. God wanted Moses to know, along with the elders, that God was about to intervene like no one on this planet could do for them. God wants you to know that He sees your pain and affliction the enemy has placed on you, and God has already ordained the exact moment that you will see your victory moment come to pass, but until that time comes, this will not stop the enemy from continuing to make you feel trapped and enslaved by the deceptive things of this world. The world wants you to praise, bow down, and become enslaved to it; and in turn, you must be who the world paints you to be. And if you're not, you are treated as the outcast of the world's view of perfection. God, on the other hand, wants us to live contrary to what the world says because the way God views us goes far beyond any expectation the world could ever possibly label us as. God has already established each one of us and has made us in His very own image; but the enemy who comes to steal, kill, and destroy has also come to contaminate and distort God's creation including us who are His greatest creation.

God is the only perfect One; and therefore, the lies and deception that come from the enemy cause many to believe that if they do not look, act, or speak a certain way, culture and society puts forth a disclaimer on that group or individual and soon after begins pushing them toward the exit door of discreditation; but this is the point that I wanted to get to regarding Egypt, Pharaoh, Moses, and God's people. While Moses was in Egypt growing up from a baby to a boy and into a man, no matter how much Moses thought he belonged in Egypt and was a part of Pharaoh's palace, the reality was that Moses's identity, along with the Hebrews, was already marked, sealed, stamped, and approved by God Almighty to be delivered and set free by the hand of God through the mouth of Moses. You see, when Moses grew up in Egypt, the culture of the Egyptians may have allowed Moses to partake and participate in the Egyptian cultural affairs; but as Moses became more and more curious about who he really was, he discovered something that no one was able to take away from him, not Pharaoh, not his adoptive Egyptian mother, and not even his own biological mother because what was already established in Moses was already embedded within him by God. I am talking about Moses's roots. Before Moses was even conceived in his mother's womb, God already knew the journey Moses would have to take to get to Egypt one day, but God also knew that Egypt was where He would establish his work through Moses. The roots that tie us back from where we came from are the very roots that God has begun his good works from. When we really analyze this and truly begin to identify ourselves with what our Creator in heaven and on earth has established from His roots, we begin to see that from God's roots being established and planted within us, Egypt is just a place where God establishes us, because this is the beginning of the root to where God wants us to trust in Him as He performs His supernatural works through us, just like we will begin to see God work through Moses.

I hope by now you are starting to see Egypt in a whole new way. As we take a deeper look into the lives of the Hebrew children of God, we are going to discover something very vital and interesting that will leave us breathless and wanting God to act in the very same way He did for his people to do in our lives as well. There is a season of God's favor that is about to take place, and when it does, that's when a great awakening is at the break of coming to pass. Moses had no idea what coming back to Egypt as a Hebrew man and not an Egyptian prince truly meant for him; and God's people, because what was about to take place next, was about to become recorded not just in heaven but here on earth for generations to come. All that you have gone through this far was not in vain. The abandonment, rejection, pain, and heartache of this world were permitted by God to mark the course of history in your life for generations to come and see what God has established within you for His honor and glory and to be revealed throughout the earth when the appointed time comes when God will work wonders and miracles in you to accomplish His will through you. Jesus says in *John 14:12*, "*Most assuredly I say to you, he who believes in Me, the works that I do he will do also; and greater works than these he will do because I go to my Father.*" Just as God had already chosen Moses to accomplish His will for that generation in time, so God has chosen you and me to rise up and become the mouth and feet of God for our generation; and just like those who were held in Egypt as slaves crying out for salvation, so are many in this generation who are held in spiritual, physical, mental, and emo-tional enslavement are waiting for you and me (who have spent time in God's word and in prayer) to come back into the world to speak out in truth and righteousness. Although many in the world are wounded and hurting from years of pain and heartache and it may seem like the world is ignoring God's message of redemption, the more we speak out in truth, the closer we are to seeing a great revival take place, which now brings me to the next chapter of Moses's life. Coming to Pharaoh not knowing that speaking out in truth would come with a heavy price for Moses and God's people. We are about to know what Moses faced as he made his way over to Pharaoh to proclaim liberty over God's people.

CHAPTER 12

⋯◦●◉●▬▬▬▬▬◉▬▬▬▬▬●◉●◦⋯

You Were Meant to Fail the First Time but Not Surrender

D o you remember as a child in school being asked by your
teacher what you wanted to be when you grow up? When we
are young, we have this image of how life would be in the future,
like being a scientist or a pathologist who would help find cures for
different diseases out there. This type of thinking as a young child
leads us to believe that one day, we can actually achieve that goal and
pursue something great. As we get older, however, we begin to realize
that confessing who we want to be is easier said than done. No one
goes from *A* to *Z* overnight. This is because as we grow in this life, we
encounter the long road it takes to make a difference in the world.

This is exactly what happened to Moses when he was commanded by God to come back to Egypt and fulfill God's purpose.
As we look upon the first encounter Moses had with Pharaoh, we are
going to see that what we perceive as failure is actually God's way of
showing us a whole new meaning to the word *failure* and *success*. God
has established in us the ability to act upon the things he commands
us to fulfill. Sometimes however, we, through a manipulating spirit
of fear, will make up all the excuses in the world to try and get out of
something that God has already predestined for us to complete. For
Moses, this was going back to Egypt to announce with all boldness
and courage the release of God's people out of Egypt. Moses must

have known that the task that lay before him was just as mighty and strong as God's people being enslaved. Moses knew firsthand what was going on with God's people because Moses was from the same family as God's people. Moses knew the hurt and agony of his people, yet Moses could not bring himself to accept the task that was before him from God to complete. How many of us fall into the same category where we see everything that is taking place, yet being called by God to rise up and be the hands and feet of God, we shrink back and think, *I can't possibly go and do what God is telling me to do*. This is our reply nine times out of ten because where there is evil taking place, war must occur, simply because God never loses a battle, and where the enemy thinks he is winning, God already predestined a strategic move to overthrow the enemy out of his place. You and I, just like Moses, have given excuses after excuses; but there will come a time when the excuses won't matter any longer and the only thing that will matter in the end are these words found in Joshua 1:9 wherein God says, "Have I not commanded you? Be strong and of good courage: Do not be afraid nor be dismayed, for the Lord your God is with you wherever you go." God is not asking us to fulfill His will; He is commanding us to go forth and fulfill His will despite our fears and anxieties, despite our faults and failures, and despite our doubts and regrets to fight the good fight of faith, knowing that if God is for us who could be against us. Unfortunately, many of us see the mountain as bigger than God, and for that reason, God continues to pursue us until we begin to believe and take God at His every word. This wasn't easy for Moses, and it certainly won't be for you and me. But the greatest news is that it is not impossible, because with God, all things are possible.

There is a hidden message within every trial and tribulation. Every trial and tribulation will cause us to come out with perseverance and determination that ultimately allows us to follow through with the assignment that was given to us by God Himself to complete until the very end. In the beginning, it may be hard to grab the concept of the assignment, but as we continue walking aligned and conformed to the will of God, we will begin to see God show up and manifest His presence in such a way that the enemy will have no choice but to watch the supernatural events take place right before his very eyes.

A Hidden Message from God to His People Revealed to Moses for Such a Time as This

> Then Moses answered and said, "But suppose they will not believe me or listen to my voice; suppose they say, the Lord has not appeared to you." So the Lord said to him, "What is that in your hand?" He said, "A rod." And He said, "Cast it to the ground." So, he cast it to the ground, and it became a serpent, and Moses fled from it. Then the Lord said to Moses, "Reach out your hand and take it by the tail (and he reached out his hand and caught it, and it became a rod in his hand), that they may believe that the Lord God of their fathers, the God of Abraham, the God of Isaac, and the God of Jacob, has appeared to you." Furthermore, the Lord said to him, "Now put your hand in your bosom." And he put his hand in his bosom. And when he took it out, behold his hand was leprous, like snow. And He said, "Put your hand in your bosom again. and he drew it out of his bosom, and behold, it was restored like his other flesh. Then it will be, if they do not believe you, nor heed the message of the first sign, that they may believe the message of the latter sign." (Exod. 4:1–8)

Everywhere we go in this life, there are signs all around, leading and directing us on where to go, where not to go, when to stop, when to slow down, when to speed up; and when we take notice of these signs, we do one of two things. We either obey them or disobey them. One thing for sure is, we cannot avoid them in any way. Behind every sign there is a message. Here, we see Moses talking with God, and God is now really zooming in on Moses's assignment by giving him signs and the hidden message behind the signs given. I read this chapter many times before, but it wasn't until I started scrutinizing the word of God that suddenly God spoke to me. He said, "Listen to what my word is saying and find the hidden meaning behind the context of this chapter." It was like a light bulb lit up my brain, and I began to understand that these two signs that God gave to Moses at Mount Horeb where not just two ordinary signs God chose to use, because God purposely used these two signs to demonstrate something that goes far beyond our comprehending mindset. The more we spend time with God, the more we will come to know that God is very strategic in what he establishes, and when He establishes something, it always serves with meaning.

God has given each one of us something to grab hold of. Something that we can all use when we have doubts, are stressed, and when we feel fearful. And that is the Word of God. It is not only breathing but is the living proof of God's very existence. When we go out into the world to speak about what Jesus has done for us, we do not go with our own words or on our own strength, but with the word of God and the strength of His Spirit. Unfortunately, we also have an enemy who, every time an assignment is given to us, he rises up to try and make us feel inadequate or unqualified. The great news is that God already knows how we will react to certain situations, and for that reason, God does not relent in getting his point across. By this point, Moses knew that God had chosen him to go back to Egypt and proclaim liberty to the captives there. Although Moses was not physically in Egypt just yet, he, being a Hebrew, was subjected to the same captivity because of the simple fact that Moses going back to Egypt would not have been to finish his earthly reign as the prince of Egypt but to be a part of something greater such as leading and interceding for his people until he would eventually lead them out of captivity and into victory. For Moses, in the beginning, it was hard to accept this concept; and so Moses tells God, "Suppose when I go and tell them all that you have told me, they say, 'The Lord has not sent you." (I am paraphrasing). And this is our Heavenly Father's response to Moses: "What is in your hand?" God is asking us the very same question. "What is in our hand?" What is it that we are holding? And is what we are holding for just our benefit or is it for the benefit of others? Sometimes we are holding something that we think is of value when in fact it's the very thing that is not allowing us to go forth until we drop it and let God use it for His benefit and for the benefit of others. God has given us a word that He wants us to release and allow His presence to make it come to pass. When God tells us to release to him what we are holding, it is never to harm us but to open our spiritual eyes to see that God is the God of the supernatural. As Moses dropped the rod, we find that the rod changed into a serpent. The first thing that Moses did, according to the Word of God, was flee from it. Here we find a picture of a serpent on its belly and Moses fleeing from it. This is none other than a picture of Adam and the serpent. For those who know the story of Adam and Eve in the garden of Eden, know that Eve was the first to bite the fruit, and then she gave it to her husband. While all this is true, we also must remember that after Adam bit the fruit, he and Eve fled. This is the natural thing for humans to do after they realize that they are in the line of danger, and this is exactly what Moses did when he saw the rod changing into a serpent. This is our human nature. But God wanted to show Moses and the readers a whole new way to overcome our natural human nature and fix our eyes on what is true. And that is, we can stand our ground and not run and hide when we are up against a serpent that is already defeated by Christ. God tells Moses to reach out his hand and take the serpent by its tail, and when Moses did, it became a rod once again. One thing God wants us to fully understand is that when God's presence is manifest, whatever we think is out to harm us, with God's command, we have the power to bring it back to its powerless state of mind. Just like Adam, Moses too was never meant to flee from the serpent but confront the serpent. As you noticed, God didn't tell Moses to speak to the serpent but to take the serpent by the tail. In other words, let the serpent know who's boss. I think this is where the phrase "action speaks louder than words" comes into play. We need to become a generation that won't flee from our temptations but confront our temptations by taking hold of God's word and letting the enemy know who is boss when it comes to fighting temptation according to the scriptures.

As we continue reading chapter 4 verse 6, God gives Moses another sign, which in turn portrayed another message. This time God told Moses to put his hand into his bosom and take it out. When Moses did this, upon taking his hand out, it became leprous. God commanded Moses once again to put his hand back in his bosom and take it out. When he did, his hand was restored to its normal state. You may not realize this—and I didn't either in the beginning—but this message, along with the first message, goes hand in hand. Because we as humans did not confront the first temptation but fled from it, we eventually reaped the consequences of our actions, and because of this consequence, we all have fallen short of the glory of God and have been separated from His presence. Notice that God told Moses to put his hand in his bosom and not behind his back. This is because the leprosy that Moses encountered came from his heart, and this is a clear image that the condition of man's heart, being evil, has caused us to become separated from God. For example, when a person was found to be contaminated with leprosy, they were banished from the town and would be considered unclean. They would have no contact with anyone, not even their own family. This was a horrible sickness that left them without any hope of a social life. In the very same way, Moses, when he pulled out his leprous hand from his bosom, found that his hand had been unclean, which in turn brought about the message of separation due to our unclean heart. But the good news is that God didn't leave Moses in that condition, and God didn't leave us in that condition either. God told Moses to put his hand once again into his bosom, and just like that, God restored Moses's leprous hand to normal again. This is how our hearts were before Jesus came and restored our lives back to normal again. We all were separated from God and His kingdom; but God, in his sovereign mercy, chose to heal us and bring us back to His presence through Jesus Christ's sacrifice on the cross. Soon we are about to discover something that from the beginning of this book I have been waiting to talk about. What God is about to do in your life goes beyond words because God has given us a clear message from this chapter. What we thought was working against us all along was God's message of redemption working for us and is now working through us. Moses, with many others in the Bible, along with all of us in this generation, has been marked by God to lead others out of their down south or Egypt moments, desert, and/or wilderness moments; and the only way to do that is by spending time with God and believing that if God has called you out, He will draw you into His very presence just like He did with Moses at Mount Horeb.

I Guess Pharaoh Didn't Get the Memo about the Press Release of God's People

> *Afterward Moses and Aaron went in and told Pharaoh, "Thus says the Lord God of Israel. Let my people go, that they may hold a feast to me in the wilderness." And Pharaoh said, "Who is the Lord, that I should obey His voice to let Israel go? I do not know the Lord, nor will I let Israel go." (Exod. 5:1 and 2)*

When God brings you into a season of speaking out with courage, along with courage from God comes discouragement from the enemy. Along with faith in believing God in His word comes fear from the enemy in trying to paralyze us from continuing to fulfill God's plan for our lives. While Moses and Aaron where right on point with their speech to Pharaoh, it goes without saying that the enemy will always try and pretend that he knows nothing about God when, in fact, his only goal is to get us to believe that he is stronger than God, so in turn, we will bow down to his kingdom and worship him and not God. The more you and I spend time in God's word, the more we will know who our God is. This will enable us to stand firm and not doubt God's very existence in our lives. Moses and Aaron were probably not expecting the results they were hoping for, but this certainly did not catch God by surprise. After all, God has established every appointed time on this earth because time is in His hand, and although it may have seemed like Pharaoh had the upper hand in all of this, the truth of the matter is, God was just getting started. Let's just say that for Pharaoh's sake, this was just the appetizer for the big entree God was about to serve, not only to Pharaoh but his entire house as well.

As God sends us out into the world to proclaim His word, this doesn't mean that everything will be like roses in the park. On the contrary, God will allow us to go to places where we will have to stand our ground and speak with courage the words God puts in our heart to speak despite the turmoil and persecution that might rise up as a result of standing up for our faith in Christ Jesus. When God gave Moses a word in the back of Mount Horeb, God told Moses that He was sure that Pharaoh (not even by a strong hand) would let God's people go (Exod. 3:19). Knowing this, God still had Moses return and proclaim liberty to God's people. The question that arises in the minds of many is, *If God knew this would happen, then why send Moses or any other person in the first place?* Great question! God has a good reason for doing what He does and everything God does is never to harm us but to prosper us and to give us a brighter future. Everything we do in this life should always be to glorify God and make His name known throughout the earth. I truly believe nothing in this life comes easy. Everything we do here on this earth always comes with a price. Moses knew that God had spoken to him regarding the captivity and liberty of His people. Yet when Moses and Aaron came to Pharaoh with the announcement of God's people, Pharaoh led Moses and Aaron to believe that he was more powerful than God and discredited the release of God's people. As we continue reading in Exodus, we are going to unfold the truth about Pharaoh, God's people, and who our God truly is. And boy, am I excited to unravel so many attributes regarding who our God is and His purpose concerning the captivity and liberty of God's people.

CHAPTER 13

The Enemy's Job Is to Keep Us Busy and Away from Worshipping God

> So, they said, "The God of the Hebrews has met with us. Please, let us go three days' journey into the desert and sacrifice to the Lord our God, lest He fall upon us with pestilence or with the sword." Then the king of Egypt said to them, "Moses and Aaron, why do you take the people from their work? Get back to your labor." And Pharaoh said, "Look the people of the land are many now, and you make them rest from their labor!" So the same day Pharaoh commanded the taskmasters of the people and their officers, saying, you shall no longer give the people straw to make brick as before. Let them go gather straw for themselves. (Exod. 5:3–8)

Here we see a clear picture of Moses negotiating with Pharaoh. Moses and the people are telling Pharaoh to let them go three days into the desert and sacrifice to the Lord. And then Moses and the people go on to say that if Pharaoh refused to let them go and sacrifice, something bad would befall them. As you can see, this had no effect on Pharaoh since Pharaoh already stated that he would not let them go and that he claimed to not know the Lord God Almighty.

The reason for Pharaoh's actions of denying the very existence of God Almighty was not because he didn't know Him but simply because the enemy has always wanted to be like God. So here we see a clear picture of Pharaoh posing to be like the only God when in reality this was only the start of Pharaoh's downfall, but Pharaoh wasn't about to go down without a fight. The enemy knows just how important worshipping God is, and for that reason Pharaoh did not let God's people go three days into the desert to worship and sacrifice to the Lord God Almighty.

If there is something we all must understand in this life, it's that worship (as I stated earlier in this book) is the key to building a solid foundation with God. This is because when we give sacrifices of praise and worship to the Lord God Almighty, we are giving a direct declaration, letting the enemy know that there is no force or power of darkness that can take away our worship to the Lord God Almighty because Jehovah is the One True Living God and there is none beside thee! This makes the enemy mad, and for that reason, he begins the battle by trying to keep us busy and distracted with either unimportant matters or causing us to work around the clock and have no time for going to church or taking time out of our busy schedule to seek God's presence. This is exactly what Pharaoh did with God's people. After Moses and God's people were denied access to go and worship God in the desert, Pharaoh made sure that they would have no time to ponder on this request. And so Pharaoh placed an even heavier burden on God's people and made them work double for their trouble. I just want to state for many of us out there who think that this was it for God's people or that the enemy had the upper hand, this was the staging ground God had prepared for Pharaoh to enter and for God's people to observe and see that God's promise to them would soon come to pass, but the only thing we see so far here is God's people walking into a dark season of heavier burdens. Oh, but that's about to change because God sees, and God fights for the victory of His children.

When a believer walks in the ways of the Lord and goes into the world to preach the gospel, many receive the word of God and become transformed by the living power of God's word. But there are those who hear the word of God and want to become transformed and renewed, yet the enemy makes it nearly impossible for them to either come to church or spend time in God's word each day. When this happens, this is the enemy's way of trying to keep us away from worshipping God. When these moments happen and we as believers know it's happening, we need to be in constant intercession for them because the enemy doesn't want them to discover the power behind seeking God and His righteousness along with worshipping His holy name. The same tactic the enemy used on God's people by overloading them with more work is the same tactic the enemy uses in this day and age to keep those who need to be set free from their bondage. And so, you'll hear them say things like, "I wish I had time to go to church but I work entirely too much" or "My day is just so busy I can barely find time to eat, let alone pray." These are the chains that need to be broken off from the kingdom of darkness. When we begin praying for them, understand that sometimes things could get worse before they get better. Remember that when we pray the war rages because the enemy will always try and intimidate us by telling us nothing has changed and nothing will get better, but what the enemy fails to realize is that the moment you and I began praying, God began listening. We will now see just how this Egypt moment plays out regarding the new rules and regulations Pharaoh has now placed on God's people.

God's people have now entered a full throttle of Pharaoh's fury toward them. They truly thought that by going to Pharaoh and making this request that Pharaoh, with open arms would let them walk right out of Egypt. Boy, were they in for a rude awakening. Not only did Pharaoh reject this request, but he also made it known to the Hebrews that the request they proposed led them to an even mightier captivity, that now instead of having straw handed to them, they would have to find their own straw and still meet the same quota every day. This only led them to become discouraged and fearful toward Pharaoh. This is exactly what the enemy wanted. When the enemy can't win, he will always pull out the fear card to intimidate, distract, and paralyze us from believing and pursuing God's will for our lives. And so, by this point, God's people were being worked to the bone without mercy from Pharaoh and his house, with all the intentions of working until they either fainted or arrived at their death. Pretty harsh, right? But this was what God's people had to endure because their deliverance was closer than they thought possible. Whenever we are about to step into a season of overflow, the enemy will always come in like a flood and give it all he's got to try and take us away from that open door that God has predestined for us to walk through. God's people could only look at what was being done to them and not what God was about to do for them. Fear has a way of gripping us especially when it comes from an order given to us directly from the kingdom of darkness. I will explain what I mean so we can get a clearer picture of what fear is when it comes from the kingdom of darkness and fear when it comes from allowing ourselves to become a slave to it. Our mind has a way of playing tricks on us. When we have a notion that something is trying to take hold of our minds, we can quickly tear down that emotion by placing truth on top of whatever lie the enemy proposes on our lives. That type of fear can be dealt with immediately. But there is another type of fear that in a moment's notice can paralyze us and leave us traumatized to the point of causing us to shrink back and believe that no solution to the problem exists and that the condition of that person will remain the same forever. The second type of fear was the fear that gripped God's people into believing that they would remain in Egypt forever with no hope of ever becoming free.

For all the frustration that God's people were experiencing, they now were looking to place the blame on Moses and Aaron by saying that God would judge them for what had happened and that now Pharaoh's aim was to work them to death. This was what God's people were subjected to all because the enemy's plan in getting us to serve him is through fear, and when he gets us to the point of becoming so scared and frightened, he has us right where he wants us: used and abused like puppets on a string hanging from his very hand. What is going on in your life right now that is causing you to shrink back and stop believing in God's promises? Has the enemy placed so much fear within your mind, heart, and soul that you can't see past your current situation? I have good news for you. Everything that the enemy has tried to keep you captivated in is seen by God, and God has never left us nor has He ever forsaken us. This season in your life is proof that God is about to do something great in your life if you do not throw in the towel and stop believing what God spoke about you and your promises that soon are to come to pass.

As God led me to write this book, I am starting to realize something: this book that is in my hands is an interceding manual for many who will one day read this book and know that their Egypt moment was just as necessary as walking into your God-given destiny. This is because no matter what we face in this life, there will always be a motivating factor to keep us going, whether it's on a telecast program, a radio station, a podcast, or in a book. Every time you and I have an Egypt or down south moment to cross, we must always know that we are not alone and that others who have gone before you, who have come out, will always have a motivating story to tell. I am one of them. If I had not visited my Egypt and down south moments, there is absolutely no way I could have ever gotten the courage to write this book. It's because of my toughest trials that I have had to face that has kept me believing that if God did it for me and gave me the victory, then I am 100 percent sure that He will do it for you over and over again until we are home and in the Father's arms for eternity, but until that time comes, you and I are the intercessors for others out there who are held in captivity and to see them out of Egypt and on in to the promised land. To do this, it won't be easy because as we hear from God, there will be those who will shrink back in their faith when the promise you declared over them hasn't come to pass like they thought it would. And so what we have here is a conflict between what God spoke and what they are seeing in the moment, which leads them to believe that what we heard from God was not true but a lie. This is exactly what happened when Moses and Aaron went in the first time to proclaim liberty over God's people. So what did Moses do? What will you and I do when we have an army of those behind us whose faith has diminished and is left hopeless, all because of the fact that God's people were so wounded that it prevented them from seeing the overall picture of their set moment of liberty. Can we really blame them for this action? Think about it for a moment. If you and I were held and enslaved for a long time by an evil force that made our lives miserable each day; and then here comes someone who has claimed to have spoken to God and has been given a direct word from the Great I Am, goes in, and proclaims liberty yet comes out with word from the government that not only was the request denied but more work was placed on them, I think we would react in the same way: of feeling the overwhelming distress that caused them to shrink back in their faith and believe that there was no hope for them. So my question to us all is this and for those who are held in spiritual bondage right now: with everything that could have gone wrong in your life, are you still willing to believe God and take Him at His word despite all the contrary situations that are against you right now? And for those who are proclaiming liberty to the enslaved yet are not seeing the results of God's word come to pass in their lives, are you going to still believe God and take Him at His word, believing that what God has placed in your heart to speak will one day come to pass? We are about to see what Moses did despite the harsh reaction he received from God's people.

Stand Your Ground Even When the Ground beneath You Weakens

So Moses returned to the Lord and said, "Lord why have you brought trouble on this people? Why is it you have sent me? For since I came to Pharaoh to speak in your name, he has done evil to this people; neither have you delivered your people at all." (Exod. 5:22 and 23)

Then the Lord said to Moses, "Now you shall see what I will do to Pharaoh. For with a strong hand, he will let them out of his land." And God spoke to Moses and said to him "I Am the Lord. I appeared to Abraham, to Isaac, and to Jacob, as God Almighty, but by my name Lord I was not known to them. I have also established my covenant with

them, to give them the land of Canaan, the land of their pilgrimage, in which they were strangers. And I have also heard the groaning of the children of Israel whom the Egyptians keep in bondage, and I have remembered my covenant. therefore, say to the children of Israel: I Am the Lord; I will bring you out from under the burdens of the Egyptians, I will rescue you from their bondage, I will redeem you with an outstretched arm and with great judgments. I will take you as my people, and I will be your God. Then you shall know that I am the Lord your God who brings you out from under the burdens of the Egyptians. And I will bring you to a land which I swore to give to Abraham, Isaac, and Jacob; and I will give it to you as a heritage: I Am the Lord."
(Exod. 6:1–8)

In today's generation, we see a lot of simple solutions to a difficult problem. Growing up, I saw how hard my mother struggled just to maintain a family of four with no father. Life back then was not like it is now. The determination level to arrive at a goal was predetermined by what that person had to face in order to see that goal come to pass. Back then, there was rarely the push of a button or the fast-track solution to the problem. We live in a generation that have relied on technology so much to the point that when it becomes hard for us to accomplish we give up at the blink of an eye and think, *If it doesn't come easy, it's not worth fighting for.* This is one of the biggest errors of our time, and technology has a lot to blame for this error in our lives. We are living in hard times, but these are the times God has placed for us to live in, not so we would run with the world's current view of what it is to find determination at the click of a button but to persevere with diligence and stamina. The only way in this life we will ever find true perseverance is when we see the struggle become real in our lives to the point of knowing that, although things may be going against us and the waves of life might be rising higher than our expectation, yet through all of this, we will choose to fight the good fight of faith by going down on our knees and seeking the kingdom of God with all diligence and perseverance. This is exactly what Moses did. As we see in the scriptures, God's people had just received bad news from Pharaoh that they would have to work harder than they ever worked before. This made them want Moses to quit interceding for them once and for all. But Moses, although He was in distress, tired and confused, still chose to come to God; and being transparent, he spoke what was in his heart. God heard Moses and responded to his agony and cry.

There is just something about being transparent that leads us to God's presence in such a way that when God responds to our cry, we can feel His warm embrace touching our very soul. God knew exactly what Moses was thinking even before Moses spoke, but God was waiting for Moses to express his feelings of emotions so that after Moses got what he needed to get off his chest, God would begin speaking truth into Moses's life concerning the Israelites and their moment of liberation that was soon to come. This was the life-changing moment that marked the life of Moses, the Israelites, and even Pharaoh and his household. There will come a moment in our lives when we see everything coming against us and will want to throw in the towel, but it's in that very moment that we need to come to God with all transparency and fall to our knees and cry out with all diligence and tell God what's in our hearts. When this happens, we will begin to operate in the supernatural and hear from God as He speaks to us with a still, small voice. This reminds me of Elijah in the *1 Kings 19*.

> *Elijah was running from Jezebel and went and stayed in a cave for a night in the Mount of Horeb. It was there when God had spoken to Elijah and said, "What are you doing here Elijah?" And Elijah responded and said, "I have been very zealous for the Lord God of hosts; for the children of Israel have forsaken your covenant, torn down your alters, and killed your prophets with a sword. I alone am left, and they seek my life." So, God told Elijah to*

go stand outside the mountain before the presence of the Lord. And the Lord passed by, and a great and strong wind tore into the mountains and broke the rocks in pieces before the Lord, but the Lord was not in the wind. After the wind there was an earthquake, but the Lord was not in the earthquake, and after the earthquake, a fire but the Lord was not in the fire and after the fire a still small voice. When Elijah heard the still small voice of God, he wrapped his face in his mantle and went and stood in the entrance of the cave. It was then when Elijah heard God's voice say to Elijah once again, "What are you doing here, Elijah."

Although the staging is different and the context of the stories differs from one another, the concept of the situation is similar. Here Elijah was in distress because he thought there was no solution to the problem at hand (after Jezebel found out what Elijah had done in Mount Carmel, in 1 Kings 18:20–40) and was forced to run from the evil decree Jezebel had placed on him. Moses was also in distress after coming in to declare liberty for the Israelites as Pharaoh made a decree that the Israelites would now have to work one hundred times harder and complete the same quota as before. This caused Moses to return to God and cry out until God responded. When Elijah finally heard God's voice, the rhetorical question God asked Elijah was, "Elijah, what are you doing here?" When God spoke to Moses before coming to Egypt, God specifically said to Moses in chapter 3 verse 19 of exodus that He was sure that Pharaoh would not let them go, not even by a mighty hand. So what happened to Moses? Did he suddenly get amnesia? Apparently, Elijah thought too that he was the only prophet left on the planet, and God had to reassure Elijah, just like God did with Moses, that regardless of how many people are left on the planet, God is pinpointing those whom he has a plan for, and although Elijah in all reality wasn't the only prophet left on the planet, God was focusing in on Elijah to fulfill His will, and God was doing the same thing through Moses. God has pinpointed his compass toward you and me to fulfill his will. No matter what has happened before or how much worse things have come to pass in your life or in the lives of your family and friends, God is calling you by name, just like he did with Elijah when God said to Elijah, "What are you doing here?" In other words, God was saying to Elijah, "You have not finished the assignment for your life, and what I am about to do next will require you to trust and believe in me to see you and my people through to the next chapter of your lives." This is exactly what God spoke to Moses concerning the liberty of God's people as well.

God had declared to Moses that He is Lord; and He had appeared to Abraham, Isaac, and Jacob as God Almighty. This was the turning point in the life of the Israelites. Although they had no idea the conversation that Moses was having with God, God was pronouncing liberty and justice for His people. Abraham, Isaac, and Jacob had only seen the great and mighty works God established for them to see; but it was now in the land of Egypt that God would establish His covenant of being Lord and Savior over the Israelites lives forever and ever. This was the pivotal moment when Moses would have to understand and truly rise up as a born leader and trust God's plan for the redemption of God's people. God has established you and me to go far beyond our own expectations and trust in God's unfailing plan. God had brought His people thus far in to Egypt not to destroy them, but to establish them as God's own people who would become the apple of His eye and would bring about, from the tribe of Judah, the one true Messiah who would one day save us from our Egypt captive moments that we would all one day encounter. Egypt has served as an instrument in the hands of God Almighty to establish his covenant with us as Lord and Savior. I am starting to believe that without Egypt moments, there is no covenant to establish. If anything we need to do in this life, it is to embrace our Egypt moments and rejoice because Egypt is the very place where we find God's covenant with us.

God had not only established his covenant with Moses and His people by declaring to be Lord and Savior over them, but God also established the ground they would all walk on and the lands that He had predestined for them to conquer once they left Egypt. Our God is a mighty God who has the power to not only save, but to bring us into a land that flows with milk and honey, and the enemy cannot do anything about it. There are seven promises (one of them is repeated twice) that God has decreed over the Israelites, and I believe these same promises apply to us today. God says,

1. I have remembered my covenant.
2. I Am the Lord.
3. I will bring you out from under the burdens of the Egyptians.
4. I will rescue you from their bondage.
5. I will redeem you with an outstretched arm and with great judgments.
6. I will take you as my people.
7. I will be your God.
8. I am the Lord your God, who brings you out from under the burdens of the Egyptians.

As we can see from these promises just how serious God is when it came to establishing His covenant with His people. Number 8 represents completion, and number 3 represents the Trinity. When we look at promise number 3 and promise number 8, we find one and the same promise repeated, letting us know that the Father, the Son, and the Holy Spirit have established His covenant with us and that everything that was established for us to walk in is complete and ready for us to take hold of. The first step to walking out our faith is taking God at His established word and believing that God has chosen us for such a time as this to go out into the world and proclaim liberty to the captives. God is speaking to you right now. Yes! Even though you are in Egypt, right where you are right now the God of heaven and earth is speaking into your heart, and He is saying, "Do not be afraid nor be dismayed because I Am the Lord your God and I am with you wherever you go." God has chosen us to fulfill the hard yet, with God, possible task that is before us.

Moses knew that this was only the beginning of what God was about to do in Egypt. As the Hebrews grew more and more weary, God was preparing Moses and Aaron for the biggest moments Egypt has ever encountered and commanding them to go and proclaim liberty despite the adversity and judgments that lay ahead for Egypt and Pharaoh's household. Liberty for God's people wasn't far from them but was much closer than they thought. But the problem wasn't in being able to see the promise come to pass; the problem was the downhearted, downcast spirit the Hebrews were experiencing. This is because they were burdened to the point of not being able to believe in the promise of one day seeing themselves leave Egypt. When Aaron spoke all the words that the Lord had spoken to Moses in the beginning, they also performed the signs in the middle of the people. The Bible says they believed, and when they found out the Lord had visited them and looked upon their affliction, they bowed down and worshipped. This was before the first encounter with Pharaoh occurred. We know from scriptures that after the first encounter, Pharaoh placed an even more harsh punishment on the Hebrews. Yet before the encounter, scripture says that "the people heard that the Lord had visited them." The word *Lord* puzzles me because in verse 3 of chapter 6, when God spoke to Moses, He says, "By my name Lord I was not known to them." So why did the Hebrews, before the encounter, receive the message and believed what Aaron and Moses spoke about? As I began to analyze the scriptures, I heard the Holy Spirit say, "Because of the signs and wonders!" Scripture tells us in verse 30 and 31 of chapter 4 that the people believed because of what they saw and not just because God spoke the established deliverance of His people. For this reason, when they had their first run-in with Pharaoh and Pharaoh rejected their request and placed upon them an even more harsh punishment, God's people could not stand firm on their faith simply because they had not known God as Lord, only as the Great I Am. And so they had no spiritual stability to understand what the name Lord truly meant. They were merely relying on the signs and wonders they saw, but in reality, God just doesn't want us to live in the spectacular. God wants us to know him for who He is, and God is our deliverer, Lord and Savior of the world. When we know

God as just God Almighty or the Great I Am, we will always seek after signs and wonders, and when we don't see it come to pass, we become like the Hebrews in Egypt who shrunk back in their faith, all because of their lack of understanding that God is not just the God of the spectacular but also the God who rules and reigns with a rod of iron, having power and authority over all and He does as He pleases. When we come to realize this, we will come to the full understanding that even when our situation takes a turn for the worse, God is still sovereign, the supreme ruler, Lord overall. And because God is Lord overall, He can take any situation that the enemy meant for evil and turn it around for the good of His glory. Let us not become like the Hebrews who only believed because of the signs they saw. As it says in *1 Corinthians 1:22*, *"Jews request a sign, and Greek seek after wisdom."* But let us believe God's promises for our lives and our family's lives because God is Lord and Savior, and when He establishes a word, that word will come to pass, and if we do not faint but fall into the arms of Jesus, He will sustain us until the very end.

Oh, how I wish God's people could have seen what God was about to do next. This probably would have saved them the heartache of unbelief, but according to the scriptures, when Moses came once again and spoke to the Hebrews, this time, without any signs, they did not heed Moses because of their anguish of spirit and being in cruel bondage. God never looks at our ability to perform or complete a task because God knows the weaknesses that we all have. God looks at our weakness, and through it, He becomes our strength. That is why when we see an impossible situation, God already has the solution, and when we rely upon His strength, we become a mighty weapon in His hands. Moses had tried once again to encourage the people, but they could not see past their anguish, and so God spoke to Moses and Aaron and gave them a command for the children of Israel and for Pharaoh, king of Egypt, to bring the children of Israel out of the land of Egypt. What was about to occur in Egypt next, no one would be ready for, not even Pharaoh and his household.

CHAPTER 14

A Hardened Heart from the Enemy Makes
for a Weapon in the Hands of God Almighty

After the first encounter with Pharaoh, it was pretty clear that the battle between good and evil was becoming more and more evident. While Pharaoh thought he had the upper hand in this situation, God was aligning His plan to overthrow Pharaoh and His household with many plagues. Egypt was about to encounter God's fury like never before. The moment had finally arrived for the plan of God's redemption to be revealed in all of Egypt. If you feel like you have been in Egypt for far too long, rejoice because the time has finally come for God to show up and show the kingdom of darkness who God is. If God is for us, who could be against us? Do you feel like your Egypt moment is never-ending? Have you been prophesied to but haven't seen the promise come to pass yet? Does it feel like the more you hope the less you see the light at the end of the tunnel? I have great news for you! The longer your Egypt process is, the bigger your victory deliverance will be. Don't think for one moment that everything that has happened to you God did not foresee happening. On the contrary, God allowed every moment of your Egypt process to occur simply because He knows the plans that He has for your life supersedes the Egypt moments you are facing right now. After Moses and Aaron went in and spoke to Pharaoh and Pharaoh now being aware that Moses was in town, this is where we are going to see change happen. Where one of God's anointed is, there is the power and glory of God's unfailing presence. The people already felt the pressure of Pharaoh's decree weighing down on them, and just like before, they had no choice but to submit to Pharaoh and his household. But this time, it was going to be a whole lot different. Although the Israelites did not know and fully understand what was taking place, God gave clear instructions to Moses regarding the next steps that would occur, and one of them was that God had made Moses to be as God and that his older brother Aaron was a prophet who would speak to Pharaoh everything God put in His mouth to speak. The reason God told Moses that he would be as God, not because Moses was God but because God's presence was within Moses, and therefore, Moses could react in such a way that fear wouldn't grip him and set him back from proclaiming the word of God throughout the land of Egypt.

God's intentions on bringing them out of Egypt were good and not of evil. The unfortunate situation had to occur in order for God's people to understand the journey later on. Right now the Israelites were undergoing the toughest and the most horrible moment of their lives. Still, with all of this mess taking place, the God of heaven and earth and all its fullness had already established a plan to see His people free and out of the land of Egypt. So why so much calamity before the great deliverance? Why didn't God just make this go all away, destroy Pharaoh, and allow His people to walk on out of Egypt? This is the question that most people have when it comes to us as Christians and followers of Jesus Christ when we talk about the awesome powers of God Almighty. In the New Testament, in Matthew 26:53, we find Jesus at the garden of Gethsemane and the Pharisees and Israelite soldiers ready to take Jesus away and later on have Him brutally beaten, scourged, and crucified. One of Jesus's disciples saw this happening and tried to stop them by cutting off the ear of the servant of the high priest. When Jesus saw this (Him being God), He went to Peter and said, "Put your sword in its place, for all who take the sword will perish by the sword. Or do you think that I cannot now pray to my Father, and He will provide me with more than twelve legions of angels? How then could the scriptures be fulfilled, that it must happen this way?" So now to answer this question. It's pretty clear that although God could stop the events from happening, what God has already established to take place must take place in order for God's redemptive plan to come to pass. As much as it pained the Father to see His Son go through all of what He went through, even God knows that without sacrifice, there is no saving, because every act of saving requires a sacrifice. And so God had established in Egypt plagues that would take place because through the process of elimination, God would cause Pharaoh's heart to become weakened, but until that time came, God would be the one to harden Pharaoh's heart and show Pharaoh that even with a hardened heart, God was still in charge. God would bring redemption to His people and bring them out of the cruel bondage they were in through various plagues that correlate with the events that took place in the beginning when God first created the heavens and the earth. Only this time we will discover that through Pharaoh's hardened heart, the curse that would be brought upon Egypt would lead to the people's redemption toward their exodus. The first plague:

> Thus says the Lord, "By this, you shall know that I am the Lord. Behold, I will strike the waters which are in the river with the rod that is in my hand, and they shall be turned to blood." (Exod. 7:17)

> Then the Lord spoke to Moses, say to Aaron, "Take your rod and stretch out your hand over the waters of Egypt, over their streams over their rivers, over their ponds, and over all their pools of water, that they may become blood. And there shall be blood throughout all the land of Egypt, both in buckets of wood and pitchers of stone." (Exod. 7:19)

God had already spoken to Moses and Aaron and let them know that through these plagues, Pharaoh's heart would become hardened. Still, this was because God had a plan to overthrow Pharaoh, but before God could do that, He needed to show Pharaoh and his household that the only God in Egypt and throughout the entire earth and universe was, is, and will always be God Almighty, the Great I Am and that there is none beside thee. God wasn't only making a declaration in Egypt just for Pharaoh and his household, but for the Israelites to also see and know that God hasn't forgotten about them and had established an exodus that would eventually lead them to the promised land. But before that time could come to pass, there were events that needed to take place. We see here in chapter 7 verses 14-21 that the first plague that took place had to do with blood. God's redemptive plan ultimately had to do with the sacrificial pouring out of blood. This is a distinction between those being washed in the blood of Jesus and those who have not received Christ into their hearts as Lord and Savior. In the beginning of Genesis (in chapter 1), the Bible says that on the first day, God separated the light from the darkness. This is a clear picture of how Jesus separated us by bringing us from darkness to the light through the shedding of His blood on the cross. When the first plague occurred, this plague took place early in the morning and occurred in the place that was most sacred to the Egyptians (the Nile River). The reason this place was sacred to Pharaoh and the Egyptians was that they considered the Nile River to be a god, and so when Pharaoh and his household would come out early in the morning, they would come out to worship the Nile River as a god of fertility. When this plague took place, this was God's way of interrupting Pharaoh's morning ritual and letting Pharaoh know that God is the God of all creation, including the rivers, streams, ponds, and pools of waters. God turned water into blood to make a statement and to also use this plague as a symbol of God's foreshadowing prophecy of what was to occur through water and blood of Christ redemption toward the human race. I'm not going to go through every single plague that occurred (although every plague mentioned plays an important role in the land of Egypt), but only of three main plagues that God has placed on my heart to talk about. We talked about the first plague regarding the water and blood, now the sixth plague:

So, the Lord said to Moses and Aaron, take for
yourselves a handful of ashes from a furnace, and

let Moses scatter them towards the heavens in the sight of Pharaoh. And it will become fine dust in all the land of Egypt, and it will cause boils that break out in soars on man and beast throughout all the land of Egypt. They took the ashes from the furnace and stood before Pharaoh, and Moses scattered them toward heaven, and they caused boils that broke out in sores on man and beast. And the magicians could not stand before Moses because of the boils, for the boils were on the magicians and on all the Egyptians. But the Lord hardened the heart of Pharaoh; and he did not heed them, just as the Lord had spoken to Moses. (Exod. 9:8–12)

This was the sixth plague that God had sent to the land of Egypt, but this plague was directed toward not only man but the animals of the earth as well. When we analyze this particular plague, we find that this plague goes hand in hand with what God had created on the sixth day. The Bible says in Genesis 1:24–31 that God created man and the cattle and beast of the earth on the sixth day. The Lord told Moses and Aaron to take a handful of ashes from a furnace and scatter it toward heaven, having them turn into fine dust in all of Egypt. With those same ashes and dust, man was formed from and will eventually return to someday. This was a clear declaration from God that as He created man and beast on the sixth day, so the sixth plague would be a symbolic act of God's sovereignty over man and beast. When it comes to studying the scriptures, I found this type of plague to also play a role in why the book of Revelation refers the number 6 as the number of man yet referring the number 666 counted as the number of the beast. Everything in this plague, including the ashes coming out of the furnace along with the boils that burned intensely, all point to the main source of the issue here: Satan, man's pride, and destruction. This plague was so intense that it prevented even the magicians from trying to imitate the same plague. Now in order for God to continue with His redemptive plan of salvation, God would once again have to harden Pharaoh's heart. In Revelation

20: 3, Satan is bound for a thousand years. Just imagine how angry and enraged Satan must be after being held in the bottomless pit for a thousand years, but after a thousand years, Satan will be released to deceive the nations once more. When it comes to God and His plan of redemption, we see that God has full control over everything that happens in heaven and on earth. Just as God will have bound Satan in the bottomless pit for a thousand years and released him thereafter knowing he would come back to deceive the nations once more, so God hardened Pharaoh's heart knowing that Pharaoh would still not let God's people go. This is pure evidence that we do not need to fear but have faith in God's plan for our lives, even when our enemies are closing in on us. From an outside view, it may look like everything is falling apart, but from an inward view, everything is becoming aligned exactly how God predestined it to be. Redemption for God's people was becoming more and more visible even though Pharaoh's heart was becoming more and more hardened. Although it may have looked as though the more plagues were being directed toward Pharaoh, the more Pharaoh's heart became hard; but the truth of the matter is, in order for God's wonders to be multiplied in the land of Egypt, the harder Pharaoh's heart had to become. This was because God was getting ready to show Pharaoh and his household that even through a hard heart, God could still fulfill His plan of redemption. We as children of the Lord must understand that when we are being faced with life's greatest challenges, God isn't just sitting back in His thrown watching us go through the storm. On the contrary, God is permitting the storm to occur so that when the storm reaches its maximum potential, God steps in and shows us that even when the storm rages (a storm that God permits to occur), no matter how big the storm may get, the storm must obey God at His command. In the very same way, no matter how hard Pharaoh's heart got, God always knew how to deal with Pharaoh's heart. After all, God did create Pharaoh for such a time as this! God will allow people or certain natural causes to occur in our lives, not to destroy us but to build us up into a vessel that brings forth honor and glory to His name. In the beginning, it was not easy for any of the patriarchs Abraham, Isaac, Jacob, Joseph, and even for Moses. Think about it, Abraham had to walk out his days always trusting God even though his family had not known the God of Abraham in the beginning. Isaac was almost sacrificed by his father, yet Isaac was spared by God and became the father of Jacob, who fled from his father, Isaac, because God had predestined Jacob to receive the inheritance and not Esau, his older brother (who sold his birthright to Jacob for a morsel of bread), which caused Jacob to flee to his uncle Laban's household (due to Esau's anger toward his brother Jacob for inheriting the blessing that Esau gave up when he gave up his birthright to Jacob) where Jacob found and married Laban's two daughters, one of whose name was Rachel, who gave birth to two sons, one of which was Joseph. Joseph had a hard life as we found out earlier in this book and was sent to Egypt to begin a revolution that would lead up to the exodus, which would in turn establish a nation under God that would one day bring liberty and justice for all who come to the cross and bow down at the feet of Jesus Christ and confess that He is Lord and Savior overall. This is the true redemption of God's perfect plan.

You see, every single part of our lives is held in the Father's hands, and until our time is fulfilled on this earth, trials and tribulations will come and at times will cause us to have doubts and questions. But through it all, when our eyes are fixed on Jesus, no matter how hard the enemy may come at us to throw us off course, God will always be by our side to fight our battles. God says to us today, "Be still and know that I am God." What God was about to do next in all of Egypt would be the last thing the Israelites would expect to happen. Don't ever think, *This is all that my life will come to*, because God always leaves His children in awe of His wonders. What God is about to do next in your life is the moment you have been waiting for, and God is about to make Himself known not only for your benefit but for the benefit of those around you. Before Moses could have ever gotten the courage to stand before Pharaoh, Moses had to know and understand that God was with him and with his brother Aaron. Together God would cause them to not shrink back in the faith but continue walking and proclaiming liberty that they had yet see come to pass. Yet, through every Egypt moment that occurred, the more God's people saw the hand of God defending them, the more they trusted in Moses and Aaron to see them through. The more you and I spend time in God's presence (like Moses did), the more we will have the courage to rise up in the midst of this dark world and proclaim liberty to the captives. As we continue to walk out our faith, others will see it and become attracted to the presence of God and in turn will be set free from the powers of the kingdom of darkness. Our job here on this earth is to proclaim liberty and announce with all boldness to the kingdom of darkness that God has already made a way, Satan has already been defeated, and liberty has come to set the captives free in Jesus's name. Oh but don't think for one moment just because Satan knows this, he won't still try to put up a fight. The good news is, just like God already knew Pharaoh's every strategic move (in pleading for Moses to intercede and have the plagues removed yet after the plagues were removed, Pharaoh's heart would return to the same hardened condition). God knows Satan's every move before Satan moves, and He uses them against his own knowledge. There will come a time when Satan can do absolutely nothing. This is where we come to see God's hand move in such a tangible way that every moment of despair, anguish, and doubts will not compare to the great deliverance that was to come for the Israelites who had suffered for far too long in Egypt—the place where Joseph was brought toward to be enslaved by the Egyptians, only to rise up with power and authority, was the same place (called Egypt) where God would rise up with great power and cause Egypt to tremble with fear as God Himself weakens Pharaoh's heart and causes His household to become distressed with pain and agony. This is the moment when all that has happened in Egypt serves as a purpose in the fulfillment of God's prophecy that would soon come to pass right before Pharaoh's eyes.

> *And the Lord said to Moses, "When you go back to Egypt, see that you do all those wonders before Pharaoh which I have put in your hand. But I will harden his heart so that he will not let the people go. Then you shall say to Pharaoh, 'Thus says the Lord: Israel is my son, the firstborn. So, I say*

to you let my son go that he may serve me. But if
you refuse to let him go, indeed I will kill your son,
you're firstborn." (Exod. 4:21–23)

The time has now come when Pharaoh would have to watch as God fulfills his very own prophecy. Although Moses may have had a hardened heart, everything was working out for the benefit of God's people, and soon God's people would encounter the biggest deliverance of their lives. When we find ourselves at the point of no return, this means that something great is getting ready to occur, but the enemy is working overtime to keep us from our exodus moment, of being set free from whatever held us in Egypt in the first place. Before Moses stepped foot back into Egypt, God had already prophesied to Moses what would occur in Egypt, and although Moses heeded the words God spoke through various trials and misfortunes, Moses ran toward the presence of God to plead his case. Yet through every moment of despair, Moses always found strength in God's presence to continue on with the task that was before him. We too need to understand that when God gives us a word or a prophecy, although we heard from God, it doesn't necessarily mean that we will always understand what God is saying. We may receive it at the moment; but just like Moses, when the going gets tough and the crowd becomes more than we can handle, we need to do exactly what Moses did and run into the presence of God Almighty and present our case. And in His unfailing mercy, God will continue to remind us of the importance of the task ahead of us. God is our strong tower, the one we can lean on when everything feels like it's falling apart or has gone completely opposite of what we thought was going to happen. God is our refuge from whom we can run and hide when we feel overwhelmed. For Moses, this was the ultimate test before the great deliverance. God had already spoken to Moses regarding the last and final plague that was to come upon the people of Egypt in 4:21–23, but the time had come for Moses to relay the message to Pharaoh and all of Egypt that there would be a great cry in all of Egypt because Pharaoh could not heed God and let the Israelites go.

In chapter 4 verse 22, God states a very important fact regarding Israel being the firstborn. Scripture tells us that Jacob's name was changed to Israel and that Israel was the firstborn. This is because when we look at the story of Jacob and Esau, we find that, in chapter 25:25 and 26 of Genesis, Esau came out first then Jacob. But Esau did not see the importance and value of his birthright, and for that reason, Esau lost it, and Jacob gained it. This in turn caused Jacob to inherit the inheritance of firstborn rights to being called God's firstborn out of Egypt. Although this is true, Scripture does also say in Genesis 25:23 that the older would serve the younger. Although Esau lost his inheritance, God still called Jacob to serve and not be served. This is a truth that even Jesus spoke about when He said to the disciples, "The Son of man did not come to be served but to serve." We know this to be true because Jesus Christ is the firstborn fruit to be raised from the dead, and He is our big brother, yet Him knowing this, He still came not to be served but to serve with all humility even to the point of death. Just like Esau gave up his birthright, we to have at one point in time or another devalued what was committed to us, yet God still says to us, "I have sent my son into the world, not to condemn the world but through Him save the world, that through His service of sacrifice on the cross, those who repent will be forgiven." When Israel came back to meet his brother, Esau, what Esau at the time gave up and lost, Jacob gained and restored. This picture that I see in the spirit was a clear picture of what Adam lost in the garden and what Jesus gained and restored on the cross. Both Adam and Jesus found themselves in a garden, yet Adam fell into temptation from lack of prayer; and Jesus, because of prayer, conquered every temptation from the serpent. What Adam should have done in the garden of Eden Jesus did in the garden of Gethsemane, and that was crushing the head of the serpent. In the very same way, we are like Esau and Adam, devaluing what God has placed in our possession; yet Jesus, being our high brother, has come to let us know that what we once lost Jesus came to give it back to us. And for that reason, just as Esau wept on his brother's shoulder after seeing why Jacob needed to be the one to inherit the firstborn rights to the inheritance, so all those who come to the knowledge of repentance fully understand the importance of forgiveness. What we were never meant to fulfill, Jesus fulfilled it for us on the cross.

Moses was now about to make the final announcement regarding the last plague that would leave Egypt and Pharaoh's household in devastation. Pharaoh and his household had just encountered many plagues, yet through all these plagues, Pharaoh still had remained hard of heart, and this time Pharaoh didn't want to see Moses's face again. Moses, being full of God's presence, found the strength to let Pharaoh know that this last plague that God would send would be because of the unbelieving hardened heart that Pharaoh possessed, and it would have ultimately been what led him to his downfall as Pharaoh of Egypt. God would show Pharaoh that he is no god and that God has been the one permitting everything thus far to take place so that in the end, neither Pharaoh nor his men would rise up against the children of God to enslave them anymore. And so Moses spoke all that God put in Moses's heart to speak and declare. Moses had given the command for everyone in God's household to take articles of silver and gold because the Lord had given the children of Israel favor in the sight of the Egyptians, Pharaoh's servants, and in the sight of the people. Moses's name was being made great throughout the land of Egypt. And as for the Israelites, the best was yet to come! I feel in the spirit someone who has been in Egypt is about to encounter a deliverance like never before. Hold fast to your faith because soon the floodgates of heaven are going to open to your victory. Celebrate because your victory is closer than you think!

The Last and Final Plague Marks the Beginning of Something New for Generations to Come

There comes a time when God will allow those used by the enemy to come in and make your life impossible. No matter what you do or say, they will remain harsh toward you. God, in his mercy, raises up those who may try to come against you and intimidate you, not because He gets a kick out of seeing His children mistreated by the enemy, but because God wants us to know and understand that the battle belongs to him, and what the enemy meant for evil in any situation, God will turn it around for His greater good. It may look as though victory may be a long distance away, but when God fights for His children, no matter how fierce the battle may be, God never loses a battle. Not ever! The greatest part about God fighting for us is that, the more the enemy continues to surround us with hate and anger, the more the enemy must watch God multiply his wonders in a land that was meant to keep us enslaved yet has become the very place that would soon give birth to a mighty nation. I don't know if you have figured it out by now, but Egypt is a birthing ground for a new beginning. When we find ourselves walking toward our Egypt moment, in our Egypt moment, or at the end of our Egypt moment, remember that what God has allowed to occur in our lives will always be used to prosper us and never to harm us. Whatever stage you are in right now, always believe that through these moments, God is establishing something great in you—and not just with you, also for those who are with you and the generations to come.

> *Now the Lord spoke to Moses and Aaron in the Land of Egypt, saying, "This month shall be your beginning of months; it shall be the first month of the year to you. Speak to all the congregation of Israel, saying: 'On the tenth of this month every man shall take for himself a lamb for a household. And if the household is too small for the lamb, let him and his neighbor next to his house take it according to the number of the persons; according to each man's need you shall make your count for the lamb. Your lamb shall be without blemish, a male of the first year. You may take it from the sheep or from the goats. Now you shall keep it until the fourteenth day of the same month. The whole assembly of the congregation of Israel shall kill it at twilight. And they shall take some of the blood and put it on the two door posts and on the lintel of the house where they eat it.'" (Exod. 12:1–7)*

The final chapter to the lives of the Israelites was looking more and more like a reality to them. After having been enslaved for far too long, the promise that God first made to Abraham was soon about to come to pass right before their very eyes. God had spoken to Moses and Aaron and had given them instruction regarding the Passover and what this would mean for generations to come. Can you just imagine being a part of something so great as being the first to participate in the Passover, the feast of the lamb. I bet the Israelites at the time had no idea exactly what was going on and what God was about to do through their obedience in receiving the instructions given to them by Moses and Aaron (who received them from God). This was the pivotal moment when they would see and know that God was with them the entire time, but now God was about to open a door that not even the Egyptians could close. We all must prepare ourselves just like God told His people to prepare themselves because soon there will be a shout; and when this occurs, we will find ourselves just like God's people leaving behind a life marked with pain, hurt, heartache, only to walk out of our Egypt moment and into a place where slavery will just be a thing of the past. And those who walk faithfully toward God's commands will one day inherit the promised land.

For those of you who have not read the book of Exodus regarding the Passover, this was given to Moses and Aaron to prepare the Hebrews for a great deliverance. They were to keep a male sheep or goat of the first year without blemish until the fourteenth day of that same exact month. Then between sunset and dusk, the Israelites, together as a congregation, were to kill the animals and spread the blood on every door post and lintel. This is a symbol of being covered with the Lamb that one day would descend from the tribe of Judah to become the atoning sacrifice the entire world would need in order to become freed from our sins and have inheritance to the kingdom of God. Along with God coming through with His promise to one day save His people from being enslaved in Egypt, there was also a price that needed to be paid in order to finally come to the end of God's perfect plan of redemption. Every firstborn of the households who did not heed the instructions (like Pharaoh and a majority of his household) would suffer the ultimate consequence of having the firstborn (from Pharaoh who reigned on the throne of Egypt to the handmaids, those in the dungeon, right down to the cattle and beast of the earth): killed instantly. This was one plague that even if Pharaoh pleaded for Moses to call upon God, would not have seen his son raised again because only through the blood of Jesus Christ can one be resurrected, and we know two things are for sure: Jesus had not come yet, and Pharaoh had not put the symbolic sign of the blood of the lamb upon his doorpost. For that reason, Pharaoh and his household suffered a major loss. God says to us today that in order for us to see redemption, we must be covered in the blood of the Lamb. The Bible says in verse 10 and 11 of chapter 12 that if there were any remains after eating that night, the remains in the morning shall be burned in the fire and eaten in haste with their belts strapped to them and their sandals on their feet. We can clearly see a picture of how we all should live our lives from day to day. We do not know the time or the hour Christ will return to take us up out of this world. Although we live in this world, we are not of this world. We are living in unprecedented times, and it's quite evident that the coming of the Lord could happen at any given moment in time. Yesterday has past, and today is a new day that brings us that much closer to the coming of the Lord, and so every morning that we rise from wherever we are, we must always seek God for fresh oil and fire from above. We must always eat the bread from heaven (the word of God) and always be on guard, not letting the enemy steel our joy and gladness, because soon, when that trumpet sounds, we will all be ready, in haste to meet the Lord Jesus Christ in the air and be with our Heavenly Father for eternity. This was the hope that Abraham had for his descendants, and this is the hope that we as believers should have for our kids, our families, and even our friends.

The Tenth Plague

The last and final plague was the tenth but the most effective one of all. As I stated before, I only talked about three plagues in the book because they were the three main plagues God wanted me to focus on in reference to the bigger picture at hand regarding Egypt, our lives, and the lives of the Israelites and how these plagues played a major role regarding the blood of the lamb, the fall of man, and the end-time events that will soon take place. I do, however, strongly advise everyone to read and study the book of Exodus and let the Holy Spirit illuminate your understanding. This will require us, however, to put in long hours of devotion and seeking first the kingdom of God and his righteousness and hearing from the Holy Spirit's revelation that only comes through prayer and fasting. This plague was like no other plague. This plague was a direct symbol foreshadowing the coming of Christ as the lion of Judah. The first plague we saw concerned blood and water, which symbolized God's redemptive plan to interrupt the enemy's agenda with the blood of Jesus's sacrifice on the cross that would mark a new way of living. When we look at the scriptures carefully, we find that the first plague go hand in hand with the first miracle Jesus did in the wedding at Canaan (John 2:1–11). Both were involved with ritual customs, yet the only difference between the two occasions was that God had interrupted Pharaoh's morning ritual (turning the waters of the Nile River to blood) to let Pharaoh and his house know that a new and tragic error had begun for Pharaoh and his household, which would end in destruction. But in the wedding of Canaan (when Jesus turned the water into wine), this was God's way of interrupting a ritual custom to bring about a new error where one day we would become heirs with Jesus Christ through His precious blood. This is no coincidence, my friend. What God establishes, there is no man on this earth that can stop the plans of God. Man can certainly try but will not prevail, because if God be for us, who can be against us? Next, we saw that the sixth plague had to do with man and beast and how these two symbols play a huge role in the sixth-day creation of God, the end-time prophecy regarding man's mark of the beast, and man's final destination should they die without Jesus Christ. These particular plagues regarding Egypt all has to do with one thing: redemption. God wants all to become redeemed from the powers of Satan, but unfortunately, many cannot come to see the truth because they are so wrapped up in a lie that even when the truth stares them in the face, they cannot bring themselves to accept the truth, let alone live out the truth. This is so evident in Pharaoh, because although Pharaoh saw the plagues, he could not bring himself to believe that the One doing all of this was mightier than him. And so most of the time, when Pharaoh would encounter a plague, he would seek Moses to intervene for him; yet after the plague had stopped, Pharaoh would continue walking as if he were still in control. We see this in one of Jesus's disciples as well. Judas in the Bible walked with Jesus and was counted as one of Jesus's disciples. He saw all the miracles Jesus did before the people; yet despite all that he saw, there was still in his heart a wickedness. And in the end, Judas, because of the condition of his heart, betrayed Jesus to his face and sold him to the Pharisees. Shortly thereafter, we find Judas Iscariot took his own life. This is all because, although they saw all that the power of God had done, they could not bring themselves to believe in the truth. For that reason, both of their lives ended in destruction. The word of God says in *Hebrews 3:12–15,*

> *Beware, brethren, lest there be in any of you an evil heart of unbelief in departing from the living God; But exhort one another daily while it is called "today," lest any of you be hardened through the deceitfulness of sin. For we have become partakers of Christ if we hold the beginning of our confidence steadfast to the end, while it is said: "Today if you will hear His voice, Do not harden your hearts as in the rebellion."*

So now, how does the tenth plague correlate with these other plagues? At the beginning of time, God already knew that his firstborn would have to come to this fallen and broken world to become the ultimate sacrifice for all humanity. What stands between the first plague (blood) and the tenth plague (death) is the sixth plague, which has to do with man and the flesh. So here we see these three plagues immerging into one single purpose, and that is, that even before the foundations were laid, there would have to be the shedding of blood (the first plague) for man's fall (the sixth plague) and the firstborn would have to die (the tenth plague) for redemption to take place (the Exodus). I don't know how much clearer of a picture we can get to see just how strategic God is when it comes to His symbolic plan of redemption, not just for his people but for the entire world who comes to the knowledge of the cross and finds redemption through the sacrifice Jesus made for us on Calvary's cross. Egypt is not only a staging ground for redemption; but I now truly believe, and I hope you will agree, that Egypt in its entirety is a symbolic movement full of God's prophetic foreshadows of what is to come to pass centuries after God freed his people from Egypt never to physically return there again as slaves.

CHAPTER 15

•••◦●◦——————●——————◦●◦•••

Exodus Was within Your Egypt Moments and Your Egypt Moments Brought You toward Your Exodus

We have now entered the chapter of this book, which is the chapter we have all been waiting to get to in order to now fully understand the entire picture of why Egypt and why God chose the south to accomplish His mission in redeeming His people. We may not know every detail of our past, like who our ancestors were, what they did, how they looked, and why they were placed on this planet for. But what we do know is that God created every one of us with an intentional purpose in mind. Whatever our ancestors went through brought us to where we are now, and if you are reading this book and have gotten this far into the book, then you'd better believe that God has allowed you to understand what it means to go through Egypt or travel down south. We all have a past, and along with our past is a testimony for the future.

I want you to take the time now to reflect on how many times you have had to go through an Egypt moment in your life and how you felt in the moment. I also want you to remember being in a situation you had no idea how you were going to get out of yet somehow you made it through. God has been there a countless number of times, but the reality is that, we don't realize it because what life's trials cause us to do is block out sometimes the truth to the matter: that through it all, God has never left us or abandoned us. And although it may feel like that sometimes, this is a lie that the enemy uses to make us believe: that God has forgotten about us. Truth be told, we may not know the truth about what our ancestors did in the past. Some could have truly fought the good fight of faith; and because they did, we see in today's society great preachers, evangelists, prophets, etc. Or maybe there are those whose ancestors came from a dark background and generational curses lingered for a long time from generation to generation. But I have great news! Although this may be true regarding where our ancestors may have come from, there is One who from eternity already predestined our lives for great victory despite our heritage or ancestral background, there is One who came to break every bondage and every generational curse from the kingdom of darkness and His name is Jesus Christ. He is the First, the Last, the Beginning, and the End; He is the Alpha, the Omega; He is the Author and Finisher of our lives; and from His lineage, we all can obtain a new beginning through the redemptive plan established, knowing that one day we all would have to go through Egypt in order to be delivered from our bondage.

The time has now come for God's people (after 430 years of cruel bondage and affliction) to see the hand of God move with favor like never before. Every single course of action that we are about to witness was already predestined by God. In other words, God rejoiced over this moment way before His people experienced it. God rejoiced over us way before you and I came to the knowledge of the cross. Therefore, when we go to the house of God, we don't go to celebrate seeking a victory; we go to partake of a victory that was already taking place before time began on earth. God will always rejoice in His redemptive plan because through it all, God always had us on His mind. You and I are not here by accident; you and I were always meant to be here and travel the long road through Egypt so in the end, we would find redemption through His son, Jesus Christ. God's people, including Abraham right down to Joseph, had to travel to Egypt in order to understand who God is, was, and will always be. Although Egypt has a bad reputation for its enslavement, Egypt also was a chosen place where the children of Israel had to experience the hand of God move in defense for His people and to know and fully understand that the God of Abraham hears, the God of Isaac moves, the God of Jacob restores, and the God of Joseph saves and redeems. Through it all, God has chosen Egypt as a place of growth and development. When we learn to endure our Egypt moment, all that is left for us to reap is promotion, favor, and victory. For the Israelites, this was becoming tremendously factual to them as God has given the command to Moses and Aaron to lead the people right out of Egypt with confidence and direction, but before this could take place, there was something that the people had to do in order to proceed in pursuit of becoming free and out of bondage.

God had established already through the shedding of blood, death, and resurrection the One who would come to set us free. He is called the Lamb of God who was slain since the foundation of the world. In chapter 13 of the book of Exodus, we find that Moses is giving instructions regarding the law of the firstborn. The people's exit out of Egypt was for them to go and inherit the land God swore to their fathers to give them, a land flowing with milk and honey. Now, regarding the firstborn, according to the scriptures, every firstborn that comes from an animal that was a male was to be consecrated to the Lord, but every firstborn donkey (which was considered unclean) was to be redeemed with a lamb. If this animal was not redeemed with a lamb, its neck was to be broken and all the firstborn males were to be redeemed. This was a sign for the children of Israel for generations to come. I'll explain why in just a moment. The scriptures say that with a mighty hand, the Lord brought the Israelites out of Egypt and out of the house of bondage. Every challenge we face in this life, God already has a prophetic outcome to the reality we are living in. We may not see it or even understand it at the moment we are facing it head on, but that does not mean that whatever was meant to come to pass won't come to pass. On the contrary, everything that was meant to pass was already prophesied by God Himself. In fact, I'll go a little further to say, God has already aligned the road map with His compass to strategically align our calling to his purpose. Our path has already been predestined and marked with the blood of Jesus. When we walk by faith, I want you to understand something very important: when you and I received Christ into our hearts, we made a final decree in letting the kingdom of darkness and Satan know that they no longer have power or dominion over what God has already established within our hearts. We have been marked with the blood of Jesus and sealed with the Holy Spirit to exit our life of bondage and enter our next level of favor and blessings. The evidence of this is within the next few verses of chapter 13. Moses explains that through Pharaoh's stubbornness of not letting the people go, the Lord brought death to the firstborn males—but not just for the firstborn males within Pharaoh's household, but also for all the firstborn male beasts as well. When we look at this picture, we see that replacing the firstborn male donkey with a lamb is a representation of Moses letting all the people know that in order for them to be saved from the destroyer, they had to place the blood of the lamb on their doorposts and lintel, and if no blood was found on the doorposts, regardless if you were a Hebrew or not, death had access to enter and kill the firstborn males both man and beast. Pharaoh, on the other hand, was as stubborn as a donkey; and for that reason, he and his household (who did not replace their stubbornness with humbleness) later found themselves in a place of devastation. For Pharaoh's uncleanness (like the donkey) and disobedience, the children of Israel were spared; but the firstborn children and males from Pharaoh's household were killed. God's people understood the instructions in regard to redeeming the donkey with a lamb, but for Pharaoh's household, this was a deliberate sign for Pharaoh that the donkey was a representation of the house of Pharaoh and that God would break the necks of all those firstborn males who had not replaced the firstborn male donkey for the lamb's blood to be placed on the doorposts and lintel of their houses to be redeemed from the destroyer. Therefore, we see God say three times in chapter 13, "For by strength of hand the Lord brought us out of Egypt." When God repeats Himself, it's because what God has established will always come to pass whether we are prepared or not to perceive it.

Then it came to pass, when Pharaoh had let the people go, that God did not lead them by the way of the land of the Philistines, although that was near; for God said, "Lest perhaps the people change their minds when they see war and return to Egypt." So, God led the people around by way of the wilderness of the Red Sea. And the children of Israel went up in orderly ranks out of Egypt. (Exod. 13:17 and 18)

They took their journey from Succoth and camped in Etham at the edge of the wilderness. And the Lord went before them by day in a pillar of cloud to lead the way, and by night in a pillar of fire to give them light, so as to go by day and night. He did not take away the pillar of cloud by day or the pillar of fire by night from before the people. (Exod. 13:20–22)

The Fearful Road of No Return That Leads Toward A Greater Destiny

It was in my midtwenties when I came to Christ and fully committed my life to Him. After everything I had been through, for the first time in my life, I felt free and fulfilled in Jesus's presence. I wanted to go to church all the time. I would spend all my time and energy reading God's Word, and I felt the change of who I was and who God said I have become so much more evident with every passing day. Still, I remember times when I would have these dreams directly from Satan himself trying to place fear within my soul. At that time, I was newly reborn again and still didn't really know how to fight my battles the correct way. I remember that in the dreams, when the enemy was getting ready to devour me, I would wake up and know that God was with me. One day, as I was in my room, I fell asleep and, all of a sudden, found myself in an empty circus tent. All the props were there, but there were no people around. It was dark, yet I could still see everything. The next thing I know, there was a short man coming my way, saying to me, "Welcome, let me show you around." As he led me up the bleachers, I felt this sense that something bad was brewing around the corner, yet I couldn't leave or escape. It was as if I had been hypnotized. As we approached the very top of the bleachers, the short man had turned into a woman. She approached me, and the closer she got to me, I noticed her mouth opening wider and wider and saw sharp teeth like I had never seen before. I remember trying to kick her with my feet when suddenly she grabbed my foot and tried to bite of my big toe. The moment it looked as if she was going to bite it off, I woke up and was drenched in my sweat. Oh, but this was not the only dream I had when I came to Christ, but the dreams became more and more tangible as the weeks and months went by. There was another dream wherein I saw a fallen angel approach me. I was lying on my stomach, and again, I was paralyzed and could not move. I remember feeling a sharp nail scraping my back from the top going down to the middle of my back, and when the fallen angel stopped midway, I felt the pain of the nail digging into my back. Then suddenly, I woke up. I knew that these were attacks directly from Satan's kingdom, because by this time I already had begun studying how the kingdom of darkness operates in the spirit. This time though the pain was not only felt in my dream. When I woke up and turned over to my side, the middle of my back also felt like someone had stuck a needle through it. Even though I was experiencing these spiritual attacks from the kingdom of darkness, I still felt the power of the Living God protecting me and letting me know that everything would be okay, because God would never leave me nor forsake me. There were countless times when I felt the enemy try and place fear within me by attacking me in my sleep. There is this one dream that quickly turned into a nightmare. I was working at the bus company as a driver's assistant, and one day I was on break, and so my mother and I went to the local church nearby to pick up some food from the pantry. I usually go in with her, but that particular day, I was so exhausted that I ended up staying in the car and falling asleep. I'm not sure if this was a demonic attack within the natural realm or if this was a dream that turned for the worst, but anyway, I felt these hands brushing up against my hair massaging my scalp. The sensation felt so good and relaxing. The touch was extremely tangible, yet I physically was not able to move from the stimulation. I was so relaxed that I felt as if I was in a trans. To my surprise, the massaging was becoming more and more intense to the point where I now started to feel pressure and discomfort, yet I could not break loose from the grip these hands had over my head. Suddenly, I felt (although I could not see who it was) my head being tossed around, and that's when I came to and realized that something had been in the car with me because when I came to, my heart was racing and my hair was a mess.

Why am I telling you these stories? And what do they have to do with the children of Israel leaving Egypt? Well, scripture tells us that when the time came for the children of Israel to leave, God did not lead them by the way of the Philistines. This is because the people of God were not ready for war just yet. God Himself already knew that, later, Pharaoh would come after the children of Israel; but for the time being, they were not ready to combat any other people who would try and come against them, lest out of fear the children of Israel voluntarily go back to Egypt, which would have defeated the real purpose why God freed them from there in the first place, which was to establish a strong and fortified nation through Egypt's trials and tribulation. Just like we have come to the power of the cross never again to become slaves of sin but children of God, to do away with our former life, so too the children of Israel have become freed from the bondage and afflictions of the Egyptians to never again to return to Egypt as slaves but to continue pressing forward toward the promised land God had established for His people to inherit. God had freed my soul from the kingdom of darkness. God already knew that Satan would stop at nothing to try and intimidate me by trying to place dreams and spiritual attacks on my life in the hopes that I would surrender and turn back to my former lifestyle, but boy was he quickly mistaken because God had already established my exodus from my Egypt moments.

There are three things God does not want us to encounter when He frees us from Satan's bondage. *The first is a changed mind.* When God has established a way out for us, He doesn't want us to stand in the doorway of doubt and regret. God wants us to walk on through and trust that He knows what's best for our lives. *The second thing God doesn't want us to encounter but still wants us to know and understand is that war will happen but only when God permits it to occur.* God never made us to war against one another. Unfortunately, a war began in heaven because of Lucifer and his fallen angels. You and I do not need to fear war because the One who never loses a battle is always on the battlefield with us. God knew that Lucifer would rebel against God; and for that reason, God permitted war to break out, knowing that one day Jesus would come to put an end to Satan and his kingdom by becoming the sacrificial lamb whose blood would set us all free. God sees what we cannot see, and for that reason, God is not slack when it comes to calling out the enemy. When God calls the enemy out, it's because God has already given us the victory. *The last and final thing God doesn't want us to encounter is a willing heart to return to the former lifestyle.* Many times we will have to face the reality of the hard life that sometimes may knock us down for the count. These are the moments when we must reflect on two things: how far we have come, and what am I sacrificing by returning to the former lifestyle that had me in bondage? God wants us to prevail and continue to press forth toward the prize. Looking back while running slows you down, and what slows you down will eventually cause you to stumble, and what causes you to stumble will eventually cause you to give up and turn back. This is what the enemy does to try and bring you back into bondage.

God already knows the danger that lies ahead. Still, God sees the outcome of the dangerous journey ahead. So God sends a pillar of cloud by day and a pillar of fire by night to demonstrate to the people that through every part of this journey, God is leading and guiding them to the next level of their faith they all have yet to encounter. Although God could have taken the children of Israel right to their destination, which would have been the more logical thing to do when it comes to the way man thinks, but if it was up to man, two things could have occurred by just leaving Egypt with no directions or means of getting to the destination that awaited the children of God. First, the children of Israel could have made it to their destination, but eventually, the Egyptians would have caught up to them and annihilated them completely. Or second, like the scripture says, coming across the Philistines, the children of Israel would have been filled with much fear and no faith to continue, which in turn would cause the children of Israel to draw back and back down and turn back toward Egypt. But God, in His eternal mercy over His people, has made a way, even when the children of Israel were walking toward a place where they would be forced to camp out and wait for God to show up and perform the wonder that would cause them to know that the God of Israel has to lead them, not into temptation to have them draw back and return to their old ways but to deliver them from the hands of the evil one who from the beginning has tried to diminish a nation that for generations to come would be called blessed in the Lord.

Numbers Count for Something

Let My People Go

Afterward Moses and Aaron went in and told Pharaoh, "Thus says the Lord God of Israel: let my people go, that they may hold a feast to me in the wilderness." (Exod. 5:1)

And you shall say to him, "The Lord God of the Hebrews has sent me to you, saying, 'Let my people go, that they may serve Me in the wilderness'; but indeed, until now you would not hear." (Exod. 7:16)

And the Lord spoke to Moses, "Go to Pharaoh and say to him, thus says the Lord 'Let my people go, that they may serve me.'" (Exod. 8:1)

And the Lord said to Moses, "Rise early in the morning and stand before Pharaoh as he comes out of the water. Then say to him, thus says the Lord, 'Let my people go, that they may serve me.'" (Exod. 8:20)

Then the Lord said to Moses, Rise early in the morning and stand before Pharaoh, and say to him, thus says the Lord God of the Hebrews, "Let my people go, that they may serve Me." (Exod. 9:13)

So Moses and Aaron came in to Pharaoh and said to him, "Thus says the Lord God of the Hebrews: 'How long will you refuse to humble yourself before Me? Let my people go, that they may serve Me.'" (Exod. 10:3)

Pharaoh's Heart Hardened

For every man threw his rod, and they became serpents. But Aaron's rod swallowed up their rods. Pharaoh's heart grew hard, and he did not heed them, as the Lord had said. (Exod. 7:12 and 13)

The magicians of Egypt did so with their enchantments; and Pharaoh's heart grew hard, and he did not heed them, as the Lord had said. (Exod. 7:22)

But when Pharaoh saw that there was relief, he hardened his heart and did not heed them, as the Lord had said. (Exod. 8:15)

Then the magicians said to Pharaoh, "This is the finger of God." But Pharaoh's heart grew hard, and he did not heed them, just as the Lord had said. (Exod. 8:19)

And the Lord did according to the word of Moses; He removed the swarms of flies from

Pharaoh, from his servants and from his people. Not one remained. But Pharaoh hardened his heart at this time also; neither would he let the people go. (Exod. 8:31 and 32)

Then Pharaoh sent, and indeed, not even one of the livestock of the Israelites was dead. But the heart of Pharaoh became hard, and he did not let the people go. (Exod. 9:7)

And the magicians cold not stand before Moses because of the boils, for the boils were on all the magicians and on all the Egyptians. But the Lord hardened the heart of Pharaoh; and he did not heed them, just as the Lord had spoken to Moses. (Exod. 9:11 and 12)

And when Pharaoh saw that the rain, the hail, and the thunder had ceased, he sinned yet more; and he hardened his heart, he and his servants. So, the heart of Pharaoh was hard; neither would he let the children of Israel go, as the Lord had spoken by Moses. (Exod. 9:34 and 35)

And the Lord turned a very strong west wind, which took the locusts away and blew them in to the Red Sea. There remained not one locust in all the territory of Egypt. But the Lord hardened Pharaoh's heart, and he did not let the children of Israel go. (Exod. 10:19 and 20)

But the Lord hardened Pharaoh's heart, and he would not let them go. Then Pharaoh said to him, "Get away from me! Take heed to yourself and see my face no more! For in the day you see my face you shall die!" (Exod. 10:27 and 28)

But the Lord said to Moses, "Pharaoh will not heed you, so that my wonders may be multiplied in the land of Egypt." So Moses and Aaron did all these wonders before Pharaoh; and the Lord hardened Pharaoh's heart, and he did not let the children of Israel go out of his land. (Exod. 11:9 and 10)

Now it was told the king of Egypt that the people had fled, and the heart of Pharaoh and his servants was turned against the people; and they said, "Why have we done this, that we have let Israel go from serving us?" So he made ready his chariot and took his people with him. Also, he took six hundred choice chariots, and all the chariots of Egypt with captains over every one of them. And the Lord hardened the heart of Pharaoh king of Egypt, and he pursued the children of Israel; and the children of Israel went out with boldness. (Exod. 14:5–8)

And the Lord said to Moses, "Why do you cry to me? Tell the children of Israel to go forward. But lift up your rod and stretch out your hand over the sea and divide it. And the children of Israel shall go on dry ground through the midst of the sea. And indeed, I will harden the hearts of the Egyptians, and they shall follow them. So, I will gain honor over Pharaoh and over all his army, his chariots, and his horsemen. The Egyptians shall know that I am the Lord, when I have gained honor for Myself over Pharaoh, his chariots, and his horsemen." (Exod. 14:15–18)

The Lord Spoke to Moses and Aaron

Now the Lord spoke to Moses and Aaron and gave them a command for the children of Israel and for Pharaoh king of Egypt, to bring the children of Israel out of the land of Egypt. (Exod. 6:13)

Then the Lord spoke to Moses and Aaron, saying, when Pharaoh speaks to you, saying, show a miracle for yourselves, 'Then you shall say to Aaron, take your rod and cast it before Pharaoh, and let it become a serpent. (Exod. 7:8 and 9)

So, the Lord said to Moses and Aaron, "Take for yourselves handfuls of ashes from the furnace, and let Moses scatter it towards the heavens in the sight of Pharaoh." (Exod. 9:8)

Now the Lord spoke to Moses and Aaron in the land of Egypt, saying, "This month shall be your beginning of months; it shall be the first month of the year to you." (Exod. 12:1 and 2)

And the Lord said to Moses and Aaron, "This is the ordinance of the Passover: No foreigner shall eat it. But every man's servant who is bought for money, when you have circumcised him, then he may eat it." (Exod. 12:43 and 44)

For by Strength of Hand, the Lord Brought Us out of Egypt

And Moses said to the people: "Remember this day in which you went out of Egypt, out of the house of bondage; for by strength of hand the Lord brought you out of this place. No leavened bread shall be eaten." (Exod. 13:3)

It shall be a sign to you on your hand and as a memorial between your eyes, that the Lord's law may be in your mouth; for with a strong hand the

*Lord has brought you out of Egypt. You shall there-
fore keep the ordinances in its season from year to
year." (Exod. 13:9 and 10)*

*So it shall be, when your sons ask you in time
to come, saying, what is this? That you shall say to
him, "By strength of hand the Lord brought us out of
Egypt, out of the house of bondage." (Exod. 13:14)*

*It shall be as a sign on your hand and as front-
lets between your eyes, for by strength of hand the
Lord brought us out of Egypt. (Exod. 13:16)*

As I began studying the book of Exodus and really pressing into the scriptures in detail, I found that the number of times God had purposely repeated the same phrases in the scripture adds up to a purpose that runs deeper than the eye sees and the mind can comprehend. Behind the intention of repeating these phrases, we find that six times in the book of Exodus, Moses says to Pharaoh, "Let my people go." The number 6 (biblically speaking) means imperfection of man. Man's heart from the beginning had been defected through the sins of Adam and Eve because of the deception and lie of the enemy. Since that moment, man has always walked with an imperfect heart. Man was created on the sixth day and just before the seventh day, showing us that we are short one day of God's rest because man was made to rest in God, but because of our imperfect will to fulfill God's desires, we become like Pharaoh at times walking around with pride and the lustful desire to fulfill our own will that eventually leads to death and destruction.

When it comes to Pharaoh's heart being hardened, we find that this took place thirteen times in the book of Exodus. The reason for this is, the number 13 represents wickedness and evil. This was the exact representation Pharaoh gave when it came to the children of Israel whenever Pharaoh and his household had encountered God's plagues. Thirteen is one above twelve yet is considered odd due to the imperfection of not being able to regroup itself into an even sum.

Twelve, on the other hand, has the capability of regrouping itself into different forms of even sums. The thirteen times Pharaoh's heart had been hardened was a sign of his wickedness and evil intentions toward God's people. The twelfth time God had hardened Pharaoh's heart, the children of Israel were already on their way toward their victory, yet when they arrived and stood in front of the Red Sea to behold its mighty waves, the last and final time Pharaoh has hardened his heart would be the thirteenth time, and this time all the wickedness and evil intentions Pharaoh and his army would demonstrate toward the children of Israel would finally be put to an end by God Himself.

When the children of Israel first came to Egypt and remained there for quite some time, it looked as if things were getting better for them. Between the time of the famine to Joseph's death, the children of Israel were brought to Egypt not as slaves but as people who for a time would live comfortably in a land where a dream quickly became a nightmare, and so for the children of Israel, their story of redemption suddenly became the story of survival. The more and more I began to analyze the book of Genesis and the book of Exodus, I started to realize that the story of Joseph and the history of Pharaoh in Egypt is all too similar to Jesus, Satan, and the world we are currently living in. I know you must be saying how, right? Well, looking back at Joseph's history, we see that Joseph was sent to Egypt to one day save, not just his house but the entire earth from a devastating famine. Next, we see that although Joseph had conquered his mission through the power and strength of God's presence, we have come to know that although Joseph fulfilled his calling and completed his purpose of saving his people, there was still a war going on behind the scenes that only God could fight and win, but this would have required the children of Israel to completely surrender to God's will. You see, when we come to Christ, we become a new creature and all old things pass away. When we make Jesus our Lord and Savior by confessing our sins and believing in our heart that He is Lord and Savior overall, Jesus comes into our heart and our name gets written in the Lamb's book of life. However, when this happens, the real war begins because although we are marked and sealed with the seal of salvation, the devil's job is to try and keep us in bondage and not allow us to step out into the unknown and into our God-given destiny. This is what happened with the children of Israel when Joseph (who represented Jesus) died. After Joseph had passed away, the children of Israel became slaves in a place they thought freedom rang for them. Unfortunately for Pharaoh and his household, this was the very place where the strength of the hand the Lord would bring the children of Israel out of Egypt and out of the house of bondage. In Exodus 13:3, 9, 14, and 16, four times God declares these words that means self-fulfillment. God did not and does not need anyone to do what only He could do Himself to make sure that although we have already been set free from sin through Jesus's sacrifice on the cross, we see the full picture of what a glorious redemption from God Himself really looks like when we trust in God's unfailing plan to bring us from glory to glory just as He did for His people in Egypt.

God's grace toward the human race has been expressed more times than we can count. God's goodness is all around us. His favor and willingness to always pursue us will always be a mystery to us, but the evidence that God cares is within his very acts of mercy toward us. When Moses kept giving God all the excuses in the world as to why he was the wrong person for the job (to free the children of Israel from Egypt), God kept pursuing Moses because God makes no mistakes when it comes to fulfilling his purpose in and through us. The number 5 represents grace of God, goodness, and favor toward humans. Unity is a key factor here as well. We have five fingers on each hand that are odd, yet when we put them together makes up an even number, which in turn allows us to pull more weight. Five times in the book of Exodus, God spoke not just to Moses but to Moses and Aaron together. Why is this, if Moses was the one chosen by God to relay the message to Pharaoh regarding the redemption of the children of Israel? Well, reading the beginning of Exodus, I found that four times Moses tries to tell God why he was unqualified, and once more, what he was supposed to say to the children of God to convince them that he was chosen by God to free the people. Five justifications lead Moses to not become disqualified for the mission, but on the contrary, this led Moses to experience God's goodness by allowing his brother, Aaron, become part of the mission that would cause them both to experience God's grace and favor over their lives like never seen before. And so, we find in the book of Exodus that God speaks to both Moses and Aaron five times; and eventually, between the two working side by side, the children of Israel were led through Egypt within the unity of Moses and Aaron's ability to work together and accomplish God's plan of redemption. When it comes to Egypt, I too have learned so much, more than meets the eye. There were things that even I had not known about Egypt, but through the leading and guidance of the Holy Spirit, I have not only come to know more about Egypt, but I have come to appreciate my Egypt moments now more than ever. There is still more to understand, but one thing is for sure, although we are coming close to the end of traveling through Egypt's encounter of God's people, the best part of their story is about to unravel in such a way that by the time this book is finished, we all will come to see and appreciate Egypt in a totally different way. Hold tight because the best is yet to come!

CHAPTER 16

The Glory of God's Hand, the Powerless Effect of Pharaoh's Army, and the Victory of God's People

Ever notice that sometimes in the blink of an eye how everything around you can change and become something you never thought could be? I think we have all gone through these moments before, or maybe this is a season your encountering right now. Writing this book has taken me longer than I thought, not because I didn't have the capability to finish the book because we can do all things through Christ who strengthens us, but simply because only God knew when in fact this book would become published and ready for the world to receive it. There were so many Egypt moments I had to face just by being obedient in writing this book for the honor and glory of God. Still with every trial and tribulation I faced while writing, this book was worth the wait. Throughout the years of writing this book, I have felt God's supernatural grace upon me like I have never felt before. There were times when I thought for sure this is the end of me, and when those thoughts crossed my mind, I then began to feel the hand of God pulling and tugging on my heart and saying to me, "I am with you wherever you go, my daughter. Whether you are on a mountaintop or in the valley, there my presence goes with you, because I will never leave you nor forsake you." Hearing those words is what motivated me to keep on writing despite what the enemy was saying or trying to do to pull me away from a victorious deliverance that would not only impact my life but the lives of those who place their faith in Christ Jesus until the very end of their journey. While I was writing this book and trying to stay within my equilibrium state of mind, God was intentionally allowing the enemy to rise up against me, making me think I would never reach my exodus moment, but little did the enemy know that everything God permitted to occur this far has served for a mighty purpose that in time would be revealed through a great deliverance and those who rise up against you and me while crossing through our Egypt moment will soon encounter God's wrath and judgment because God has gone before us to already execute judgment on every ungodly tongue that has risen to make war against God's people. In a little while I will explain what I mean when it comes to God executing judgment on Pharaoh and his army and why this had to take place before God's people could further their journey into the wilderness, but first, I want to go back to when the Israelites began their journey toward the Red Sea.

Like I had stated in the previous chapter, the Israelites when coming out of Ramses (Egypt), scripture says they left with boldness and triumph. Now I don't know about you; but in high school, when we had a pep rally and we would celebrate and cheer one another on, there was lots of noise and loud shouts going on. So you can just imagine the shouting and praising that must have been going on at the time of the exodus. So my question is, due to the number of Israelites and the amount of noise being made, how is it that Pharaoh and his army just let them walk right on out? And when the children of Israel marched on out in victory, why did God take them the long way around just to bring them to a place where they would be cornered on all sides with no tangible or visible exit in sight? These are good questions, and the answers will surprise you like it did to me when God gave me a clear understanding as to why He permitted His people to walk the strategic path God had predestined for them to walk through. In Exodus 14:1 and 2, scripture says that the Lord spoke to Moses, saying, "Speak to the children of Israel, that they turn and camp before Pi Hahiroth, between Migdol and the sea, opposite Baal Zephon; you shall camp before it by the sea." This was no coincidence that God had purposely brought His people to these three places that have three different identities in their own location, yet these three locations play a huge role and has become the turning point for what God was about to do to Pharaoh and his army. The first thing God says to Moses is to tell the people to turn and camp before Pi Hahiroth. Pi Hahiroth was the place the children of Israel were to go ahead and camp at until the time of the parting of the Red Sea took place, yet they still had no idea what was about to take place. They were literally stepping into the unknown, which is exactly what Pi Hahiroth means (place of the unknown). God will often bring us to the place of the unknown not to scare us, but to show us that in all the places we perceive as the unknown, God Himself has already placed His feet there and has trodden on an uncharted territory to show us that although we may not know or recognize the unknown, God does and He will see us through to the very end. This particular location was not a place God stumbled upon and told the people to camp out there. No this was a place where God would purposely and strategically appoint His people to remain, and so the children of Israel were encamped in this location between another location named Migdol. Migdol was a location that had a watch tower. Its name means fortress. The Israelites were in a place where they could see the watchtower yet still with no understanding of what is taking place or what their next move would be. This specific place where God brought them was also a symbolic move of God's action to let them know that although they were in a place of the unknown, they were also not alone. God sees us right where we are, and although it may seem like we are not being watched and everything is closing in on us, God is and will always be our strong tower who watches over us. So here we see the children of Israel camped out at Pi Hahiroth between Migdol and the last location is Baal Zephon, which is on the opposite side of Migdol. Looking at where the Israelites are placed (Pi Hahiroth) and the two directions they are looking at, Migdol is directly opposite of a place that has the meaning idol or possession of the north or hidden secret. The biblical reference to Zephon is the one who sees and observes, one who expects or covers. Baal means Lord. The place of Baal Zephon was a place of observance. If we look back at the scriptures, we see that God purposely mentions Migdol first and then Baal Zephon second. I believe this was because we first must come to the full understanding that God is our fortress, our strong tower who watches over us (Migdol), and second, the place after we understand who God is, is a place of observance to what God is about to do in the midst of His people (Baal Zephon). To the Egyptians, these places may have been a symbolic attribute, but in all reality, everything in heaven and on earth belongs to God Almighty and God is the one who builds up and tears down. And that is exactly what God was intending to do with Pharaoh and his army. Where God plants our feet, we must come to understand something very important. Where God places us, there is meaning and purpose in that place. We must seek God in order for us to discover the hidden message beyond where our feet are planted because it's in the very place we are standing that God is trying to tell us something that will bring about our victory. You see, in the moment that the Israelites were camped out waiting for Moses to lead them, they were not able in that moment to see beyond the seashore or beyond the hidden message that was right around the corner for all of them because of fear and doubt. They just had a massive victory parade while exiting Egypt, only to arrive at a place where fear gripped them and doubt got the very best of them. Oh, but this was just about to reach its climax very quickly because what was unraveling rapidly was making its way over to the Israelites like a bullet coming out of a gun.

Pharaoh did not heed the victory party that was going on while the Israelites danced their way out of Egypt, having plundered the Egyptians. So what was going on with Pharaoh and his household that made them not stop the children of Israel as I had mentioned before and come after them with such hate in their hearts? Well, we found the missing piece to the puzzle in the scriptures: Numbers 33:3 and 4. The essential reason Pharaoh could not hear the celebration of the Israelites was because Pharaoh and his household were too busy mourning the deaths of their firstborn and burying them. During that time, according to the scriptures, God was also executing judgment on all their gods for what Pharaoh had done to the children of Israel. So while there was a celebration going on as the children of

Israel were making their way out of Egypt, there was mourning and judgments occurring in Egypt. Wow! This is powerful. In fact, this is so powerful that I feel the presence of the Holy Spirit saying to me right now, this picture you see of the children of Israel walking triumphantly out of Egypt, Pharaoh mourning, and judgments being executed is none other than a picture of the rapture occurring, the celebration of the marriage supper of the Lamb taking place in heaven, the mourning, shouting, and crying that will be taking place on earth after those who have believed in the one true living God has been raptured and the judgments that will be poured out in the tribulation time for all the sins committed on earth. This representation did not catch my attention until I began scrutinizing the word of God carefully. Egypt represents the world we live in, which is full of sin and idols. Pharaoh represents Satan, and his armies are the fallen angels who follow after Satan. The children of Israel represent all those who become sons and daughters of the Most High God through believing in their hearts that Jesus is Lord and Savior and being covered in the blood of the Lamb. The Exodus represents the rapture taking place. The mourning Pharaoh and his household encounter was none other than the great tribulation taking place after the rapture. The celebration of the exodus represents the marriage supper of the lamb taking place, and, not to say the least, the final representation of the judgments God poured out on the gods of Egypt clearly is the judgments that will be poured out upon the earth for all its wicked idolatry. Not only will we be with the Lord Jesus Christ for eternity; but also while we are in heaven, on earth, along with mourning, will be the ultimate judgments God will execute on the earth for all the wickedness of those who chose to live an ungodly life while on earth. In the very same way, God executed judgments on the gods of Egypt, so God will also bring about judgments on all those who chose to serve Satan instead of God. So now we find the source of why Pharaoh couldn't stop the exodus from happening. And just like Pharaoh couldn't, so Satan won't be able to stop the rapture from occurring. If we look at all of this from a bird's-eye-view, we can start to understand that the book of Exodus is not just a book that tells the story of the life of a people enslaved by Pharaoh for many years and sought victory through an exodus, no. This goes so much more beyond the headlines. This is a story that everyone on this planet will soon be a part of because this story has a record of repeating itself time and time again, only this time we are living in the end times where everything that is getting ready to happen will be the final exit of mankind's life here on this earth, and just like Pharaoh and God's people, some will be destined for eternal life and some for eternal condemnation. But one thing is for sure, we are so much closer to our exodus than our own minds can comprehend right now.

Pharaoh and his army, after mourning the loss of their firstborn and burying them, came to the realization that every slave in Egypt was set free by a great deliverance. And so Pharaoh (by God Himself) once again hardened the hearts of Pharaoh and his army to go after the children of Israel. This was the final attempt Pharaoh and his army would have against the children of Israel because what was to occur soon would leave Egypt with a new reputation and God's people with a new beginning. We know that the children of Israel are in a place where they are awaiting instructions as to where they are to go next, and from a distance, they see Pharaoh and his army storming through with rage to make war with the children of Israel. But this is where we see God show up and take over and defend His people whom He has called the apple of His eye. Because the children of Israel were cornered on every side, Pharaoh was sure to count his victory before all was said and done. Isn't that just like the enemy, always thinking he has the upper hand when in fact he has been dealt the lowest hand in the deck. When it comes to the enemy trying to destroy what God has already accomplished in you and me, always remember that the good works God has started in us, He is faithful to complete it all the way through. God started a good work through Abraham, and God's promise was about to be fulfilled through Moses; and from Moses all the way to Jesus, God's establishment in saving the world through the sacrifice of Christ has been fulfilled and completed through the Messiah, who was, is, and will always be the Lamb of God and the Lion of Judah who rises up to defend His people. Although it may seem as though we are being cornered by the enemy, always look beyond what meets the eye and look to the one who holds our greater destiny in His hand, because the one who made the seas is the One who has the capability to order the seas to approach and recede with power and dominion, only the children of Israel could not see past their fear of Pharaoh and his army coming toward them. It may have looked as though God's people were out of Egypt, but the truth is, Egypt came following after them to swallow them whole.

When God brings us through our Egypt moment, we need to always be on guard because the enemy will always try his very best to either make life nearly impossible to enjoy our victory or, worse, try and bring us back to that place of enslavement. This is what happened to the children of Israel when they saw Pharaoh and his army coming straight for them with no place to escape from. The quickest theory the children of Israel could come up with was "all the graves were taken in Egypt so you Moses brought us out here to die in the wilderness." After watching God perform all the wonders in Egypt and then give the people such a victorious deliverance, this is what the children of Israel came to, all because they thought that this would be how God intended for their lives to end. God never loses a battle, and that day God had no intention of leaving or forsaking a nation whom He had established and set free by a mighty hand. God was getting ready to save His people from a fierce battle that God's people had no intention of fighting but surrendering to the enemy out of fear. God knows our fears and doubts, and for that reason, God is never slack when it comes to rescuing His people at just the right appointed time that will leave us all in awe of His wondrous ways. That moment has come for God's people, and soon God was about to do something that would change the course of history for everyone on this earth to know: that when God intervenes, no one, not even Satan himself, can stand against the force of God's power. In fact, Satan knows this all too well! The final war of Armageddon must occur between Jesus and His heavenly hosts and Satan and his evil armies after the seven years of tribulation at the Euphrates River. At this point, God will come in and intervene to destroy the armies of Satan, and Satan will be cast down to the bottomless pit. So Pharaoh will also try to make war one last time against the Israelites before

God executes the final judgment on Pharaoh and his army. Now we find Pharaoh leaving Egypt enraged and full of anger as he has come to the realization that the children of Israel will never return to Egypt as slaves again, which has now caused him and his army to go after Israel and make war against them. Pharaoh now knows where they are, and according to the scriptures, Pharaoh is gloating over the fact that the children of Israel are bewildered and closed in. Yet Pharaoh has no idea that, although his heart has been hardened once again by God to go and make war against the children of Israel, his last and final moments along with his army are about to come to an end. In Revelation 16:16, the word of God says that they gathered together to the place called in Hebrew, Armageddon, which means Hill of Megiddo, which in turn is a reference for the demonic leadership that will wage war on the forces of God at the end of history. Before this war takes place, the sixth bowl of God's wrath will be poured out, and this is the drying up of the Euphrates River, where the last and final war will take place, and thereafter evil will be destroyed. In the very same way Pharaoh gathers his army to go out enraged toward the children of Israel, there will be a drying of the seabeds, and God will show up to defend his people from Pharaoh's army.

We must look back at a couple of things that occur before this great event takes place. These are the things that occur in our lives as well when it comes to seeing God's glorious hand move in favor of His children. Many times we want a miracle, but what it takes to see that miracle has to do with how far in we are to truly need that miracle to come to pass. When we are in need of a miracle, we are making a bold declaration that we ourselves are not enough to make it happen and that we need God to intervene on our behalf or all will be lost. This is what the children of Israel needed at the moment. They were at their last stages of coming to the beginning of a whole new chapter, but this would require them to bring their true colors to Moses so Moses could bring them to God. At the beginning, when Moses had his first encounter with Pharaoh, thereafter the people came to Moses and complained to Moses, saying, "Let the Lord look on you and judge because you have made us abhorrent in the sight of Pharaoh and in the sight of his servants to put a sword in their hand to kill us, was the same people at the exodus who spoke and said, because there were no graves in Egypt, you have taken us away to die in the wilderness? Why have you so dealt with us, to bring us up out of Egypt? Is this not the word we told you in Egypt?" I don't know about you, but I see a pattern here, and it has to do with doubt and defeat. The people had it in their minds that every time things looked like they were taking a turn for the worst, this automatically meant that they were destined for destruction; but the truth is that, in this life, we need people to push us to the edge sometimes so that we can bring it all to the One who is waiting to do the impossible. But it's only when the one chosen by God brings all the chaos to the One who has the capability to make a desert from the raging waters and the capacity to destroy the enemy in the process. Despite what the people may say or think, God has called you and me to step in the gap for them to see the glory of God's presence manifest in the moments we think all is lost. When Moses first heard their complaints in Egypt, Moses did not try to justify his actions to the people but went straight into the presence of God, and when he did, God said these words that caused Moses to rise up once again and keep fighting the good fight of faith. God said to Moses, "Now you shall see what I will do to Pharaoh." Moses, through it all, did not stop believing that God would leave them in this condition but that God would come through. We know this because of what Moses tells the people next despite the fact that Moses may have been crying in the process because let's be real and totally honest, Moses was under a lot of pressure; yet Moses still found it within himself to encourage the people by declaring these three phrases that the people needed so desperately to hear and believe. Moses said, "Do not be afraid," "Stand still," "See the Salvation of the Lord, which He will accomplish for you today." These are the very same words that God is telling every pastor and every leader in the church that has struggled within their leadership to declare over the congregation who come with doubts, fears, worries, and anxiety due to the spiritual warfare that takes place every day of our lives. The enemy's number one target is to get the people to turn on their leaders so that the congregation will become divided. It is up to the leader to take initiative action and bring the greater issue to the Lord. No matter how it comes out, God hears. When we bring the problem up to the Lord, however, He responds, we too must respond to the instruction that He gives us. For Moses however, God tells him, "Stop crying and start walking because that declaration you proclaimed to the people has already taken effect, only take the rod in your hand and lift it up and stretch it over the sea and divide it." Moses had told the people that the Lord would fight this battle for them, so why do we find Moses crying to the Lord thereafter? This may sound crazy, but I believe that even though God calls leaders to lead, they have no idea what God is doing. And so just like the people, they too have to put their faith into action even if they are scared and fearful in that moment, which is exactly what Moses did. Moses kept his eyes on God and took the rod that he had in his hand and stretched it out over the Red Sea. I believe at that moment, God gave Moses an authority that we could not comprehend even if we tried. As leaders, we must understand that when we put our faith into action despite the things that may be going on around us, faith in its own entirety has the power to move mountains. That's why Jesus in Mathew 17:20 said, "I say to you, if you have faith as a mustard seed, you will say to that mountain, 'Move from here to there,' it will move, and nothing will be impossible for you." When it comes to faith and fear, we see a fight for the title, but in this case, size doesn't matter because although fear can become as big as a mountain and try everything in its power to intimidate us when it comes to faith, it can become as little as a mustard seed and still have the power to move that giant mountain from one place to another. This is what Moses did after crying. He took the little bit of faith he had and put it into action not knowing that God would fulfill his promises and bring them through to a victory that would mark generations to come. This was the pivotal moment where everything that God had intended to occur would happen according to what God had spoken over Abraham from the beginning. A great awakening was happening, all because the fathers of faith, like Abraham, stepped out and believed God in His word. Men like Isaac who didn't question the very act of sacrifice but was a representation of Jesus who, although wasn't that sacrificial Lamb, but out of obedience to his father was willing to get on the altar of sacrifice. Or like Jacob whom God gave the twelve tribes of Israel to, of whom one of them called Joseph became the intercessor for his house, and not only for his house but became a representation of Jesus coming not only to save the house of the lost sheep (Jews) but to save another flock of sheep (Gentiles) as well. Right down to the one chosen by God, chosen to bring about a great deliverance through obedience and courage to believe that through every Egypt moment of affliction, hurt, pain, rejection, calamity, loneliness, hard bondage, and the never-ending feelings of desperation and despair of hopelessness was all coming to an end and a new beginning was rising up from the faith Moses had in raising the rod that was given to him from the beginning and spreading it over the mouth of the Red Sea. Every Egypt moment led to this one moment, a moment that became the start of an establishment that would run all the way through to the Messiah and would reach beyond the ends of the earth. Just as the parting of the Red Sea was a supernatural event that only God could have done to intervene, so the sacrifice made on the cross through Jesus Christ was a supernatural event that took place that only God could have done to intervene and rescue us from the powers of darkness. The symbolic parting of the Red Sea being split right down the middle was a representation of the veil that was torn from top to bottom in the temple. The Bible says in Mathew 27:50–51 that right before the veil was torn, Jesus cried out again with a loud voice and yielded up his spirit. Then behold, the veil of the temple was torn in two from top to bottom, and the earth quaked, and the rocks were split. Wow! Moses standing by the Red Sea crying just before the parting of the Red Sea is a representation of what Jesus did just before the veil was torn and the earth quaked with trembling and fear. I truly believe with all of my heart now more than ever that God is in the details of our lives. No matter how small we may see the view of what we are going through, God sees the fine print, and within the spaces of our lives is the details that we cannot see. Yet when it's all said and done, God will show us every detail we either missed or could not see within that moment because of our fear, faults, and failures. Still God will show us not to condemn us but to show us that in the littlest of the details that we thought were of no importance, God was actually using them to bring us into a new season of our lives.

God has already written the story of our lives. Nothing needs altering, because with God, the plans that He has for our lives are not to harm us nor are they of evil intentions. On the contrary, they are to give us a future, a hope, and a new beginning; but before we can step out into our calling, we all must face Egypt in order to become who God has intended for us to become. Remember that even Jesus, in coming to earth, knew he would have to go through his own Egypt moments and suffer harshly. But what we could not see in the details of Jesus's life was that although Jesus came to this earth as a man, He also understood the mission of His Heavenly Father who was in Him, and so what we could not see in the details of Jesus's life was already established by God, and in due season, we were able to see the finished works of God's unfailing plan to redeem the world through His Son Jesus Christ. Through every journey into the lives of those whose lives were written in the Bible who reflected and represented the life of Jesus was predestined by God for all to see and know that within every detail of our forefather's lives was a mere reflection of what intentions the coming Messiah would have in coming down to this earth to save us from the powers of the evil one who has come to steal, kill, and destroy. But Jesus, in His mercy and grace, has come to give us life in abundance. Every story we have encountered from the book of Genesis to the book of Exodus has all pointed to the main topic at hand, Jesus Christ, and what He would have to endure just to rescue us from our sinful ways and bring us from darkness to light. Yes, our forefathers have risen to the occasion and have triumphed over many trials, but we all must remember that every trial they faced in their lifetime was all because of the hidden message that was revealed to us through the coming of the Messiah, but for them, the obstacles they faced within their era was a saving victory for what was to come for all who believe in the One True Living God, and that through the power of the cross, all who come to Jesus with a repented heart and follow after Him will be led into victory and walk the rest of their lives out in victory despite the accusation from the enemy, despite our past mistakes, despite the journey that lies ahead, nothing from this point on can separate us from God's presence because it's only within the details of our worship can we truly come to know the evidence of the Father's plan through what God has been doing from the very beginning, which started with God's creation that resembles a finished masterpiece. You and I will always be the center of God's focus, and when we learn to cherish not just the noticeable moments of our lives but the final details, we will begin to understand for the very first time that within every detail of our lives, God has given us grace and mercy to bring us through to the other side.

> *Now it came to pass in the morning watch, that the Lord looked down upon the army of the Egyptians through the pillar of fire and cloud, and he troubled the army of the Egyptians. And He took off their chariot wheels so that they drove them with difficulty, and the Egyptians said, "Let us flee from the face of Israel, for the Lord fights for them against the Egyptians." (Exod. 14:24 and 25)*

> *Then the Lord said to Moses, "Stretch out your hand over the sea, that the waters may come back upon the Egyptians, on their chariots, and on their horsemen." And Moses stretched out his hand over the sea; and when the morning appeared, the sea returned to its full depth, while the Egyptians were fleeing into it. So the Lord overthrew the Egyptians into the midst of the sea. (Exod. 14:26 and 27)*

As far as we know from these verses, we see that God had allowed his people to walk on dry ground through the Red Sea. God from above was looking down upon the Egyptians and sees something in the details that we cannot see; yet God, who sees everything, goes on ahead to do something that caught my attention for the first time among the many times I have read this passage. Let's see these verses from end to beginning. In verse 27, Moses stretched out his hands and the sea returned to its full depth while the Egyptians were running toward the sea, which caused them to drown. In verse 26, God gives Moses the command to stretch out his hand over the sea so that the waters may come back upon the Egyptians, horsemen, and their chariots. When I was studying these two verses, I found that in order for the Egyptians to fall into the Red Sea (v. 27), the Red Sea had closed behind them (v. 26), and if that is true, then that means Moses and the people saw the Red Sea from a distance come crashing down from behind the Egyptians right before their very eyes, bringing the Egyptians, horsemen, and their chariots right into their own destruction. That was the most obvious event that took place and will always be remembered for generations to come: that God in His mighty powers caused the Red Sea to fall upon the Egyptians, the horsemen, and their chariots. But there is a small detail that is in fact the key detail to why the Egyptians could not reach the other side before the sea came crashing down on them and destroyed every last one of them. God had done something that we all, if not paying enough attention, would miss. If God had not placed this minor yet essential detail within the history of this book, we would all have thought the same and kept on thinking that it was the sea that destroyed the Egyptians when in fact it's the minor detail of what God had done before the closing of the Red Sea that changed the course of action the Egyptians took in trying to catch up to the children of Israel. The children of Israel were busy crossing over to the other side of the Red Sea with heavy carts, wagons, and loads of cargo; yet they were all able to cross over with no problem. But now we find the Egyptians with their horsemen and chariots running after the children of Israel with chariots that were made to withstand the adversity of the ground they were running on. If the children of Israel made it to the other side with more cargo and heavier carts than the Egyptians, then why couldn't the Egyptians speed up and catch the children of Israel? It's in the very details of verse 25 that we find that God had purposely taken off the wheels of the chariots so that in the process of them trying to catch up and conquer the children of Israel, this would cause the Egyptians to slow down and come to the realization that without this important detail to their chariots (the wheels), they had no chance of catching up to the children of Israel. And so we find the Egyptians declaring God's victory before the Red Sea swallowed them up whole. The enemy will always have to announce God's victory before the actual victory takes place because even the enemy knows that when God gets into the details of our lives, it's because God is up to something. Within the details of what we cannot see happening, the enemy sure sees it, and for that reason, even the enemy cannot help but give God what belongs to God, and that is the victory that only belongs to God. Those who have gone before us have experienced victory upon victory as they passed through their Egypt moments, trusting in God's unfailing plan to redeem what the enemy has stolen. Every trip our forefathers took to Egypt was a memorial of what was to come for us, and it was in the details of every Egypt moment that we can now see the greater overall purpose of why every single one of us at one point or another will have to cross Egypt in order to capture the overall view and purpose of why God called us to travel on through Egypt and what God has planned and destined for us to do when we finally come out of our Egypt process. But always remember that life is in the details, and the details of our lives are what make up the overall view, and the overall view will become the very masterpiece God so patiently waited for us to come and see that only in His presence can everything make perfect sense.

When it's all said and done, the songs that we sang in the midnight hour as the pain becomes our blanket, our tears become our pillow, and our dreams quickly turned into our greatest nightmare. Still God will never forget that in every song we sing along with every note of despair, every tune sung out discouragement or every word spoken out of sadness and sorrow will never escape God's throne room because He holds every tear in His hands; and at the moment when we thought all was lost never to be traced, God shows us the DNA of his scars that represents the lifeline that will always bring us back to his birthing place where it all begins again and again and again. The word of God says that in the day that God destroyed the Egyptians, the horsemen, and their chariots, God allowed the children of Israel not only to see the great works of the Lord come to pass, but they would come to sing a new song that in all its entirety proclaims the mighty works God has done to save His people by a mighty hand. There is nothing greater than when we have seen the hand of God fight for us in such a way that before our very eyes, we see our enemies who once persecuted us with such harsh persecution go down from where they came from. God alone is our victory. When we encounter God, we encounter a triumphant life filled with songs of salvation and thanksgiving in our hearts. God is our exceedingly great reward, and I believe within our Egypt moments and having to travel down south at times, if we allow ourselves to surrender to the calling and place our faith in God's unfailing plan, we will see far greater works being done through us than what is being done to us in the moments we think that the waiting period is just too long for us to endure. Within Egypt's moments, there is a promise given to us by God, that although it may take a while for the promise to come to pass within the waiting period, God gives us the privilege of seeing the great and mighty works He is doing to one day set us up for a victory so big that right before our very eyes, we will see the enemy fall into the very same net he constructed for our downfall. You and I may have had to endure much while in our Egypt or down south moments, but I promise you this according to *Exodus 15:9* and *10*, which says, the enemy said: "*I will pursue, I will overtake, I will divide the spoil; my desire shall be satisfied on them. I will draw my sword, my hand shall destroy them, 'you blew with your wind, the sea covered them; they sank like lead in the mighty waters.*" The enemy, as we can see, is all talk and no game. Six times the enemy professed what he would do to the children of Israel (which amounted to nothing in the end), yet God in His mighty powers declared three works that He would perform to bring the enemy to his destruction, and every last word God decreed over the enemy came to pass exactly how God proclaimed and established it to be. Our victory is already in the hands of our Creator. He has given us the victory song so we can boldly proclaim what God has done from the beginning of time to save His people and rescue us from the forces of evil that lie low and brings deception and seeds of fear to all those God has chosen to rise up and become a chosen generation. And with triumph and victory, through what Jesus has done for us on the cross, we can in the end proclaim and sing, "*The*

Lord is my strength and song, and He has become my salvation; He is my God, and I will praise Him; My father's God, and I will exalt Him. The Lord is a man of war; The Lord is His name" (*Exod. 15:2 and 3*). The song that is deep down within the core of your spirit is a song of victory, but before that song can become manifest and flourish, the songs of sorrow and sadness must be planted in the depths of God's presence so that God can cause (through our prayers, tears, reading of His word, worshipping even when it hurts) that indestructible seed to sprout up to encounter and behold the beauty within God's creations and become the very thing that was once hidden in darkness, rejected and forgotten about by man, but carefully and intricately designed by God to do great and mighty works here on this beautiful planet called earth. After God had called Abraham and his family to step out into the unknown and travel toward a place called Egypt, only to discover that within Egypt's borders lay the very foundation for God's purpose, to one day be fulfilled through Moses to establish a nation and that through the established nation of God, the Lion of Judah would come forth and bring salvation to every nation on this planet. What started with Abraham's first journey toward Egypt enabled the rest of the family down the line to know and believe that through Egypt, we have the capacity to measure the length of our faith as we wait upon the Lord to fight our battles and give us victory no matter how long we remain in Egypt.

I want you to know that whatever event leads us toward our Egypt moment, we are that much closer to seeing what God has in store for our remaining time in Egypt; and instead of complaining about our stay, we ought to know and understand by now that within every Egypt moment, there is favor and that God's glory will be revealed within every encounter we have going forth until God says it's time to leave and that's when we will see the hand of God move in such a supernatural way that when it's all said and done, you will come out of Egypt singing, praising, and declaring just as the children of Israel did, "The Lord is a man of war; the Lord is His name." And through it all, we will know beyond a shadow of a doubt just how important and vital it will always be for us to encounter our Egypt and down south moments.

CONCLUSION

I hope and pray that this book has inspired you to go out and face your Egypt moments with a whole new perspective. Life is all about how we view the uncertain times of our lives. If someone has told you bad moments come because of bad luck, by simply reading this book, you can look them in the eye and say, "What you call bad moments, I call them my Egypt moments, and luck has absolutely nothing to do with the process I am encountering right now." This is how we can shut the enemy up and put him in his place. God has so many wonderful blessings for us to reap, but if we are not willing to surrender to our Egypt moments, we cannot inherit what can only be given to us through encountering the hardship of walking out our journey in Egypt, only to find that, in the end, more strength and courage is needed to keep on walking until we reach the promised land. So as we have journeyed into the lives of those who, by God's grace and mercy, had to encounter their very own down south and Egypt moments just to fulfill God's greater purpose, remember that all of their Egypt moments were not for them to glory in but to bring honor and glory to the One True Living God who, through every Egypt encounter, brought forth His blueprint map of redemption that would soon become the establishment of God's perfect plan revealed through the Messiah, Jesus Christ. So why the south? why Egypt? Because it's not until we have traveled the long road that we can start our journey into the destiny that awaits us. Where God calls us to, He will also see us through, and as God created Egypt, He also has designed a specific path we would all have to take to arrive and exit according to the will of God's perfect plan and purpose designed to bring us from glory to glory. Whether you are about to enter into your down south experience or are in the experience of feeling like you've been in Egypt for too long or you may be coming out and are experiencing the warfare of your life just before the victory arrives, just know that whatever season you are in, God is in that season with you, leading you on in, comforting you through the hard times, fighting your battles for you, and will remain with you until the very end.

Printed in the USA
CPSIA information can be obtained
at www.ICGtesting.com
LVHW031113230224
772606LV00042B/488